China Debates Its Global Role

What do China's scholars make of the nature of China's global rise? And what is the significance of academic debates for Chinese policy goals and preferences?

In this book, leading Chinese specialists outline how their colleagues are studying and interpreting different dimensions of China's evolving global role, opening these Chinese language debates to a new audience. Collectively they show that while some ideas and ways of thinking are more prominent than others, there is no homogeneity of scholarship and no single conception of what China thinks and wants. Not only has the range of issue areas under discussion actually increased as China's global role and impact has changed, but there also remains considerable diversity when it comes to thinking about what China can, might, and should try to do as a global power, and how China's global role should be studied and theorized.

The chapters in this book were originally published in the journal, *The Pacific Review*.

Shaun Breslin is Professor of Politics and International Studies at the University of Warwick and Senior Research Fellow, The Wong MNC Center. This collection was completed while he held a Leverhulme Major Research Fellowship to study the nature of China as a global power.

Ren Xiao is Professor of International Politics at the Institute of International Studies at Fudan University in Shanghai, where he is also Director of the Center for the Study of Chinese Foreign Policy.

China Debates Its Global Role

Chinese Scholars on Chinese Scholarship

Edited by
Shaun Breslin and Ren Xiao

Routledge
Taylor & Francis Group

LONDON AND NEW YORK

First published 2022
by Routledge
2 Park Square, Milton Park, Abingdon, Oxon, OX14 4RN

and by Routledge
605 Third Avenue, New York, NY 10158

Routledge is an imprint of the Taylor & Francis Group, an informa business

© 2022 Taylor & Francis

British Library Cataloguing-in-Publication Data
A catalogue record for this book is available from the British Library

ISBN13: 978-0-367-71293-8 (hbk)
ISBN13: 978-0-367-71294-5 (pbk)
ISBN13: 978-1-003-15020-6 (ebk)

DOI: 10.4324/9781003150206

Typeset in Myriad Pro
by codeMantra

Publisher's Note
The publisher accepts responsibility for any inconsistencies that may have arisen during the conversion of this book from journal articles to book chapters, namely the inclusion of journal terminology.

Disclaimer
Every effort has been made to contact copyright holders for their permission to reprint material in this book. The publishers would be grateful to hear from any copyright holder who is not here acknowledged and will undertake to rectify any errors or omissions in future editions of this book.

Contents

Citation Information

The chapters in this book were originally published in *The Pacific Review*, volume 33, issue 3–4 (2020). When citing this material, please use the original page numbering for each article, as follows:

Introduction
China debates its global role
Shaun Breslin and Ren Xiao
The Pacific Review, volume 33, issue 3–4 (2020) pp. 357–361

Chapter 1
The study of Chinese scholars in foreign policy analysis: an emerging research program
Huiyun Feng and Kai He
The Pacific Review, volume 33, issue 3–4 (2020) pp. 362–385

Chapter 2
Grown from within: Building a Chinese School of International Relations
Ren Xiao
The Pacific Review, volume 33, issue 3–4 (2020) pp. 386–412

Chapter 3
Striving for achievement in a new era: China debates its global role
Ling Wei
The Pacific Review, volume 33, issue 3–4 (2020) pp. 413–437

Chapter 4
Chinese conception of the world order in a turbulent Trump era
Zhimin Chen and Xueying Zhang
The Pacific Review, volume 33, issue 3–4 (2020) pp. 438–468

Chapter 5
Chinese perception of China's engagement in multilateralism and global governance
Hongsong Liu
The Pacific Review, volume 33, issue 3–4 (2020) pp. 469–496

Chapter 6
China debating the regional order
Dong Wang and Weizhan Meng
The Pacific Review, volume 33, issue 3–4 (2020) pp. 497–519

Chapter 7
Foreign aid study: Chinese schools and Chinese points
Meibo Huang and Jianmei Hu
The Pacific Review, volume 33, issue 3–4 (2020) pp. 520–549

Chapter 8
International law debates in China: traditional issues and emerging fields
He Zhipeng
The Pacific Review, volume 33, issue 3–4 (2020) pp. 550–573

For any permission-related enquiries please visit:
http://www.tandfonline.com/page/help/permissions

Notes on Contributors

Shaun Breslin, Department of Politics and International Studies, University of Warwick, Coventry, UK.

Zhimin Chen, School of International Relations and Public Affairs, Fudan University, Shanghai, China.

Huiyun Feng, School of Government and International Relations Griffith University, Brisbane, Australia.

Kai He, Griffith Asia Institute and Center for Governance and Public Policy, Griffith University, Brisbane, Australia.

Jianmei Hu, School of Economics and Management, Hebei University of Technology, Tianjin, China.

Meibo Huang, International Development Cooperation Academy, Shanghai University of International Business and Economics, China.

Hongsong Liu, School of International and Public Affairs, Shanghai Jiaotong University, China.

Weizhan Meng, China Institute and Development Institute, Fudan University, Shanghai, China.

Dong Wang, School of International Studies, Peking University, Beijing, China; Institute for Global Cooperation and Understanding, Peking University, Beijing, China.

Ling Wei, Zhou Enlai Diplomatic Studies Center, China Foreign Affairs University, Beijing, China.

Ren Xiao, Institute of International Studies, Fudan University, Shanghai, China.

Xueying Zhang, School of International Relations and Public Affairs, Fudan University, Shanghai, China.

He Zhipeng, School of Law, Jilin University, Changchun, China.

Introduction: China debates its global role

Shaun Breslin and Ren Xiao

The very simple and straightforward aim of this special issue is to outline and analyse how debates over international politics and China's global role have evolved in China in recent years. In particular, we want to open up debates that can be found in the Chinese language literature to an audience that might not normally be able to access or understand them. To be sure, there is now a relatively large cohort of Chinese academics publishing in English in high quality outlets and participating in international conferences. Their scholarship and insights have done much to increase knowledge and understanding of Chinese thinking. Even so, we think the time is right for a collection that looks in depth at Chinese debates and discourses for five main reasons.

First, China matters. Of course, China has mattered in different ways for a number of years. But with China's economic interactions expanding in size and scope, and China's leaders enunciating a desire to take the lead in global governance reform (in some issue areas at least), it is hard to disagree that Chinese interests and objectives matter more to the way the global order functions today than at any other time in recent history.

How academic thinking affects and is affected by policy making and strategic objectives is the specific focus of the contribution by Feng Huiyun and He Kai, and so will not be repeated here. However, it's not really a plot-spoiler to suggest that we think that how Chinese analysts think about the world and China's place within it helps shape the way that China matters now, and how it will matter going forward. In particular, conceptions of the shifting nature of the global order (detailed here by Chen Zhimin and Zhang Xueying) and changing understandings of what China could and/or should try to achieve given these power shifts (the subject of Wei Ling's contribution) help us understand the directions that Chinese policy could take in the future.

Second, there has been a massive change in the nature of international relations (IR) scholarship in China in the first two decades of the twenty-first century; certainly compared to the last two decades of the previous century. It is worth remembering that the academic study of IR in China (rather than, for example, training international relations officials) is still a *relatively* new endeavour. So is not surprising, then, that it is still in a process of evolving and expanding from its original rather limited basis in the immediate post-Mao years. But even compared to a decade ago, the Chinese IR community has expanded considerable, both in terms of the number of individuals involved, and the number of Universities that have established IR schools and departments and/or research institutes and centres. Rather than being a minority activity undertaken by a relatively small group of people in a few places, it has become increasingly prominent and has emerged as a mainstream academic undertaking across the country as a whole.

As already noted, many of these scholars seeks to publish their work in international journals; particularly those in the SSCI. A number of Chinese universities and research institutions have also established their own international journals, primarily in English, but also with publications in Japanese, Korean and Russian. At the same time, there has been an outpouring of domestic-facing journals too, and notwithstanding the contribution that Chinese scholars make outside China, the overwhelming majority of Chinese scholarship is published in China in Chinese language outlets. The major IR centres all publish their own journals and a number of them have for some years now; alongside the flagship Chinese Academy of Social Sciences journal *shijie jingji yu zhengzhi* (World Economics and Politics), Beijing University has *guoji zhengzhi yanjiu* (Journal of International Studies), China Foreign Affairs University has *waijiao pinglun* (Foreign Affairs Review), Qinghua (Tsinghua) University has *guoji zhengzhi kexue* (Quarterly Journal of International Politics), China Institutes for Contemporary International Relations has *xiandai guoji guanxi* (Contemporary International Relations), and the China Institute of International Studies is home to *guoji wenti yanjiu* (China International Studies). The social science editions of other universities' in-house journals (*xuebao*) now also frequently carry IR papers too.

The number of outlets increases even further when you add on those more area studies focussed journals that primarily deal with IR issues. There are, for example, at least four major and well-respected journals that focus on Southeast Asia alone. And while relations with countries in China's regional backyard(s) and relations with the USA still tends to dominate, the third reason for looking anew at Chinese debates is that the geographic focus of Chinese IR scholarship has also expanded too. Not least because

China's international interactions and interests are much more globally encompassing than in previous eras, countries and regions in "non-core" parts of the world that previously had little notice paid to them now receive significantly more attention.

Fourth, and very much related, the issues that fall within the remit of IR scholarship has changed too. For example, while security considerations used to solely focus on war and conflict, the extension into non-traditional and human security issue areas is very much a product of this century. The importance and potential of regional forms of governance covered in this collection by Wang Dong might have emerged before the turn of the millennium, but it's fair to say that this too has increased in significance as China's potential to influence regional forms has also increased. The same is true when it comes to studies of multilateralism and global governance, as discussed here in detail by Liu Hongsong. Here, alongside the papers on global order by Chen and Zhang and Chinese strategic objectives by Wei, one collective conclusion is that the global financial crisis in 2008 marked a key turning point in shaping conceptions of shifting power resources, and what this meant for China's ability to "strive for achievements".

In the process, the changing nature of Chinese international interactions has blurred the dividing lines between IR and other forms of international scholarship. For example, debates over the nature and utility of international law in China outlined and analysed by He Zhipeng are, as he argues, "closely related to China's national interests and national policies", and thus of considerable significance to IR scholars (as well as interesting and important in the international law field itself). China's rather rapid emergence as a globally significant provider of overseas aid and aid-type finance has also shed a new light on the study of foreign aid too and, as Huang Meibo and Hu Jianmei show, debates over what Chinese aid might or should seek to achieve.

Fifth, there is an increasing theoretical plurality and sophistication in scholarship too. To be sure, overall, varieties of realism remain the most often used and referenced theoretical preference, but there is much more to Chinese scholarship than just realism. This might in part be a result of the extensive overseas training that many Chinese scholars have undertaken overseas, particularly at the doctoral level, before returning to take up academic positions in China. Or perhaps simply in part through a wider engagement with a broader range of theoretical starting points too. But Chinese scholars are not just theory-takers. As Ren Xiao shows in his contribution, they are increasingly theory modifiers and innovators too, both challenging the basic assumptions of existing theories and calling for them to be adapted to reflect the experiences of non-Western countries, and also looking to China's own experiences and philosophical traditions to develop new more indigenously based theories too.

Add these five reasons together, and the overall picture is of a new self-confidence in Chinese IR scholarship as a whole. It is also a picture of a body of scholarship that is large and diverse, and as a result unsurprisingly not fully represented by publications in English in international journals. In fact, in the writers' workshop we held in Shanghai in July 2019, it was very clear that not even the Chinese experts presenting papers themselves had full knowledge and awareness of the extent or content of the debates in all of the other sub-areas covered in this collection. So in addition to providing access to the range of debates to a non-Chinese reading audience, the papers might collectively also be useful for some Chinese scholars in China itself as well.

This should not be surprising. Scholars in other countries would not be expected to know the full range of debates in all sub disciplines. The reason that it *might* be slightly surprising in the Chinese case is the wide held belief that under Xi Jinping, pluralism is gradually being challenged as some researchers chose to align their research with official positions and preferences. And there is some truth in this. Proposing to study Xi Jinping's Thought increases the chances of getting research funding, and there has been a proliferation of publications that elucidate a number of Xi's favoured concepts and projects; the New Type of International Relations, the Community of Shared History for Mankind, the China Solution, Great Power Diplomacy with Chinese Characteristics and so on. Studies of the Belt and Road are also rather abundant; though as the editors of any non-Chinese language journal will attest to, it's not just in China that there has been an explosion of Belt and Road papers, and it's not just Chinese scholars that are writing them. It's probably fair to assume that some scholars who might not share the government position have also decided to keep their opinions to themselves. This creates a real dilemma for students of Chinese academic debates. How do you study what is not being written and said, and do the amount of publications providing exegeses of Xi's thinking accurately reflect the real extent of alignment with them in the academic community as a whole?

Given the importance of what we might call leader-influenced scholarship, one question the editors asked all contributors to consider in their papers was the extent to which scholarship in their specific area was shaped or driven by the preferences of top leaders and leadership changes. Collectively, the contributions show that the specific and immediate focus of scholarship does often respond to new and/or prominent policies and initiatives. Indeed, it would be odd if they didn't given that the aim is to study debates over China's global role and this role is very much shaped by what top leaders think, do and want.

However, what the papers also show – individually and collectively – is that this has not resulted in the eradication of diversity and plurality and the emergence of sub-disciplinary mono-cultures. To be sure, some positions and approaches might dominate in some areas. But overall, there is no single Chinese position, and no single set of aims and objectives. Today the Chinese IR community is engaged in truly serious studies and producing sophisticated arguments and viewpoints. As a result, and fortunately for us, our assumption that a collection outlining and explaining difference was necessary proved to be correct. So on to the papers.

Funding

This special issue was partially funded by Leverhulme Trust Major Research Fellowship no. MRF-2016-103, "China risen? What is global power (and in what ways does China have it)?

The study of Chinese scholars in foreign policy analysis: an emerging research program

Huiyun Feng and Kai He

ABSTRACT

A review of studies of China's foreign policy reveals three dominant methods: the area studies approach, the IR theory method, and the integrated approach. We suggest that it is time to pay close attention to an emerging research program focusing on the study of Chinese international relations (IR) scholars, especially their internal debates, as a new venue to understand China's foreign policy. Although Chinese IR scholars are normally quoted as valuable sources in the study of Chinese foreign policy in general, there is no systematic study of China's IR scholars *per se*. In order to transform the study of Chinese IR scholars to a full-fledged research program, researchers need to pursue theoretical innovations on the relationship between different types of IR scholars and foreign policy inquiries, advance multi-method research designs across the different methods of field interviews, textual analysis, and opinion surveys, as well as encourage international collaboration between Chinese scholars and non-Chinese scholars.

Introduction

The rise of China and its profound implications for world politics have turned Chinese foreign policy into a fascinating field of study for scholars and policy makers alike. The study of Chinese foreign policy, however, is a tough enterprise. Due to its unique one-party political system, China's policy making, especially on foreign policy, is a mystery in the eyes of outsiders. On the one hand, China's foreign policy is clear and simple to understand because almost all Chinese officials and public media seem to follow the same official line on major foreign policies and present one voice predetermined by the central government. As China's first Premier Zhou Enlai famously put it, 'there is no small thing in foreign affairs' (外事无小事). It means that the government is extremely sensitive to anything related to foreign policy, including the articulation and interpretation of China's foreign policy to the outside world. Therefore, it is easy to discern what China's foreign policies are because of the high-level control of the subject matter by the Chinese Communist Party (CCP).

On the other hand, it is quite difficult to analyze the sources of Chinese foreign policy, especially regarding how and why China has made a particular policy decision at a certain time as well as when and under what conditions China will change its foreign policy behavior in the future. The reason is also simple, because scholars and policy analysts have limited access and resources to investigate the decision-making process of Chinese foreign policy. For example, the famous bureaucratic politics model in the study of foreign policy has some inherent difficulties to be well operationalized because scholars have limited evidence about bureaucratic infighting in China.[1] There is no public policy debate among officials or different bureaucratic units on foreign policy. This hierarchical, top-down, decision-making system makes China's foreign policy more than a monolith. It is clear and simple outside, but opaque and complicated inside.

Through examining three dominant methods in the study of Chinese foreign policy—the area studies approach, the IR-theory method, and the integrated approach—in this essay we suggest that it is time to pay close attention to an emerging research program on the study of Chinese international relations (IR) scholars, especially their internal debates, as a new venue to understand China's foreign policy. We suggest that this emerging research program should be taken seriously, because it will complement and enrich the existing three approaches in the study of China's foreign policy behavior.

The following paper has four sections. First, we briefly review the strengths and weaknesses of the three dominant research traditions in the study of China's foreign policy. We argue that although Chinese IR scholars are normally quoted as valuable sources in the study of Chinese foreign policy, there is no systematic study of Chinese IR scholars per se. In the second section, we discuss the fourth research approach, which treats Chinese IR scholars as a subject of inquiry in studying Chinese foreign policy. There have been two waves or directions of scholarship in the study of Chinese IR scholars in foreign policy since the end of the Cold War. The first wave focuses more on exploring dominant views or the consensus among Chinese scholars, especially the America Watchers—scholars specializing on US-China relations, so that reliable inferences can be drawn from what America Watchers have perceived regarding what Chinese leaders believed in guiding China's foreign policy toward the United States. The second wave, however, places more emphasis on the divergent views of Chinese IR scholars on broader issues beyond US-Chinese relations, and this perspective opens a new window for the outside world to understand the dynamics of Chinese ideas and perceptions of international relations.

In the third section, we discuss how to move this scholar-focused research approach forward. We argue that more attention should be paid to theoretical innovations regarding the relationships between different types of IR scholars and foreign policy inquiries, the conduct of multi-method research designs across the different methods of interview, textual analysis, and opinion surveys, and the emerging international collaboration between Chinese scholars and non-Chinese scholars. In conclusion, we argue that this new research program—the study of Chinese IR scholars in the area of foreign policy analysis—will not only deepen the world's understanding of China's rise but also bring prominent Chinese IR scholars to the world stage.

Three approaches and the role of Chinese IR scholars

There are three research traditions in the study of Chinese foreign policy.[2] One is the traditional area studies approach, which emphasizes the idiosyncratic features of Chinese foreign policy. China experts in this research tradition are normally equipped with Chinese language skills and familiarity with Chinese culture and history. Their research is mainly based on extensive field work in China, gathering original materials and conducting interviews with Chinese policy elites, normally in Chinese. More importantly, the success of this approach depends highly on personal networks between outside researchers and the different levels of Chinese society from government officials to the scholarly community.

For example, David Lampton, a leading scholar of China's foreign policy and US-China relations, states that his book *Same bed different dreams: Managing US-China relations* (2001) 'reflects his unique opportunity to interact with Chinese people and leaders from the People's Republic of China (PRC), Hong Kong, and Taiwan for nearly thirty years as a scholar, as the head of a policy-oriented exchange organization, and as director of Washington think-tank research programs dealing with China.' The Chinese leaders with whom Lampton interacted as the president of the National Committee on US-China Relations for his book include Zhu Rongji—later Chinese Premier, Wang Daohan—Jiang Zemin's close friend, as well as a member of Deng Xiaoping's family. These kinds of personal interactions and interview experiences make Lampton's book one of the most authoritative sources in the study of China's foreign policy, because no other scholars have had similar access to such high-level policy makers or politicians in China.

Similarly, David Shambaugh, another prominent China scholar from the United States, spent one year as a Fulbright senior visiting scholar at the Chinese Academy of Social Sciences to conduct field research and interviews in China during 2009–2010 for his book *China goes global* (2013). His interview list is also impressive in that he interviewed a politburo Central Committee member, State Councilor Dai Bingguo, Executive Vice Foreign Minister Zhang Zhijun, Vice Foreign Minister Cui Tiankai, and a dozen other high-level officials as well as leading policy analysts and IR scholars in China. Consequently, it is not a surprise that one of the reasons that his book was selected as a best book of 2013 by *The Economist* and *Foreign Affairs* was its 'masterful survey' of China's foreign policy. Again, the privileged access to Chinese officials is one key factor for the success of Shambaugh's work. However, it is clear that not all researchers can get such high-level access to Chinese officials when studying China's foreign policy.[3]

One criticism of the area studies approach is that area-specific knowledge and findings are hard to generalize and apply to other cases due to their limitations on theoretical contributions. To a certain extent, this research tradition is closer to the disciplines of the humanities than to the social sciences. Consequently area studies have declined in the United States and other countries after the Cold War, especially in the context of the scientific and behavioral movement in the field of comparative politics in particular and political science in general.[4] The study of Chinese foreign policy, as Johnston (2006) points out, is also marginalized within the academic field in the United States as we can see from the declining number of university faculty positions on China's foreign policy in American universities.

The second approach in the study of China's foreign policy is to explicitly apply IR theory to examine China's foreign policy behavior. This is deductive modelling from theory to fact rather than inductive reasoning from fact to theory. For example, John Mearsheimer (2001) applies his offensive realism theory to explain and predict China's foreign policy behavior after the rapid rise in its economic and military capabilities. His famous analogy is to compare China with the United States in the 19th century by suggesting that China will model the American Monroe doctrine to pursue regional hegemony. In other words, China is not a unique country in its foreign policy behavior compared to other major powers in the eyes of Mearsheimer or other IR scholars. Instead, it is a normal state that intends to maximize its interests in terms of power or security within an anarchical international system.

One advantage of this IR approach is that researchers do not need any China-specific knowledge to analyze Chinese foreign policy behavior. By treating China as a rising power in the international system like other states,

IR scholars can apply different theoretical frameworks, such as realism, liberalism, and constructivism, to shed light on China's foreign policy behavior. Realism, especially Mearsheimer's offensive realism, seems useful to explain China's assertive turn in diplomacy after 2010, because the more power China has, the more assertive its policy will be (Mearsheimer, 2010). China is a revisionist state just because of its rising military and economic capabilities. On the contrary, according G. John Ikenberry—a leading liberalism scholar, China has no reason to become a revisionist state because China is the greatest beneficiary of the current liberal international order (Ikenberry, 2008). The utility of a general IR theory, like realism and liberalism, in explaining China's foreign policy highlights the weakness of the area studies approach, which emphasizes idiosyncratic explanations for China's foreign policy behavior.[5]

However, the problem of the IR theory approach is that it ignores many culture-latent variables in shaping China's foreign policy behavior. For example, it is debatable whether China's foreign policy has indeed turned in an assertive direction or not as some media portrayed it in the 2010s (He & Feng, 2012; Johnston, 2013). In addition, it is too simplistic to argue that China is pursuing regional hegemony like the US did in the 19th century if we consider the positive impacts of China's Belt and Road Initiative (BRI) and its charm offensive toward its neighboring states. We do not suggest here that China does not want to expand its influence in the region. Instead, how China pursues its influence might be different from others.

For example, David Shambaugh (2005, p. 94) points out that 'both the logic and application of offensive realism [in China's case] are … unsustainable,' and China's rise does not necessarily lead to US decline or to inevitable conflicts between the two nations. In a similar vein, David Kang (2003, 2007) echoes and extends Shambaugh's critique by pointing out that IR theory, especially realism, is always 'getting Asia wrong,' because the realist assumption of an anarchical international system is not compatible with the traditional hierarchical nature of Asian international order.

The third approach to China's foreign policy is to integrate the area studies and the IR theory approaches. Two leading China experts, Thomas Christensen and Alastair Johnston, are pioneers in promoting this approach in the field. Although their own works are based on China's foreign policy behavior, they synthesize and advance various IR theories with their China-specific case studies. Therefore, their works not only shed light on China studies but also contribute to general theory-building in the IR field. For example, Christensen (1996) is seen as a leading scholar in building neoclassical realism—a realist theoretical framework that integrates both systemic effects and domestic transmission belts in the study of foreign policy, according to Gideon Rose (1998). Similarly, Alastair Johnston (1995, 2014) is a leading scholar with his work on socialization theory and constructivism although his main case studies focus on China's strategic behavior and its multilateral diplomacy after the Cold War.[6]

One notable institutional contribution of Christensen and Johnston is their joint effort in building a post-doctoral research program to train a new generation of China scholars with solid IR theoretical foundations and area studies skills.[7] For example, Kai He (2008a, 2008b; 2017; 2018; 2019) develops an institutional balancing theory to explain how states use different institutional strategies to pursue influence and power in the era of globalization (also see He & Feng, 2019; Feng & He, 2018; Feng & He, 2019b). Todd Hall (2015) integrates emotion theory with IR theory to shed light on the role of state-level emotional behavior in states' strategies and interactions with other states. Ja Ian Chong (2012) enriches state formation scholarship by examining the role of foreign intervention and external rivalries in affecting the institutionalization of governance in weak states. One feature of this new generation of China scholars is that they no longer concentrate on China as their sole research focus, as traditional area studies scholars do. Instead, China is only treated as a case study or an important source in their theory-building endeavors.

It is not our purpose in this essay to evaluate which approach in the study of China's foreign policy is better or the best. As mentioned before, both the area studies approach and the IR theory method have their respective strengths and weaknesses. While the area studies approach can go deeper culturally and socially in understanding China's policy behavior, the IR theory approach can reach a wider generalization in their arguments. The third integrated approach seems to maximize the strengths of the previous two methods, but it has a very high standard for scholars to achieve in both theoretical reasoning and language training.

Another important, but sometimes ignored, approach in the study of China's foreign policy is to systematically examine Chinese IR scholars. To be fair, the above three methods all take Chinese IR scholars seriously because Chinese IR scholars' comments and publications are important original sources in the study of China's foreign policy. Area studies scholars rely heavily on interviews to substantiate their findings. Because of China's one-party political system, Chinese IR scholars might be one of the most important, if not the only, interviewees who can be approached for most researchers, even though Lampton and Shambaugh did reach top policy makers for their research. Due to the language barrier, researchers with an IR theory approach might not be able to conduct interviews freely with Chinese IR scholars in China. However, they can still rely on printed materials, such as commentaries and scholarly publications written by Chinese scholars to support their arguments.

However, there is a 'utilitarian bias' regarding how to cite Chinese IR scholars in the study of Chinese foreign policy. Most research treats Chinese IR scholars as an important source of evidence for substantiating theoretical arguments or empirical findings. Although Chinese IR scholars have diverse views and internal debates, outside researchers might or might not be aware or fully understand what these different perceptions among Chinese IR scholars really mean. Consequently, a cherry-picking practice seems common when scholars selectively cite some Chinese scholars' publications in supporting their arguments but ignore others.

For example, if a scholar intends to argue for China's burgeoning nationalism, he or she can easily cite some commentaries written by Chinese scholars in the *Global Times*, which is a flagship nationalistic newspaper in China. It is not to suggest that the writings in the *Global Times* should not be cited at all. Instead, just like in any country, Chinese scholars have different views on diverse issues. How to wisely use Chinese scholars' commentaries in the *Global Times* is a judgment call for researchers studying Chinese foreign policy. One thing is certain, however, and that is that merely citing Chinese scholars publishing in the *Global Times* will not be good enough to gauge a complete picture of Chinese nationalism in the whole of society.

Another concrete example can be drawn from Michael Pillsbury's popular book *The hundred-year marathon: China's secret strategy to replace America as the global superpower* (2015). The main argument of the book is to suggest that China has set a secret plan to surpass the United States in the 100 years since the 1950s. This book has been seen as a roadmap of Trump's confrontational policy toward China (Schreckinger & Lippman, 2018). However, as Johnston (2019, pp. 189–190) points out, the whole book is built on a 'shaky foundation,' because

> the evidence that Pillsbury supplies, however, does not sustain this narrative. Indeed, the claim appears to rest on a misreading of one of his major sources—a book by Colonel Liu Mingfu entitled *The China Dream: Great Power Thinking and Strategic Posture in the Post American Era*. Liu is a People's Liberation Army (PLA) political work officer—that is, a propagandist, and not a strategist or commander.

In other words, Pillsbury seems to have become a victim of Chinese propaganda, in that he chose the wrong evidence to reach the wrong conclusion about China's foreign policy strategies.

The study of Chinese IR scholars—a research program in the making

Treating Chinese scholars as a subject of study, instead of a source of evidence, paves a new path in the study of China's foreign policy. There have been two waves or two directions in the study of Chinese scholars in foreign policy. The first wave is led by David Shambaugh (1991), who published his pathbreaking book, *Beautiful Imperialist,* in which he examines how China's 'America Watchers' perceived the United States between 1972 and 1990. Using China's America Watchers—Chinese IR scholars working on US-China relations—as a proxy measure of Chinese policy elites, Shambaugh argues that China's distorted and biased perceptions of the United States contributed to the fluctuations in bilateral relations between the two nations during the Cold War. Shambaugh's book is an exemplar of the area studies approach in the study of China's foreign policy with its extensive use of primary sources and interviews in China.

In the 1990s and early 2000s, other scholars followed Shambaugh's example in exploring Chinese IR scholars' perceptions of the United States (e.g., Callahan, 2008; Chen, 2003; Glaser & Medeiros, 2007; Wang, 2000; Zhang, 2005). For example, Yong Deng (2001) examines Chinese scholars' perceptions of US global strategy after the Cold War. Deng suggests that Chinese analysts have overall perceived a consistent and malign US strategy of global domination as well as the predatory nature of US hegemony. This perception of 'hegemon on the offensive' can well explain China's balancing efforts against the United States in the post-Cold War era.

In a similar vein, Rosalie Chen (2003) explores Chinese IR scholars' changing perceptions of the United States from the mid-1990s to the early 2000s. She suggests that Chinese IR scholars have seemingly reached a consensus on the hegemonic nature of US foreign policy, particularly its intention of containing a rising China. This negative perception of the United States from Chinese IR experts can also count for the troubled bilateral relations between the United States and China.

In 2012, based on their extensive interviews and fieldwork in Beijing, Andrew Nathan and Andrew Scobell (2012) published an article, 'How China sees America,' in *Foreign Affairs,* in which they examine 'the sum of Beijing's fears' toward the United States. They suggest that 'the Chinese believe the United States is a revisionist power that seeks to curtail China's political influence and harm China's interests' (Nathan & Scobell, 2012, p. 33). However, they point out that 'mainstream Chinese strategists do not advise China to challenge the United States in the foreseeable future' (Nathan & Scobell, 2012, p. 45). Therefore, they suggest that Washington should adopt a reassurance policy toward Beijing to expand common interests between the two nations.

While the first wave of scholarship on the study of Chinese scholars somehow looks for more consensus in Chinese perceptions and views, especially regarding the United States, the second wave of scholarship pays close attention to diverse views, especially the debates among Chinese scholars over various issue areas beyond the United States. For example,

Mingjiang Li (2008) investigates the Chinese IR scholars' debate on soft power. Because of the diverse and contending views on the sources, utilities, and means of soft power among Chinese scholars and pundits, Li suggests that it will be still a long way for China to use its soft power effectively to challenge the international order.

Daniel Lynch (2015) investigates how Chinese academic elites debate China's economics, politics, and foreign policy through intensive content analyses of Chinese publications and elite interviews. One interesting finding of Lynch's book is that Chinese IR scholars are more optimistic about China's future, including its economic and military power and standing in the world, than are Chinese economists. This self-confidence in the field of international relations might partially account for the assertive turn in Chinese diplomacy after the 2008 global financial crisis. Through examining how Chinese scholars debate the construction of a Chinese school of IR theory, Noesselt (2015, p. 444) also suggests that 'the search for a "Chinese" paradigm of IR theory [thus] finally reveals itself as part of China's global positioning ambitions.'

Shaun Breslin, as a leading scholar in the second wave of the study of Chinese scholars, is worth noting in particular. Relying on original Chinese scholarly publications and commentaries, he and his colleagues thoroughly examine Chinese perceptions of human security, the global order, core interests, plus China's international identity and power. For example, Breslin (2015) examines the evolution of China's perceptions of human security by delving into scholarly works and media publications. Through exploring how the concept of human security has been 'Sinicized' by Chinese scholars to reflect Chinese contexts and preferences, Breslin concludes that China might pursue an 'anti-norm' policy in the future global order.

In his widely cited article in *International Affairs*, Breslin (2013) argues that Chinese scholars hold five different views on China's role in the future global order and these different identities can explain China's diverse strategies toward different audiences in different issue areas. Breslin's findings further Shambaugh's argument on China as 'a deeply conflicted rising power with a series of competing international identities.' According to Shambaugh (2011, p. 7), 'understanding these competing identities is crucial to anticipating how Beijing's increasingly contradictory and multidimensional behaviour will play out on the world stage.'[8]

Besides China's role identity, Breslin and Jinghan Zeng dig into the Chinese debates over the so-called 'new type of great power relations' proposed by Xi Jinping in 2012 (Zeng & Breslin, 2016). By analyzing 141 Chinese language articles, they argue that 'the mainstream discourse views China as both a Great Power and a rising power at the same time' (Zeng & Breslin, 2016, p. 775). This double identity makes it hard to pin down what

China really wants strategically. However, they argue that China will not behave as a 'norm taker' dictated to by the outside powers. Instead, China will become a norm contester or even a norm shaper in the future international order (Zeng & Breslin, 2016, p. 775).

Another notable project on the study of Chinese scholars' internal debates regarding international relations is led by Kai He and Huiyun Feng (Feng & He, 2015; Feng & He, 2016; Feng, He, & Yan, 2019; Feng, He, and Li, 2019). With support from the MacArthur Foundation in the United States, the 'He and Feng project' conducted a three-year project entitled, 'understanding China's rise through the eyes of Chinese IR scholars.'[9] One part of the project is to systematically examine Chinese IR scholars' debates on China's key foreign policy perceptions, principles, and strategies, including the future international structure (国际格局), soft power, international status, comprehensive power, national interests, the non-interference principle, responsibility to protect, use of force, non-alliance strategy, maritime strategy, and economic diplomacy (see Feng et al., 2019).[10]

One interesting feature of the 'He and Feng project' is that all the contributors are Chinese IR scholars or originated from China (while holding teaching positions outside China). As mentioned before, one difficulty in the study of Chinese IR scholars is the language barrier, because it will need extensive research on original Chinese scholarly publications and related written sources. One added value of this project, therefore, is to 'let Chinese IR scholars tell their own stories' regarding their internal debates on international relations (Feng & He, 2019a). Moreover, the guidelines for the project explicitly asked all contributors to examine whether and how the Chinese IR scholars' debates have any influence on China's foreign policy (Feng & He, 2019a).

In particular, the 'He and Feng project' (Feng & He, 2019a) proposes four models to illustrate the relationship between Chinese scholars and foreign policy. The first model is the 'epistemic community' model suggesting that some Chinese scholars might have some direct influence in shaping China's foreign policy through shared policy beliefs within an epistemic community. The second model is the 'free market' model, in which scholars produce knowledge and make policy recommendations for the policy makers (consumers) to adopt (purchase) in a free marketplace of ideas.

The third model is called a 'policy signaling' model, because scholars can help policy makers test and signal some bold and controversial policy ideas and proposals to both domestic and international audiences. It helps the government to measure possible impacts and consequences of certain policy changes or new policies. The last model is called a 'policy mirroring' model, in which scholars' debates can reflect China's policy deliberations within the government as well as domestic political dynamics in the broader Chinese society.

The project's findings suggest that all of these four models have some purchase in China although the 'free market' model is the most popular one in explaining the relationship between Chinese scholars and foreign policy. Some prominent scholars, such as Wang Jisi, Yan Xuetong, Qin Yaqing, Shi Yinhong, and Wu Xinbo, are good examples of the 'epistemic community model,' in which people can draw some direct linkages between individual Chinese IR scholars and some policy outcomes. Qin Yaqing lectured on global governance at a Politburo study session. Shi Yinghong served as an advisor for the State Council. Yan Xuetong's 'moral realism' philosophy is seen as a major theoretical backbone of Chinese foreign policy transformation under Xi Jinping (Feng et al., 2019). One widely circulated story is that Wang Jisi's policy proposal of a 'moving West strategy' might have had some direct influence on China's Belt and Road Initiatives, because both emphasize the strategic importance of Central Asia (on the western side of the China) for China's grand strategy (Wang, 2012).

An illustration of the 'free market' model can be drawn from Wang Yizhou's 'creative involvement' theory and Yan Xuetong's 'China-needs-alliances' argument. Wang (2011, 2017) suggests that China needs to modify its 'non-interference' policy principle in order to cope with new challenges in the era of globalization. Yan (2011, 2013a, 2013b) argues that China needs to change its non-alliance policy and consider forming a military alliance with Russia due to its increasing competition with the US as well as system-level pressures. Both arguments are highly controversial and contested in the marketplace of ideas in Chinese academia. However, it seems that Wang's 'creative involvement' was 'purchased' by the government as seen from China's proactive involvement in the UN peacekeeping missions. Yan's 'China-needs-alliances' proposal, however, gets the cold shoulder from Chinese policy makers, because China's then Vice Foreign Minister Fu Ying insisted in her article in *Foreign Affairs*, that China's relationship with Russia is not an alliance, but a partnership (Fu, 2016).

The 'policy mirroring' model also has some empirical support. For example, the intense public debates on China's non-interference principle might reflect China's policy changes from 'keeping-a-low-profile' to 'striving-for-achievements.' However, the 'policy signaling' model seems to be not very popular among the contributors to the project. Scholars sometimes seem reluctant to admit that they are playing a signaling role for the government, which might jeopardize their academic integrity and scholarship. However, there are some exceptions. For example, Dingli Shen, a well-known IR scholar at Fudan University, published an article in July 2010 entitled 'Don't shun the idea of setting up overseas military bases' on www.China.org. (Shen, 2010).

Shen's idea of building military bases overseas is very controversial due to China's defensive military doctrine and ideological constraints. Five years after Shen's article, China opened its first military base in Djibouti in 2015. According to the *Financial Times*, Shen believed that 'the lack of international reaction to his article, which was published in English, might have been a factor in the Chinese decision to go ahead with a foreign base' (Clover & Lin, 2016). It is a good example of the 'policy signaling' model. However, it is not clear whether Shen sent this policy signal for the government voluntarily or accidentally.

This special issue of *The Pacific Review* 'China debates its global role,' co-organized by Shaun Breslin and Xiao Ren, is a commendable effort in expanding the study of Chinese IR scholars. Seven papers written by leading and emerging Chinese IR scholars in this special issue cover various aspects of scholarly debates over China's global role, including the contending views on world order (Chen and Zhang, this issue), the different perceptions of regional order (Wang and Meng, this issue), the various analyses on China's multilateral diplomacy and global governance (Liu, this issue), the dynamic quests for a Chinese School of IR (Ren, this issue), the divergent understandings of policy principle, diplomatic style, and tactics (Wei, this issue), the distinctive understandings of international law and China's diplomacy (He, this issue), as well as the contending schools of thought on foreign aid (Huang and Hu, this issue).

In particular, Ling Wei (this issue) examines three nuanced adjustments of China's foreign policy doctrine after the 2008 global financial crisis through Chinese scholarly debates. She suggests that Chinese scholars in general advocate a more balanced foreign policy, a cooperative relationship with the US, and deeper integration into the current international system. Dong Wang and Weizhan Meng (this issue) echo Wei Ling's argument but from a different regional order perspective. They suggest that Chinese scholars have not accepted the concept of '*Tianxia*/tributary system' proposed by a Chinese philosopher Zhao Tingyang. Instead, most Chinese scholars emphasize the importance of mutual accommodation between the United States and China and prefer a 'concert of great powers' for regional order.

If the debates of Chinese scholars can be seen as a proxy measure of the views of Chinese policymakers as mentioned before, it seems that the deep-seated American concern over China's challenge to the liberal international order is unwarranted. China's global role as discussed in this special issue is not only benign in orientation but also constructive in substance. However, the harsh reality is that Washington has labelled Beijing as a strategic competitor and rival in Trump's 2017 National Security Strategy. The prolonged trade war and the related technological war on 5 G and Huawei have signified an inevitable strategic competition or even rivalry between the two nations in the future. The intriguing question is: why do most Chinese scholars, as seen from this special issue, still seem to be optimistic about the future of US-China relations as well as China's international relations? In order to answer this question, we need to think about how to move this emerging research program forward, theoretically, methodologically, and internationally.

Moving forward—theory, method, and collaboration

This scholar-focused approach faces both theoretical and methodological challenges along the way to becoming a full-fledged research program in the study of China's foreign policy. First, the relationship between Chinese scholars and China's foreign policy still needs to be further theorized. Most research in the study of Chinese IR scholars focuses on the 'face value' of exploring the diverse or consensual views of Chinese scholars on a specific issue. To be fair, even 'face value' research is already a notable academic contribution because it assists the non-Chinese speaking world to better understand China's domestic discourses and debates. In order to answer Jeffery Legro's (2007) question: 'what China will want,' we need to open the black box of the Chinese society and explore its ideational dynamics, especially among Chinese IR scholars. As Shambaugh (2013, p. 16) points out, 'the IR discourse in China offers a "window" into official policy thinking, even if it is difficult to decipher (requiring the venerable Sinological tradition of 'tea leaf reading).'

However, merely presenting what Chinese scholars' views are and how they debate is only the first step of inquiry in the study of China's foreign policy. The relationship between scholars and policy is a highly debated question throughout the whole world. There is no simple causal link between Chinese scholars and foreign policies. We can neither argue that Chinese scholars have a direct influence on foreign policies, nor assume that Chinese scholars are simply influenced by the government's policies. As we have illustrated above, there are intense debates among Chinese IR scholars on various issues although this might or might not be known to the outside world.

The 'He and Feng project' (Feng & He, 2015, 2016, 2019a) has made some preliminary, hopefully inspiring, contributions by exploring the relationship between Chinese scholars and policy outcomes. In order to advance the research program, we need to make more theoretical efforts in deepening our understanding of the link between scholars and policies. For example, it might be useful to classify different types of Chinese IR scholars based on their professions. Bonnie Glaser and Philip Saunders (2002) examined the role of Chinese civilian research institutions, mostly think-tanks, in China's foreign policy decision-making process. Apparently, think-tank scholars perform a different function from what university-based scholars do in influencing China's foreign policy. In addition, there is a third type of scholar—'media scholars'—who are actively involved in the public media space, such as op-eds for newspapers, TV shows, radio broadcasting as well as various social media. These scholars might or might not publish articles in academic journals. However, their influence in society and the policy community cannot be ignored.

After typologizing different IR scholars, we need to draw the theoretical linkages between Chinese scholars and the study of China's foreign policy. The main job for think-tank scholars is to provide policy analyses and pro-posals to the Chinese government through internal reporting channels. These internal reports are not accessible for ordinary researchers. However, these think-tank scholars might also publish some academic articles and commentaries. Although these publications are not their major everyday work products, they might entail some signaling messages for the outside world, intentionally or not. In other words, the 'policy signaling' model should be taken seriously when studying the works of Chinese think-tank scholars.

Regarding university-based scholars, academic publication is one of the most important criteria in evaluating their research quality. Although Chinese scholars also intend to conduct policy-relevant research, they might not have direct channels like think-tank scholars to offer policy rec-ommendations or proposals for the policy community. Therefore, the 'free market' model will apply to university-based scholars in that they can have more time and energy to produce knowledge-based research and scholar-ship for the consumer—policy makers— to purchase in the marketplace of ideas. However, as we have discussed above, Chinese university-based scholars will not be able to control how and whether their research is val-ued or purchased by policy makers or not. Therefore, when we examine scholarly publications by Chinese university-based scholars, we cannot sim-ply draw a causal linkage between scholarly recommendations and China's policy orientations. However, we can capture the most controversial, but brightest, policy ideas on China's foreign policy in this marketplace of ideas.

As for the so-called 'media scholars,' they deserve some special attention in the study of China's foreign policy. Although Chinese media have been commercialized in recent years, the party still tightly controls the main-stream or official media in society. Therefore, scholars in this category have the most direct link with government bureaucracies in that they can help interpret and justify China's official policy to society as well as to the out-side world. However, this type of scholar might also serve a propogandist function, and their works might be highly politicalized for domestic purposes. Liu Mingfu, author of *The China Dream* mentioned above, is one of the media scholars in China who advocate strong ultra-nationalism in China. Although ultra-nationalism might serve some political agenda items of the Chinese government, it is by no means the only political and strategic thought that influences China's foreign policy. Researchers, therefore, need to learn a lesson from Pillsbury's eye-catching but flawed argument on China's secret 100-year strategic plan, because it would be misleading to read too much into this kind of propagandist work.

However, researchers should not ignore these 'media scholars' at all. In the study of this type of scholars, the 'policy mirroring' model might be useful. Since the main function of 'media scholars' is to justify China's foreign policy, we will not be able to get any critical insights on China's foreign policy from their commentaries and even publications in scholarly spaces. Academically and intellectually, their writings might have limited research value. Nonetheless, the rise and fall of their appearances and rhetoric in the media might reflect possible policy changes of China's foreign policy. Hypothetically speaking, if Liu Mingfu and other media scholars advocating ultra-nationalism appear less frequently in various media outlets, we can infer that the Chinese government might be constraining the influence of nationalism in foreign policy. If continued hype of ultranationalist works is seen from the frequent appearance of the 'media scholars' in various major media outlets, we can infer that China's foreign policy might be moving in a more nationalistic direction.

It is worth noting that we do not draw a link between the 'epistemic community' model and any type of Chinese scholars. It is not to suggest that the 'epistemic community' model is not valid in the study of Chinese scholars. Instead, we argue that this model might apply to any scholar who has a direct and personal connection with the policy community, no matter to which group of scholars in our typology he or she belongs. *Guanxi* 关系 or personal network might be one of the most important factors for scholars to exert influence in the policy community. However, this type of relationship might not be openly observable or known in public. It is definitely useful for researchers who study China's foreign policy to interview the most famous and notable IR scholars in China. However, we might need to take it with a grain of salt when we are tempted to equate scholars' fame with their influence in foreign policy.

We also need to emphasize that the proposed theoretical frameworks for different types of Chinese scholars in this essay are just illustrative or hypothetical in nature. Not only is serious empirical work needed in order to test these models, but also more creative theoretical models need to be introduced and proposed by other scholars. For example, beyond their job affiliations researchers might consider how other factors, such as theoretical inclinations and even geographical locations, might shape the different roles of Chinese IR scholars in influencing China's foreign policy. In addition, the relationship between scholars and social media as well as how scholars use social media to influence foreign policy are also worth exploring.

Besides theoretical innovation, we also need to consider how to advance the methodology in the study of Chinese scholars in foreign policy. The most traditional approach is to conduct interviews with Chinese scholars and perform textual and content analyses, qualitatively and quantitively, on Chinese scholarly and policy-related publications. As mentioned before, this traditional approach requires a high level of Chinese language skill, both in conversation and writing. In Shambaugh's words, it will require 'tea-leaf-reading' skill. It is why area studies scholars with intensive language training background are better equipped to pursue this approach than general IR scholars. It is also the reason why this special issue written by Chinese IR scholars on the internal debate on China's global role is exceptionally valuable, because the insights from these articles are not normally accessible to the English-speaking world.

Opinion surveys of Chinese scholars were also used by the 'He and Feng project' although the implementation of such a method has become more and more difficult in China given the tightened control of the government over survey research. He and Feng conducted four years of opinion surveys at the annual conference of the Chinese Community of Political Science and International Studies (CCPSIS) hosted by Tsinghua University in 2014–2017. Although the findings were inspiring and intriguing, one challenge was the limitation of the sample because the participants at the CCPSIS cannot fully represent the whole population of IR scholars in China (Feng, He, and Li, 2019). Nevertheless, their project paves a new methodological path for the study of Chinese IR scholars in foreign policy, which may encourage other scholars to follow in the future.

One methodological innovation of the 'He and Feng project' was to compare their survey findings with textual analyses of Chinese scholarly publications in five major Chinese journals during a similar time period (2013–2018). One interesting finding was that there are some discrepancies between what scholars said in surveys and what they published in their writings. For example, more than half of the survey participants state that they support changing China's non-alliance policy during their four-year surveys. However, in scholarly publications, only a few publications touched on this topic implicitly. In addition, a majority of the survey participants thought that China should have changed its policy toward North Korea in 2014–2017.

In contrast, scholarly publications seem to be silent on this topic although there are some public debates in popular media (Feng, He, & Li,

2019). This result from the 'He and Feng project' illustrates the value of encouraging more cross-methodological innovation in studying China's IR scholars in the future. This discrepancy attests to the fact that Chinese scholars might face 'double pressures' from both the government's censorship and self-censorship in their publications. It is understandable because all scholars, no matter whether they are Chinese or not, might be more cautious in writing than in anonymous surveys. Therefore, researchers who study Chinese IR scholars as a subject of inquiry should consider how to reduce such censorship effects on their findings.

Finally, international collaboration, especially between Chinese scholars and non-Chinese scholars, is of utmost importance for the success of this research program—the study of Chinese scholars in foreign policy analysis. This special issue, co-led by Breslin and Ren, is a good example of such an effort. In a similar vein, the 'He and Feng project' would not have been successful without support from Tsinghua University, especially from Professor Yan Xuetong and the Institute of International Relations, who co-sponsored the multi-year scholar surveys as well as international conferences. In the study of Chinese IR scholars in foreign policy analysis, there is an inherent advantage for Chinese scholars to tell their own stories due to their unique understanding of the Chinese way of conducting scholarly debates influenced by Chinese culture and tradition. However, since onlookers may also see most of the game, non-Chinese scholars can provide extra insights that contribute to theoretical development and methodological sophistication in the study of Chinese scholars.

Conclusion

China is one of the most defining actors in world politics in the 21st century. How to understand what Chinese policy makers think and grasp how China will behave is an imperative task for IR scholars, China specialists, and policy analysts. Traditional area studies methods, IR theory approaches, and an integrated approach employing the best of both academic traditions have made significant contributions to the study of China's foreign policy. One emerging research program, the study of Chinese IR scholars, also deserves special attention in the field due to the unique role that Chinese scholars play in the decision-making process inside China's one-party political system.

As Daniel Lynch (2015, p. x) points out, 'studying these (Chinese scholars') images can be useful in trying to assess what trajectory is likely to emerge, precisely because the elites are operating inside parameters imposed by the (still) awesomely powerful Party-state.' There is no direct or easy causal linkage between Chinese IR scholars and China's foreign policy;

however, we can use Chinese scholars to make sense of the policy boundaries and future directions of China's foreign policy. Through examining the existing research on the study of Chinese IR scholars in foreign policy, in this essay we have proposed three ways to move this emerging research program forward.

First, we need to identity different types of IR scholars and employ specific theories about their research implications. For example, in the study of university-based scholars a free-market model is appropriate to gauge new ideas and proposals in China's foreign policy. The writings and works of think-tank scholars might serve as policy signaling for the Chinese government. Writings and publications by media scholars might reflect China's domestic political dynamics as well as international aspirations. The principle of 'horses-for-courses' should be considered in theorizing the role of IR scholars in China's foreign policy decision-making processes.

In addition, the study of Chinese IR scholars in foreign policy needs to encourage a multi-method approach in which personal interviews, textual analysis, and survey research can complement one another in exploring what Chinese IR scholars think and how they can influence China's foreign policy. Moreover, international collaboration between Chinese scholars and non-Chinese scholars is also necessary for advancing the level of theoretical and methodological sophistication of this emerging research program. As China becomes a global actor in the future, the study of Chinese IR scholars in foreign policy will also deserve global efforts and international endeavors. It will thereby provide an opportunity to bring Chinese IR scholars and their works to the world stage. Therefore, the rise of Chinese IR scholars will likely accompany the rise of China.

Notes

1. There are some exceptions, for example, please see Jakobson and Knox (2010), International Crisis Group (2012), Lai and Kang (2014), Zhang (2016).
2. Here, we simply classify the major research traditions in the study of Chinese foreign policy for analytical purposes. In practice, scholars might conduct research across different traditions. For more detailed discussions of research methodology, such as Pekingological analyses of statements and discourses, historical analysis, qualitative and quantitative behavioral analysis, content analysis, interviews, surveys and structured interviews, and formal modelling, please see Johnston, (2006) and Johnston and Ross (2006).
3. For examples of other works by China experts, see Whiting (1960), Oksenberg (1978), Harding (1984), Foot (1995), Sutter (2013), and Kim (2015).
4. For criticisms of area studies, see Shea (1997).
5. For examples of other works with the IR-theory method, see Legro (2007), Buzan (2010), Allison (2017).
6. For examples of other works with an integrated approach, see Ross (1994), Goldstein (2005), Shirk (2007), Feng (2007), Fravel (2008), Kastner (2009), He (2009, 2018), He and Feng (2014, 2020), Liu and Liu (2019), and Pu (2019).
7. The postdoctoral program was first called 'Princeton-Harvard China and the World Program.' Later, it was renamed 'Columbia-Harvard China and the World Program,'

because Thomas Christensen moved from Princeton to Columbia in 2018. For details about the program and related scholars and publications, see https://cwp.sipa. columbia.edu/

8. One related topic that Breslin and his associates focus on is China's internal debate over 'core interests' (Zeng, Xiao, and Breslin, 2015). They suggest that Chinese scholars hold contending views on what constitutes China's core interests. This vague conceptualization of China's core interests 'makes it difficult to predict Chinese diplomatic behaviour.'

9. For details about this project, see https://www.griffith.edu.au/asia-institute/our-research/how-china-sees-the-world

10. In addition to the edited volume (Feng et al., 2019), the He and Feng project also published a special issue at the *Chinese Journal of International Politics* in 2017, see Pu (2017), Liu and Liu (2017), Mao (2017), and Qi (2017). The *Chinese Journal of International Relations* has become a major academic platform for Chinese IR scholars to present their views and perspectives on world politics. Other notable examples include Li (2019), Zhao (2019), Zhao and Zhang (2019) and Zhou (2019).

Disclosure statement

No potential conflict of interest was reported by the author(s).

Funding

This project is supported by the Australian Research Council [grant number FT160100355] and a policy-oriented research grant from the Korea Foundation.

References

Allison, G. (2017). *Destined for war: Can America and China escape Thucydides's trap?* Boston, MA: Houghton Mifflin Harcourt.

Breslin, S. (2013). China and the global order: Signalling threat or friendship? *International Affairs, 89*(3), 615–634. doi:10.1111/1468-2346.12036

Breslin, S. (2015). Debating human security in China: Towards discursive power? *Journal of Contemporary Asia, 45*(2), 243–265. doi:10.1080/00472336.2014.907926

Buzan, B. (2010). China in international society: Is 'peaceful rise' possible? *The Chinese Journal of International Politics, 3*(1), 5–36. doi:10.1093/cjip/pop014

Callahan, W.A. (2008). Chinese visions of world order: Post-hegemonic or a new hegemony? *International Studies Review, 10*(4), 749–761. doi:10.1111/j.1468-2486.2008.00830.x

Chen, R. (2003). China perceives America: Perspectives of international relations experts. *Journal of Contemporary China, 12*(35), 285–297. doi:10.1080/1067056022000054623

Chong, J. I. (2012). *External intervention and the politics of state formation: China, Indonesia, and Thailand, 1893–1952.* Cambridge: Cambridge University Press.

Christensen, T. J. (1996). *Useful Adversaries: Grand Strategy, Domestic Mobilization, and Sino-American Conflict, 1947–1958.* Princeton, NJ: Princeton University Press.

Clover, C., & Lin, L. (2016, September 5). China's foreign policy: Throwing out the rule book? *Financial Times.*

Deng, Y. (2001). Hegemon on the offensive: Chinese perspectives on US global strategy. *Political Science Quarterly, 116*(3), 343–365. doi:10.2307/798020

Feng, H. (2007). *Chinese strategic culture and foreign policy decision-making: Confucianism, leadership and war.* London: Routledge.

Feng, H., & He, K. (2015). America in the Eyes of America Watchers: Survey Research in Beijing in 2012. *Journal of Contemporary China, 24*(91), 83–100. doi:10.1080/10670564.2014.918404

Feng, H., & He, K. (2016). How Chinese Scholars think about Chinese Foreign Policy. *Australian Journal of Political Science, 51*(4), 694–710. doi:10.1080/10361146.2016.1202191

Feng, H., & He, K. (2018). Prospect theory, operational code analysis, and risk-taking behavior: A new model of China's crisis behavior. *Contemporary Politics, 24*(2), 173–190. doi:10.1080/13569775.2017.1407986

Feng, H., & He, K. (2019a). Why do Chinese IR scholars matter? In H. Feng, K. He, & Xuetong Yan (Eds), *Chinese scholars and foreign policy: Debating international relations* (pp. 3–19). London: Routledge.

Feng, H., & He, K. (2019b). A dynamic strategic culture model and China's behavior in the South China Sea. *Cambridge Review of International Affairs*, 1–20. doi:10.1080/09557571.2019.1642301

Feng, H., He, K., & Li, X. (2019). *How China sees the world: Insights from Chinese international relations scholars.* Basingstoke: Palgrave.

Feng, H., He, K., & Yan, X., eds. (2019). *Chinese scholars and foreign policy: Debating International Relations.* London: Routledge.

Foot, R. (1995). *The practice of power: US relations with China since 1949.* Oxford: Oxford University Press.

Fravel, M. T. (2008). *Strong borders, secure nation: Cooperation and conflict in China's territorial disputes.* Princeton, NJ: Princeton University Press.

Fu, Y. (2016). How China sees Russia: Beijing and Moscow are close, but not allies. *Foreign Affairs, 95*(1), 96–105.

Glaser, B. S., & Medeiros, E. S. (2007). The changing ecology of foreign policy-making in China: The ascension and demise of the theory of 'peaceful rise. *The China Quarterly, 190*, 291–310. doi:10.1017/S0305741007001208

Glaser, B. S., & Saunders, P. C. (2002). Chinese civilian foreign policy research institutes: Evolving roles and increasing influence. *The China Quarterly, 171*, 597–616. doi:10.1017/S0009443902000372

Goldstein, A. (2005). *Rising to the challenge: China's grand strategy and international security*. Stanford, CA: Stanford University Press.

Hall, T. H. (2015). *Emotional diplomacy: Official emotion on the international stage*. Ithaca, NJ: Cornell University Press.

Harding, H. (1984). *China's Foreign Relations in the 1980s*. New Haven, CT: Yale University Press.

He, K. (2008a). Institutional balancing and international relations theory: Economic interdependence and balance of power strategies in Southeast Asia. *European Journal of International Relations, 14*(3), 489–518.

He, K. (2008b). *Institutional balancing in the Asia Pacific: Economic interdependence and China's rise*. London: Routledge.

He, K. (2017). Explaining US-China Relations: Neoclassical Realism and the Nexus of Interest and Threat Perceptions. *The Pacific Review, 30*(2), 133–151. doi:10.1080/09512748.2016.1201130

He, K. (2018). Role conceptions, order transition and institutional balancing in the Asia-Pacific: A new theoretical framework. *Australian Journal of International Affairs, 72*(2), 92–109. doi:10.1080/10357718.2018.1437390

He, K. (2019). Contested multilateralism 2.0 and regional order transition: Causes and implications. *The Pacific Review, 32*(2), 210–220. doi:10.1080/09512748.2018.1465455

He, K., & Feng, H. (2012). Debating China's assertiveness: Taking China's power and interests seriously. *International Politics, 49*(5), 633–644. doi:10.1057/ip.2012.18

He, K., & Feng, H. (2014). China's bargaining strategies after the Cold War: Successes and challenges. *Asian Security, 10*(2), 168–187. doi:10.1080/14799855.2014.914496

He, K., & Feng, H. (2019). Leadership transition and global governance: Role conception, institutional balancing, and the AIIB. *The Chinese Journal of International Politics, 12*(2), 153–178. doi:10.1093/cjip/poz003

He, K., & Feng, H. (2020). The institutionalization of the Indo–Pacific: Problems and prospects. *International Affairs, 96*(1), 149–168. doi:10.1093/ia/iiz194

He, Y. (2009). *The search for reconciliation: Sino-Japanese and German-Polish relations since World War II*. Cambridge: Cambridge University Press.

Ikenberry, G. J. (2008). The rise of China and the future of the West—Can the liberal system survive. *Foreign Affairs, 87*(1), 23–37.

International Crisis Group. (2012, April 23). *Stirring up the South China Sea*. Report, Author.

Jakobson, L., & Knox, D. (2010, September 26). *New foreign policy actors in China*. SIPRI Policy Paper.

Johnston, A I., & Ross, R., eds. (2006). *New directions in the study of China's foreign policy*. Stanford: Stanford University Press.

Johnston, A. I. (1995). *Cultural realism: Strategic culture and grand strategy in Chinese history*. Princeton, NJ: Princeton University Press.

Johnston, A. I. (2006). 中国外交政策研究：理论趋势及方法辨析 [Trends in theory and method in the study of Chinese foreign policy]. 世界经济与政治 [World Economics and Politics], (8), 64–73.

Johnston, A. I. (2013). How new and assertive is China's new assertiveness? International Security, 37(4), 7–48. doi:10.1162/ISEC_a_00115

Johnston, A. I. (2014). Social states: China in international institutions, 1980–2000 (Vol. 144). Princeton, NJ: Princeton University Press.

Johnston, A. I. (2019). Shaky foundations: The 'intellectual architecture' of Trump's China policy. Survival, 61(2), 189–202. doi:10.1080/00396338.2019.1589096

Kang, D. C. (2003). Getting Asia wrong: The need for new analytical frameworks. International Security, 27(4), 57–85. doi:10.1162/016228803321951090

Kang, D. C. (2007). China rising: Peace, power, and order in East Asia. New York, NJ: Columbia University Press.

Kastner, S. L. (2009). Political conflict and economic interdependence across the Taiwan Strait and beyond. Stanford, CA: Stanford University Press.

Kim, S. S. (2015). China, the United Nations and world order. Princeton, NJ: Princeton University Press.

Lai, H., & Kang, S. J. (2014). Domestic bureaucratic politics and Chinese foreign policy. Journal of Contemporary China, 23(86), 294–313. doi:10.1080/10670564.2013.832531

Lampton, D. M. (2001). Same bed, different dreams: Managing US-China relations, 1989–2000. Berkeley: University of California Press.

Legro, J. W. (2007). What China will want: The future intentions of a rising power. Perspectives on Politics, 5(03), 515–534. doi:10.1017/S1537592707071526

Li, M. (2008). China debates soft power. The Chinese Journal of International Politics, 2(2), 287–308.

Li, W. (2019). Towards economic decoupling? Mapping Chinese discourse on the China–US Trade War. The Chinese Journal of International Politics, 12(4), 519–556.

Liu, F., & Liu, R. (2019). China, the United States, and order transition in East Asia: An economy-security Nexus approach. The Pacific Review, 32(6), 972–995. doi:10.1080/09512748.2018.1526205

Liu, R., & Liu, F. (2017). Contending ideas on China's non-alliance strategy. The Chinese Journal of International Politics, 10(2), 151–171.

Lynch, D. (2015). China's futures: PRC elites debate economics, politics, and foreign policy. Stanford, CA: Stanford University Press.

Mao, W. (2017). Debating China's international responsibility. The Chinese Journal of International Politics, 10(2), 173–210. doi:10.1093/cjip/pox006

Mearsheimer, J. J. (2001). The tragedy of great power politics. New York, NJ: WW Norton & Company.

Mearsheimer, J. J. (2010). The gathering storm: China's challenge to US power in Asia. The Chinese Journal of International Politics, 3(4), 381–396. doi:10.1093/cjip/poq016

Nathan, A. J., & Scobell, A. (2012, September/October). How China sees America. Foreign Affairs, 91(5), 32–47.

Noesselt, N. (2015). Revisiting the debate on constructing a theory of international relations with Chinese characteristics. The China Quarterly, 222, 430–448. doi:10.1017/S0305741015000387

Oksenberg, M. (1978). Dragon and eagle: United States-China relations: Past and future. New York, NY: Basic Books.

Pillsbury, M. (2015). *The hundred-year marathon: China's secret strategy to replace America as the global superpower*. New York, NY: Henry Holt and Company.

Pu, X. (2017). Controversial identity of a rising China. *The Chinese Journal of International Politics, 10*(2), 131–149. doi:10.1093/cjip/pox004

Pu, X. (2019). *Rebranding China: Contested status signaling in the changing global order*. Stanford, CA: Stanford University Press.

Qi, H. (2017). Disputing Chinese views on power. *The Chinese Journal of International Politics, 10*(2), 211–239. doi:10.1093/cjip/pox005

Rose, G. (1998). Neoclassical realism and theories of foreign policy. *World Politics, 51*(1), 144–172. doi:10.1017/S0043887100007814

Ross, R. S. (1994). *Negotiating cooperation: The United States and China, 1969–1989*. Stanford, CA: Stanford University Press.

Schreckinger, B., & Lippman, D. (2018, November 30). The China Hawk Who Captured Trump's 'Very, Very Large Brain', Politico.

Shambaugh, D. (1991). *Beautiful imperialist: China perceives America, 1972–1990*. Princeton, NJ: Princeton University Press.

Shambaugh, D. (2005). China engages Asia: Reshaping the regional order. *International Security, 29*(3), 64–99. doi:10.1162/0162288043467496

Shambaugh, D. (2011). Coping with a conflicted China. *The Washington Quarterly, 34*(1), 7–27. doi:10.1080/0163660X.2011.537974

Shambaugh, D. (2013). *China goes global: The partial power* (Vol. 111). Oxford: Oxford University Press.

Shea, C. (1997, January 10). Political scientists clash over value of area studies. Chronicle of Higher Education.

Shen, D. (2010, January 28). Don't shun the idea of setting up overseas military bases. *China.org.cn*. Retrieved from www.china.org.cn/opinion/2010-01/28/content_19324522.htm

Shirk, S. L. (2007). *China: Fragile superpower*. Oxford: Oxford University Press.

Sutter, R. G. (2013). *US-Chinese relations: Perilous past, pragmatic present*. Lanham, MD: Rowman & Littlefield.

Wang, J. (2000). *Limited adversaries: Post-Cold War Sino-American mutual images*. Oxford: Oxford University Press.

Wang, J. S. (2012). 王缉思: "西进", 中国地缘战略的再平衡, ['Moving West' is China's geostrategic rebalancing], 环球时报 [*Global Times*], 10–17. Retrieved from https://opinion.huanqiu.com/article/9CaKrnJxoLS

Wang, Y. Z. (2011). 创造性介入: 中国外交新取向 [*Creative involvement: A new direction in China's diplomacy*]. Beijing: Peking University Press.

Wang, Y. Z. (2017). *Creative involvement: A new direction in China's diplomacy*. London: Routledge.

Whiting, A. S. (1960). *China crosses the Yalu: The decision to enter the Korean War*. Stanford, CA: Stanford University Press.

Yan, X. (2011, June 8). 中国可以考虑改变不结盟政策. [China may consider changing its non-alliance strategy], 国防时报 [*Defense Times*].

Yan, X. (2013a). 历史的惯性 [*The inertia of the history*]. Beijing: Zhongxing Publisher.

Yan, X. (2013b). 从韬光养晦到有所作为: 中国崛起势不可挡 [From keeping a low profile to striving for achievements: China's rise is unstoppable]. 中国经济周刊 [*Weekly Journal of Chinese Economy*], 43, 44–47.

Zeng, J., & Breslin, S. (2016). China's 'new type of Great Power Relations': A G2 with Chinese characteristics?. *International Affairs, 92*(4), 773–794. doi:10.1111/1468-2346.12656

Zeng, J., Xiao, Y., & Breslin, S. (2015). Securing China's core interests: The state of the debate in China. *International Affairs*, *91*(2), 245–266. doi:10.1111/1468-2346. 12233

Zhang, B. (2005). Chinese perceptions of American power, 1991–2004. *Asian Survey*, *45*(5), 667–686. doi:10.1525/as.2005.45.5.667

Zhang, Q. (2016). Bureaucratic politics and Chinese foreign policy-making. *The Chinese Journal of International Politics*, *9*(4), 435–458.

Zhao, K., & Zhang, H. (2019). Projecting political power: China's changing maritime strategy. *The Chinese Journal of International Politics*, *12*(2), 229–261. doi:10.1093/cjip/poz004

Zhao, M. (2019). Is a new Cold War inevitable? Chinese perspectives on US–China strategic competition. *The Chinese Journal of International Politics*, *12*(3), 371–394. doi:10.1093/cjip/poz010

Zhou, J. (2019). Power transition and paradigm shift in diplomacy: Why China and the US March towards strategic competition? *The Chinese Journal of International Politics*, *12*(1), 1–34. doi:10.1093/cjip/poy019

Grown from within: Building a Chinese School of International Relations

Ren Xiao

ABSTRACT

Over the years, this author has been involved in the 'Chinese school of International Relations (IR)' debate. In this article I try to reflect on these discussions or debates from which some insights can be retrieved to inform future research and further growth of a Chinese School of IR. Should a Chinese school be set as the goal? If so, how should this be pursued? This debate and the relevant efforts have proved to be a promising movement in the Chinese IR community, demonstrating that a Chinese school of IR is inevitable and it actually is evolving. A theory is a generalization or cluster of generalizations. This article argues that from the 'Tsinghua approach', a 'moral realism' has sprung up. Qin Yaqin's theorizing is centered around relationality and has been productive. A theory of symbiosis in the world community is being developed by a group of Shanghai-based scholars, and a 'symbiosis school' has grown up. Overall, four distinct theories of Chinese origins, i.e., relational theory, moral realism, *tianxia* theory and *gongsheng*/symbiotic theory, have appeared. Thus, IR theory-building in China in the first two decades of the 21st century has rendered the question 'why there is no IR theory in China' obsolete.

There has been a growing interest in International Relations (IR) scholarship outside the Anglo-American world in recent decades (Kristensen, 2015, p. 162; Tickner & Waever, 2009). This should be seen as a positive development in fostering greater understanding and appreciation of non-Western theories and worldviews. In Asia, the Chinese IR community has made impressive progress in terms of making a Chinese contribution to the discipline of IR during the first two decades of the 21st Century. This progress deserves a careful examination; and that is what this article plans to do.

Since the mid-1990s, the Chinese IR community has been undergoing a process of reflecting upon the state of IR studies in China, analysing its progress, defects, and possible future agenda. This process is epitomized by articles appearing in major Chinese international studies journals and discussions in local or national IR conferences.[1] While the progress and achievements over the past quarter of a century are positively acknowledged, there are also expressions of dissatisfaction and debates about what the desirable goals should be and what kinds of efforts need to be made.

These discussions in turn must be viewed against the backdrop of the global attention paid to China's rise in the world arena, and the essential question of how China sees its relations with the global community. Those reflections show that IR in China now has more self-consciousness than ever and a growing sense of autonomy. In this article, it is argued that of all the new developments in China's IR studies, the most important and valuable has been the explorations for building a 'Chinese school' of international relations. The purpose of this article is to analyse the movement and its achievements, and to look into its implications for the future of Chinese IR.

The quest for a 'Chinese school'

At the outset, this quest was just a lonely call for an upgraded, more autonomous form of Chinese IR that might be called a 'Chinese School.' Later on, this appeal won supporters and proponents while arousing criticisms and disagreements as well. Today, it is becoming a mainstream view, if not a consensus, for the Chinese IR community.[2]

As early as August 1987, a different but related appeal was made for an 'IR with Chinese characteristics.' During the first national conference on international relations theory held in Shanghai, Huan Xiang, then Director-General of the China Center for International Studies and a long-time foreign policy advisor to Chinese leaders, put forward the need for China's own IR theory with Chinese characteristics (Shanghai Society of International Relations, 1991). Among the proponents who followed, Liang Shoude, a Peking University professor, is a leading representative. Since the early 1990s, Liang has advocated that Chinese international political theory-building should stress 'Chinese characteristics.' This means recognizing specific characters of IR in individual countries as well as diversities among them, but also emphasizing a pioneering spirit and the pursuit of excellence (Liang, 1997). He elaborates, 'The Chinese characteristics of the study of International Politics refer to basing oneself upon China and to face up to the world, as well as to study objective laws of the evolution and development of international politics from a Chinese perspective' (Liang, 2000, p. 31). He explained that stressing 'Chinese characteristics' is to bring to light true features of international politics and to build well China's own discipline of International Politics through autonomous studies (Liang, 2000, p. 33). But what a 'Chinese perspective' was, and how work of that kind should be carried out, were among the issues not sufficiently explained.

For some of the sceptics, an 'IR with Chinese characteristics' was more or less a transplant from the well-known political slogan 'socialism with Chinese characteristics.' For others, Chinese studies of international relations, theory or not, are necessarily conducted in the Chinese way and therefore it is unnecessary to appeal. For instance, Wang Yizhou of the Chinese Academy of Social Sciences (CASS) 'tends to refrain from saying so [that there is a Chinese IR] at this stage', due to the reason that 'thus far we have made little contribution to International Politics as a discipline' (Wang, 1995, pp. 11–12). Another basis for scepticism was concern that Chinese IR needed to distinguish ideological pursuit from the search for national interests, and policy analysis from academic research.

If the contention surrounding 'Chinese characteristics' tended to be hollow, the proposition of a 'Chinese school' and its winning of support are apparently a pursuit that is more self-conscious, more serious, and much richer in contents. This initiative is also more solidly-based than the former 'Chinese characteristics' contention.

The early calls for a 'Chinese school of international relations theory' came in 2000, from two younger generation scholars who were with Peking and Fudan Universities. In Peking University scholar Mei Ran's view, 'the students of IR theory in China should make their research have creativeness and independence in order to breed a "Chinese school of international politics".' He argued, 'To display a "China brand" is to expose the unreasonable circumstances of the current global IR community and to stress the significance of transforming this situation, as well as to demonstrate the courage of the Chinese scholars to participate in this change' (Mei, 2000). For Mei, one country's (i.e., the United States') domination of a discipline was an abnormal phenomenon and was not favourable to its healthy development. Therefore, 'Single-centeredness' had to become multi-centeredness.

In August 2000, Fudan University scholar Ren Xiao published an article in Beijing-based journal *Ou Zhou* (*Europe*). The article argued that Chinese specialists must have aspirations to put forward Chinese theoretical viewpoints and propositions. They should then proceed to develop systematized theories of international politics. This objective can appropriately be called a 'Chinese school of international relations theory (Ren, 2000)'. The article went on, '[we] can be cautiously optimistic about the invention of a Chinese school of IR theory. To erect Chinese theories is not simply to seek the opposite to the Western theories, or to search for a difference for difference's sake, but rather means that we Chinese, instead of just absorbing and transplanting, should have a spirit of thinking independently and should not always follow others. In a word, the Chinese should forge their own theoretical contributions (Ren, 2000).'

The article aroused mostly sceptical responses from Chinese colleagues. Su Changhe pointed out that any school as such was not self-proclaimed but rather needed to be recognized by others, while Zhang Xiaoming held that a school appeared to be too remote a goal.[3] Undoubtedly, scepticism should be given some credit. At the same time, while it is true that a school does not simply come into being when it is given a name, subjective efforts do matter for it to take shape. To defend the value of a 'Chinese school' as a goal, this author published another essay in 2003 titled 'Learning from the English School.' The article insisted that it is a desirable objective and worthwhile effort 'to construct a Chinese school' (Ren, 2003).

In September 2002, Qin Yaqin of China Foreign Affairs University wrote a general preface for a translated series of books on international relations theory published by Peking University Press. The preface said:

> Hope this book series will turn into 'stones from other hills that serve to polish the jade of this one', and will enable colleagues of the Chinese IR community, through learning, thinking, and criticizing, to put forward original IR theories and to establish a Chinese school of international relations theory (Qin, 2002).

In this way, Qin explicitly concurs and advocates the value of the objective of creating a Chinese school of IR.

In a similar fashion, some other scholars call for 'indigenization' (ben tu hua) of IR. One of them, Li Bin of Nanjing University, argues that:

> The key to the indigenization of Chinese international relations theory is to put forward a systemic explanation of international relations that is in China's core national interest... An indigenized Chinese IR theory, in a sense, is to link the revival of the Chinese nation via the country's economic development with cooperation and conflict in the world... A Chinese theory should neither be some footnotes of what the leaders say, nor a 'cartoon-style' illustration of Chinese foreign policy. Instead, it has to be a product that is deduced from scientific paradigms, or enlightenment that is naturally and deliberately obtained through a process of telling 'historical stories.' To me this is the most crucial objective and format requirement for China's IR theoretical innovations (Li, 2003).

Here, Li Bin emphasizes what a Chinese IR theory *is* and *is not*. He points out that people must go beyond just 'adding footnotes' or 'illustrating' the doctrines of Chinese foreign policy which used to be the case in the past. However, it is unclear what he means by 'indigenization', a term his article fails to explain in a more detailed way. As will be discussed later, the issue turns out to be a crucial one, and not without debate.

It is Qin Yaqing who has most fully elaborated upon and conducted the most comprehensive exploration so far of the 'Chinese school' issue. He also appears to be its most optimistic proponent, stating that the formation of a Chinese school of international relations is not only plausible but also destined (Qin, 2006). He provides three bases for his optimism.

First, a Chinese school is possible because a social theory differs from a natural theory in that the former has a distinct geo-cultural birthmark. In other words, any social theory is by nature built on a particular geo-culture, which is different from so-called indigenization. The indigenous conscious-ness and characteristics that he himself argues stress that a theory grows in the context of a certain culture and it further develops and gains universal-ity by interacting with other cultures. Second, three sources can provide a basis for a potential Chinese school, namely, the *tian xia* worldview and the practice of the tributary system, the revolutionary thoughts and practices in China's search for modernity, and the ideas and practice of the reform and opening-up. Third, over the past century and a half, China's greatest prob-lem has been its identity dilemma vis-à-vis the international system. Nowadays, the rapid development, the great social transformation, and the fundamental ideational changes have enabled China to begin solving this dilemma fairly successfully. China's interactions with the international sys-tem and the resultant debates will inevitably lead to the emergence of a Chinese school of International Relations Theory (Qin, 2006).

The growing self-awareness of the Chinese IR community has to do with the attention paid to the English School, as well as American IR. American theories have exerted widespread influence in China. To a large extent, this kind of US influence is inevitable and the reasons are obvious. American IR scholars are many, they have access to substantial funding, products and numerous journals, and there are opportunities for Chinese scholars to study or to spend a research stay in American universities. No other country can match the US on these fronts. As a result, it is not surprising that American IR theories and schools of thought have had, and are still having, a considerable impact upon many other countries. China is certainly no exception. Therefore, the stage of experiencing American IR influence is impossible to bypass for a country whose scholars are latecomers to IR theory.

Nonetheless, China differs from smaller countries. It is a major power and a civilization-state with a long continuous history and rich culture. It should not be a surprise that scholars in such a country may be more cul-turally and academically self-conscious than in a country such as South Korea.

As Chinese IR scholars became aware of the enormous influence of American IR, they began to tap into the products and thoughts of the English School of international relations. Leading scholars of the English

School, such as Martin Wight, Hedley Bull and Barry Buzan and their works became well known in Chinese academic circles and their theories drew much attention in China. Chinese IR scholars realized, with some surprise, that outside the US there has also been IR research of a high quality which is no less in standard, and perhaps even greater, than US research. Consequently, major books by the English School scholars, such as Bull's *Anarchical Society*, Wight's *Power Politics*, Buzan and Richard Little's *International Systems in World History*, and John Vincent's *Human Rights and International Relations*, were translated into the Chinese language. The English School's humanistic orientation and its historical perspectives come to be much appreciated among the Chinese IR community and its influence continues to expand.

The works of the English school were important on several basic counts. These works were of interest in their own right and served as an alternative to American IR. At the same time, they highlighted the question of whether there might be a Chinese school of IR – if there could be an English school, why not a Chinese school?

Chinese IR scholars' wariness of the dominance of American IR is a further reason why the 'Chinese School' thesis has been put forward. As Wang Yizhou notes, 'Professor Chen Lemin[4] has criticized the Chinese IR research community for permitting the American IR to exert too much influence and counseled attention to scholarships from other regions such as Europe' (Wang, 2003). Wang agrees with Chen and asks 'how to go beyond the America-centered situation?' He points out, 'there has to be a direction we are moving to, no matter whether it is feasible at the moment. We must try to do so self-consciously' (Wang, 2003). The feeling that 'there is too much American sort of thing' seems to be common within the Chinese IR community. Seeking novelty by whatever means characterizes the American academic culture, and if one just follows the new developments of others, one would always lag behind other people and forever. A logical question then is, 'how to establish China's own perspective, style, and language in international relations theory?' (Wang, 2003).

With discussion and research ongoing, 'Chinese school' explorations are unfolding and deepening. Below I will attempt to analyze them in turn.

What is a 'Chinese school'?

What is a 'Chinese school'? For Pang Zhongying, a 'Chinese school' is a cluster of IR theories with Chinese characteristics, rather than referring to a single school. In other words, there can be two or more schools of thought within a Chinese school. The English school of international society theory tells people that pursuing a 'Chinese school' may not be that far away. He asks, 'China has its own long-standing political ideas, philosophy, and history, why can't we construct our own IR theory by relying on so rich historical accumulations?' (Pang, 2003). In other words, the Chinese have favorable conditions to build their own IR theory.

But how should scholars proceed to build China's own IR theories, and by what means? Pang further proposes an 'open-style autonomous development' approach. He explains that openness means a readiness to learn from the methods, concepts, and knowledge of others, and to participate in worldwide dialogues and exchanges as well as to diffuse Chinese views. Autonomous development means to integrate Chinese political ideas, social science traditions, historical experiences, and East Asian international relations practice into IR theoretical considerations. In this way, the situation of Western theories dominating world IR theory will hopefully be altered (Pang, 2003) and a healthy Chinese alternative perspective may emerge.

Others also argue that the development of Chinese theory itself is to be achieved by exchanges among what might be called differing Chinese schools. For example, Yu Zhengliang of Shanghai Jiaotong University suggests that Chinese IR theory should not be a unified or sole IR theory. Its development depends on the learning that will come from contention among differing schools. For Yu,

> A 'school' refers to a specific research group, who share similar research orientations, inclinations, and academic styles. It comes into being because of specific academic inheritance, specific perspective on observing matters, and distinct judgment of reality and future. Schools of thought are essential for activating academic studies. Interactions between them give rise to theoretical innovation. Forming schools of thought plays a very important part in inheriting academic cream and bringing up academic masters. No schools, no masters (Yu, 2005).

For Lu Peng, one fundamental question remains to be answered: Why is a Chinese school or Chinese IR theory necessary and possible? (Lu, 2006). The question involves how people understand the possibility of social sciences. Proponents of Monism argue that both natural science and social science are sciences with no fundamental difference between them. Proponents of Dualism argue that the natural world and the social world are different. The fundamental difference between them is that in the social world, both the subject and object are human beings, and hence there is no possibility for being value-free.

The proponents of monism believe that IR theory is trans-border, and anything that can be called theory is universal, because the existence of law does not change as time and/or space change. By contrast, the proponents of dualism believe that natural science theory does not vary across borders, while, they say, social science theory can differ from one country to another. The reason is that in the social science field, 'understanding' as an important way of obtaining knowledge is confined by culture – which differs from place to place. The differences in geo-culture, history, ways of thinking and collective memory can lead to differences in human understanding. Therefore, a national label for an IR theory is not only possible, but also inevitable (Qin, 2006).

While Qin and this author are on the dualism side, Yan Xuetong and others are on the monism side. For Yan, all IR theories are universal and they have no national characters. Therefore, the goal of building a Chinese IR theory is not achievable (Yan, 2006). This appears to be an extreme viewpoint. Of course, a theory is a generalization to explain and decode wide-ranging phenomena. However, inevitably there exists subjective orientation, by no means unrelated to what country one comes from. One's national environment and living conditions undoubtedly affect the concrete shape and contents of his/her theoretical construction. Therefore, the situation is much different from natural sciences.

Inevitably, an answer to the question 'Why is a Chinese school necessary at all?' is that the Chinese IR circles, dissatisfied with the status-quo, aspire to 'become a producer of knowledge' (Wang, 2006). In Wang Zhengyi's view, just as countries might be labelled 'core' or 'periphery' in the sphere of economics and politics, countries may also be considered core or periphery in the production of intellectual concepts and models – with the periphery countries consuming core area products. However, this situation is not unchangeable. Through scholars' efforts, countries of the peripheral areas may also become producers of knowledge (Wang, 2006). Therefore, it is the Chinese IR community's dissatisfaction with the current situation, the aspiration to change the imbalance between its consumption and production of knowledge, and to become a producer of knowledge itself, that have stimulated the call for and initiation of Chinese theory and even a 'Chinese school'.

Yu Zhengliang correctly points out that pioneering spirit, courage and insight will be needed to invent and build China's own IR theory. Yu questions the widely held international anarchy hypothesis in IR theories. He argues that since nation-states came into being, the international order has in fact been undergoing an evolutionary process with the commitment of the international community to the establishment of norms for nation-state behavior. Those efforts include international laws, and many kinds of international covenants and international institutions. Global value convergence has been brought about by three major developments; namely scientific revolution, informational revolution, and global interconnectedness. Though the anarchical nature of the international society has not yet been entirely overcome, these three developments have catalyzed the increased orderliness and great transformation of international society (Yu, Yugang, & Changhe, 2003, pp. 225–226).

Yu argues that when international politics becomes global politics, a world order characterized by anarchy is undergoing a far-reaching transformation. The system is no longer just a combination of fully independent and separate actors. The system and its many kinds of actors are mutually dependent and penetrable, and impact upon and constrain each other, and that has led to a multi-dimensional networked structure. As a result, the fundamental assumption of the mainstream schools of Western IR could turn invalid (Yu et al., 2003, pp. 225–226). This is a bold and theoretically courageous argument.

Consequently, between 'destruction' (po) and 'construction' (li), what is to be erected? What should be the theoretical starting point of a new theoretical paradigm? For Yu et al. it is a paradigm of global shared governance. The core principle of this new paradigm is simply joint governance; i.e., shared governance based on global multilateral cooperation. According to this paradigm, state-centeredness gives way to cooperative common governance as the center of gravity. The purpose of the paradigm is to mobilize resources worldwide to resolve a crucial problem; i.e., the serious shortage of supply of global management capability, as well as to accomplish the shift of authority from state monopoly to societal power sharing (Yu and Chen 2005). If this line of argument is on the right track, hopefully the theory will be further developed.

The issue of 'question' or 'core question'

Chinese IR scholars generally agree that to build Chinese theory requires asking China's own original questions. In that case, what are those questions? Chinese IR scholars' understanding has experienced a process of gradual deepening.

In a 1998 article on the state of Chinese international studies, this author noted critically that 'in our research process, sometimes even questions are imported from abroad' (Ren, 1998). Su Changhe, agreeing with that observation, further noted that theory building has to be based on research into important and meaningful questions. For Su, 'question consciousness' is the most significant component for scientific research and quality for researchers. Although those who find questions may not be able to answer, meaningful questions can inspire further research by others (Su, 2003).

In the same issue of the journal, *World Economics and Politics*, Zi Zhongyun published an essay titled 'Theoretical innovation comes from studying new questions'. Zi argued that some Western 'IR theories' actually are detached from reality and simply are created and circulating within universities. Academics invent jargon that appears profound, but makes little sense (Zi, 2003). For Zi, 'new questions' must come from real life.

At about the same time, Pang Zhongying proposed considering core concepts that might lead to the birth of one or a couple of 'Chinese schools' (Pang, 2003). The development from 'question' and 'question consciousness' to 'core concept' illustrates the trajectory of thinking of Chinese IR researchers. Zhang Zhizhou sees question awareness and academic self-consciousness as the basic premises of Chinese IR theory-building, which need to be strengthened and promoted. In combination, they will enable Chinese IR scholars to rethink their 'indigenous' IR theoretical resources and to increase their self-confidence in the use of Chinese culture to inform theory (Zhang Zhizhou 2005).

For Shi Yinhong, the efforts for the Sinicization of IR theory should be grounded in three components: first, Chinese questions, values, sentiments, and even partial 'Chinese discourse' (*zhongguo huayu*); second, understanding of the fundamental currents in the world and the healthy direction for China's development; and third, study of and selective borrowing from IR theories in the West. To combine the above is exactly the direction in which the Sinicization of IR theory should be moving. Based on the current status of the IR theory research, a particular emphasis has to be put on 'Chinese questions', especially those significant questions for China as a country (Shi, 2004).

Again, it is Qin Yaqing who has most systematically examined the issue to date. Qin points out that although Chinese IR achieved rapid development over the past two decades, there still has yet to emerge original theory and a theoretical school – important symbols of a discipline. According to Qin, an original Chinese IR theory must have three basic characteristics: first, its growth must be based on partial (Chinese) culture, historical tradition, and contemporary experience; second, it must be of generalized nature, i.e., achieve a kind of universality beyond partial tradition and experience; and third, its core theoretical assumption must be of incommensurable nature with other IR theories. By these three criteria, there is still no original theory in China today that can be called the basis for a school. Why? One key reason is the absence of a core theoretical question (Qin, 2005).

What should be the core theoretical question of Chinese IR? Qin argues that China's peaceful integration into the international community can become such a core question. With regard to the process of peaceful socialization of a rising power, realism largely holds a negative attitude, while neither liberalism nor constructivism has conducted genuine empirical studies. Thus, the theory is lacking in empirical basis.

However, China provides the best case for studying peaceful socialization of a rising power. Regarding China's peaceful integration into the international community as the core question and theorizing on it means to theorize about the process of peaceful socialization of a rising world power.

Consequently, a series of concrete questions – whether China will peacefully become integrated, what conditions will prompt China to become integrated in a peaceful way, and what being a responsible member of the international community implies for China – will spring up from the core question and should constitute a significant part of the Chinese IR research agenda (Qin, 2005: 166). In this way, Qin has given his answer to which core question a Chinese school should grasp, and he has accordingly outlined the corresponding research agenda. Qin has obviously pushed the study of the 'core question' issue forward. Since China's rise continues to impact upon the twenty-first century world politics and economics to a great extent, and as this has raised a number of questions for China itself, there is surely great potential for Chinese-style theory to grow.

Scientific vs. humanistic approaches

How valuable are the scientific and humanistic approaches respectively for constructing a Chinese school of IR? There has emerged a debate that is rarely seen in Chinese IR circles. The debate was vividly epitomized in a symposium on 'Research Methods in International Relations', held in September 2003 in Beijing. The symposium was jointly organized by two leading scholarly journals, *Chinese Social Science* and *World Economics and Politics*.

In the debate, Yan Xuetong of Tsinghua University, who has been a leading figure strongly advocating the 'scientific method,' argues that to promote Chinese understanding of international relations, there is no better and more effective method than the scientific one. What is the 'scientific method'? For him, the scientific method stresses objective and empirical studies. Aspects that characterize a scientific method and distinguish it from other methods are that it emphasizes procedures, is empirical and those who employ it observe common rules (Yan, 2004a). Though the scientific research method has its own limitations and cannot solve all problems, it is able to solve problems that other research methods are not able to (Yan, 2004a). First, by controlling variables, it helps understand the relationship between relevant factors. Second, in contrast to qualitative analysis, which provides insight into the direction of change, quantitative analysis can help grasp the degree of change. Third, it has the accurateness of a forecast. The scientific research method has obvious advantages, including, but not restricted to, these three (Yan, 2004b).

However, this author holds that in international studies, as in other social science fields, different research methods, including the so-called 'scientific method', have both strengths and weaknesses. Methods other than the 'scientific method' (e.g., comparative historical analysis) are not necessarily less useful. I do not agree to the 'there-is-only-one-road' style view and instead advocate methodological diversity and mutual tolerance. For me, methodological diversity will not impede the development of IR research at all. To the contrary, it will only foster the development of IR (Ren 2004).

The critics argue that, in social science research, it is impossible for a researcher to be 'value-free' because it is not possible to detach oneself from viewpoints and/or feelings stemming from social connections. Moreover, social sciences are about man and his/her activities, rather than the natural world. International politics is a social phenomenon and a social construction. Events that take place in a particular cultural context have to be explained in line with their particular cultural meanings. It is impossible to do this by a natural science method. Furthermore, there exist a number of internal difficulties in using scientific method in IR studies. For instance, it is not possible to repeat controlled experiments, and many variables cannot be measured effectively. Finally, all social and historical phenomena are distinct and particular and thus researchers have to be careful to make generalizations (Zhou, 2006, pp. 432–433).

To defend their position, some proponents of the scientific method admit that for some issues it may not be quite appropriate to perform controlled empirical research, and instead, to adopt a humanistic approach may be more suitable to achieve good analysis. However, this does not invalidate the usefulness of empirical research in social sciences, which is much closer to natural science research. The impossibility of being fully 'value-free' does not constitute the rationale not to use scientific method. In economics and in other subjects, scientific method is widely employed although researchers are not totally value-free.

Qin Yaqing adopts a middle ground by proposing a 'third culture' and seeking an intersection of the scientific and humanistic approaches. He states that in the West there have been lots of debates on 'scientific vs. humanistic' alternatives and now the same debate has taken place in China. This is a good thing. In a sense, no methodological debate; no disciplinary development. In the mid-1990s, because Chinese IR was still mixed with policy studies and was largely lacking methodological consciousness at the time, some Chinese IR scholars began to stress the importance of research methods on the basis of scientific realism, and to make the case for its employment in IR research. He particularly points out that as a matter of fact, the scientific and humanistic approaches can converge fully on some aspects and should be combined and integrated. That is exactly what he advocates: to find a third way that can be called a 'third culture' and to pursue a fusion of the scientific and humanistic approaches. For Chinese IR, the combination and integration of the two approaches appears to be a more meaningful middle ground (Qin, 2004). In that regard, the Beijing symposium turned out to be a useful dialogue and exchange between the exponents of the scientific and humanistic approaches in the Chinese IR community.

On the 'humanistic' side, this author further argues that social science research certainly *needs* subsidiary of the humanities. Not just this, it cannot be without subsidiary of the humanities. The same is also true for International Relations. The proposition in China for 'scientization' (*ke xue hua*) has been deeply influenced by American behaviorism, and yet behaviorism actually has serious defects. Because of the pursuit for a 'pure science', a lot of studies along the line of behaviorism step onto an 'ahistorical' road. As a result, history disappears. Enormously rich and colorful linguistic, social, cultural, and religious phenomena are sacrificed for the sake of 'scientization'. However, in the final analysis, all the humanities and social sciences are 'studies of man.' Social sciences without humanistic subsidiary make no sense. After all, elements of humanities are essential for IR theory-building (2004b).

The 'scientific vs. humanistic' exchanges prove to be a useful debate, for it propels the two sides to think more thoroughly about their own arguments and to improve their respective discourses. The two contending views also provide room for a constructive third way. To me, well-designed empirical studies are still much needed in Chinese IR today. In this sense, Yan Xuetong and his associates have been making interesting and meaningful efforts for more 'scientific' work to grow. That being said, it would be misleading to overstate the value of 'scientific' method and depreciate other methods. Instead, methodological diversity will better serve Chinese IR.

For Shi Yinhong of the humanity-oriented camp, almost all truly brilliant IR theorists emphasize the necessity to extract nutrition from history; otherwise he or she would merely be a 'technique' person. IR theory builders should regard history as their teacher, and should familiarize themselves and understand history well. At the same time, they should be able to theorize on historical facts and materials (Shi, 2004). This emphasis on history is clearly shared by the humanity-oriented IR scholars in China.

Dissatisfied with a prevalent circumstance in IR theoretical research in China recently, Shi feels that it is crucial to properly define 'international relations theory'. In the eyes of many students of IR, only those that emerged after IR as a discipline had came into being in the early twentieth-century in Anglo-American countries, or even those sprang up since Hans Morgenthau, can be called 'IR theories'. Shi stresses that this assumption is incorrect. Those pre-twentieth century and pre-Morgenthau theoretical considerations of international relations (or even relatively systematic efforts made for theoretical construction) should by no means be excluded from the 'IR theory' category. Chinese researchers should not chiefly pay attention to, introduce, and review those 'newly emerging' theories. The newest things are sometimes, or even often, not the best things. Therefore, the main focus of theoretical studies in China should not become studies of the existing IR theories, especially contemporary theories, or even today's American IR theories. Rather, they ought to be theoretical explorations of international relations. 'IR theory' should be broadly defined, and it is a kind of theoretical thought or thinking about international studies (Shi, 2004). These views are indeed a very important alert for the IR theoretical research community in China. In recent years, younger generation Chinese scholars and research students have shown a strong interest in IR theory. Some of them have a mistaken impression, as if IR theory is realism plus liberalism plus constructivism and let those labels eclipse lots of specific topics that are extremely rich and worth being studied. According to Shi, this situation is not conducive for the healthy development of theoretical research and therefore has to be adjusted.

All of these debates stimulated Chinese IR scholars to rethink and further refine their ideas. After calls had been repeatedly made for creating 'Chinese theory' in both singular and plural, or making a Chinese contribution to world IR, they became well aware that they must take the next steps to invent Chinese theory or innovative theoretical thinking for international relations. The world is faced with enough problems, and a better world as an ideal has to be pursued. However, very often questions about 'the good life' are off the table, and international theory is limited to discussions of survival (Snidal & Wendt, 2009, p. 1). As a result, IR theories risk becoming trivial and are far removed from thinking about the big questions the world situation raises. Emanating from the movement for a 'Chinese school of IR', IR scholars working in different Chinese institutions, either for or against the notion of a 'Chinese school', realized that they should make their own real efforts to theorize on world politics. Over more than a decade, four kinds of original theories with Chinese characteristics have sprung up on the horizon. They are relational theory, moral realism, *tianxia* theory, and *gongsheng*/symbiotic theorization. I will proceed to discuss them respectively.

Relational theory

In the Chinese school of IR movement, Qin Yaqing pioneered in theory-building by employing *guanxi*/relationality and this has yielded important theoretical products (Qin, 2016; 2018). For Qin, what constitutes the nucleus for much of mainstream Western International Relations Theory is individual rationality, which is a key concept abstracted from Western culture. In contrast, his 'relational theory of world politics' centers around the concept of 'relationality' as the metaphysical component of its theoretical hard core. It conceives the IR world as one composed of ongoing relations, assumes international actors are actors-in-relations, and takes processes defined in terms of relations in motion as ontologically significant. The relational theory rests on three important assumptions. First, the IR world is a universe of interrelatedness. Second, actors are and can only be 'actors-in-relations'. And third, 'process', a key concept in the relational theory, is defined in terms of relations in motion.

According to Qin's relational theory, distinguishing from mainstream IR theories that center on, more or less, the concept of individual rationality, a crystal of the cultural sediments especially since the Enlightenment, the relational theory is cultivated and sustained by relationality. It does not deny rationality, but argues for rationality conditioned by relationality. Moreover, a balanced and mutual inclusiveness of rationality and relationality can produce a healthy synthesis for both theoretical and practical purposes. Qin's relational theory puts forward the logic of relationality, arguing that actors base their actions on relations in the first place. It uses the Chinese *zhongyong* dialectics as its epistemological schema for understanding relationships in an increasingly complex world. This theoretical framework enables us to see the IR world from a different perspective, reconceptualize key elements such as power and governance, and make a broader comparison of international systems (Qin, 2016).

Separately from Qin's work, Chih-yu Shih and his associates, who are based in Taipei, have also carried out innovative research and developed a theory of 'balance of relationship' (BoR) (Shih, et al., 2019; Shih & Huang, 2016). BoR is a concept that explains the limited relevance of differences in ideas, institutions, identities and material forces as variables that matter in IR. It is also a general theory of long-term IR. The strategy of balance of power (BoP) or bandwagoning is often triggered by fear. The classical realist assumption in IR theory has unremittingly followed the idea that 'the strong do what they can and the weak suffer what they must' (Thucydides quoted in Shih & Huang, 2016, pp. 181–182). By contrast, the rationale for applying BoR is to achieve reciprocation and harmony. Such a rationale could only appear when the state's need for survival can be met by an enhanced sense of relational security. In fact, the BoR theory is rich in content and has the potential for further development.

Building on relationality or BoR, Qin and Shih have fruitfully developed their theories respectively, and their products combined have become established as an emerging theory and have significant influence. Looking into the future, their relational theories may well travel to different parts of the world as well.

The Tsinghua approach and moral realism

A group of Chinese scholars, based at Tsinghua University and led by Yan Xuetong, have developed the so-called 'Tsinghua approach'. Two kinds of work or espousal are characteristic of the approach. One is that they attach much importance to the role of 'scientific method' in the study of IR. And two, for years they devoted enormous energies and time to refining the thoughts of pre-Qin (founded in 221BC) Chinese thinkers. Throughout the process, they formed a distinct style that came to be called the 'Tsinghua approach'. According to Zhang Feng, three features characterize the Tsinghua approach. First, its motivation originates in a desire to enrich modern IR theory and, no less importantly, to draw policy lessons for China's rise today. Second, it seeks to do this by drawing upon China's political thought from the golden age of Chinese philosophy in the Spring and Autumn and Warring States period (770-222 BC). And third, it applies Yan's own brand of scientific method to the analysis of ancient Chinese thought (Zhang, 2012).

In the process, Yan, a self-identified realist and a firm believer of realism of IR, was inspired and somewhat reshaped by ancient Chinese thought. While studying power transition and enlightened by Xunzi and other thinkers, Yan came up with what he calls 'moral realism'. For Yan, moral realism is an international relations theory which emphasizes that political leadership determines power balance between major forces and shifts in the international systems. The core question this theory studies is how rising powers displaced existing dominant world powers, namely, the principles of world center shift. Throughout human history, there have been numerous cases of power shift. When the world was no longer divided into multiple separate regions, world center shift became one of the central questions for the study of international relations. This includes the causes for the leading countries to lose their leadership status and the causes for the corresponding shift of the international system. Moral realism's key explanation for these two questions is that the rising country's political leadership exceeds that of the existing leading country (Yan, 2014, pp. 102–103).

For Yan, while based on the realist assumptions of strength, power and national interest, his theory has rediscovered the role of morality in the rise of great powers at the unit level. Moral realism considers national political leadership and national power to be the two core factors that decide the orientation of a state's foreign strategy. Political leadership is distinguished into four categories: 'inaction', 'conservatism', 'activism' and 'struggle'. When a state's national power has reached the level of a leading or rising country, whether it possesses morality and the level of it can have a significant impact on the result of national strategy, especially in terms of establishing international norms. Moral realism differentiates itself from other strands of realism by acknowledging a different means to power shift. It introduces two key variables of political leadership and strategic reputation, and sees political leadership as a key factor for strategic choice and in determining either the success or failure of a rise. While affirming material power as the foundation of a successful rise, it goes one step further by pointing to political leadership as the fundamental for international power balance. A rising power's morality or strategic reputation can increase its international power of political mobilization, which in turn reshapes the international power configuration and may even help establish a new international norm or order.

In his article 'International Leadership and Norm Evolution', Yan argues that dominant states influence the evolution of international norms through three means, namely, 'a process of demonstration-imitation; a process of support-strengthening; and a process of punishment-maintenance'. Of these three processes, the first (demonstration-imitation) is the traditional Chinese approach, as at its essence is 'lead by example'. Demonstration-imitation refers to the dominant power setting an example through its own behavior, which other states may find appropriate to follow and eventually accept as a behavior norm (Xu & Sun, 2016).

The policy ramifications of moral realism differ from those of either structural realism or offensive realism (Yan, 2014, pp. 126–127). Yan holds that China should base the establishment of a new international order on the values of 'fairness', 'justice' and 'civility'. According to Yan, borrowing from ancient Chinese thought of 'political determinism', realist theorists (himself in particular) have reintroduced the variable 'political leadership' and invented a theory of 'moral realism'. This theory categorizes types of 'national leadership' to explain changes in the international power configuration, and types of 'international leadership' to explain changes in international norms. This theory can not only explain the objective international phenomena at present, but also has certain predictive power for the trends of international political development (Yan, 2016).

Moral realism is essentially a newly revised form of widely acclaimed realism. Adding 'moral' to 'realism' with which Yan identifies himself, like 'defensive realism' some Chinese IR scholars espouse, is interesting but may face difficulty in advancing very far. Its value-added needs to be further justified.

Tianxia theory

The conception of 'tianxia' has reemerged recently and is undergoing a debate both within and outside China. In April 2005, a Chinese philosopher, Zhao Tingyang, published a short but important book Tianxia Tixi (Zhao, 2005). It soon aroused lively discussions and drew considerable attention from the Chinese IR community. By reviving the tianxia idea, Zhao attempted to rediscover and emphasize the usefulness and significance of China's intellectual legacy, i.e., the *tianxia* idea. For Zhao, the *tianxia* idea is such a significant conception not only for China, but also for the whole world. Through his rediscovery and reinterpretation, Zhao has promoted *tianxia* to 'a philosophy for the world institution'. Zhao's supporters have warmly embraced his reinterpretation and development, while his critics have offered sharp criticisms.[5] Later Zhao further developed his thoughts. For him, the world needs a new order of being, an order of the internalized world, and that is what he calls the '*tianxia* system'. In any case, these exchanges provide researchers with an excellent opportunity to reexamine the traditional Chinese concept of *tianxia* to see how useful it can be for the world's future.

Tianxia is both an idea and an ideal at the same time. As an idea, it is a framework that incorporates geographical, political, and cultural elements. As an ideal, it aims at eventually heading for '*tianxia yijia*' ('one family under the sun') which is an all-inclusive (*wuwai*) order. Within the framework, no difference is made between the internal and external, but rather simply a process of extending the same principles and ideals from inner to outer as a continuum, which ends up with a whole of combining the near and the distant, namely, a *tianxia* order.

The Chinese view of *tianxia* has a long history and a rich tradition. The idea originated in the Zhou period and matured in the Qin and Han periods. As an intellectual framework in which position, level, and cultural perspectives converge into one concept, it lasted for over two thousand years and maintained an amazing continuity. Its prominent feature has been that the Chinese always keep with them an ideal beyond reality (Xing, 1983). Given that, there is indeed a rich Chinese tradition of *tianxia*, the question now becomes: building on the historical *tianxia* idea, what should be inherited and further developed? In that regard, Zhao's efforts of reinterpreting the *tianxia* idea and adapting it to today's world therefore should be given credit. William A. Callahan criticized Zhao by stating that 'proposals for a "post-hegemonic" system often contain the seeds of a new (and often violent) system of inclusion and exclusion: *tianxia* presents a popular example of a new hegemony where imperial China's hierarchical governance is up-dated for the twenty-first century' (Callahan, 2008, p. 759). However, this criticism is mistaken because the *tianxia* idea is unquestionably inclusive rather than exclusive. Also, Callahan wrongly takes it for granted, without the necessary supporting evidence, that a reinvigorated *tianxia* concept is politically related to, if not geared toward, a 'new hegemony.' In fact, the transformed *tianxia* idea has intellectual and theoretical value exactly because it is a scholarly rather than a political enterprise.

As his point of departure, Zhao argues, 'because China is increasingly an integral part of the world, we must discuss the implications of Chinese culture and thought for the whole world'. 'What needs to be studied are the contributions China can possibly make to and the responsibilities China should bear for the world' (Zhao, 2005, pp. 2–3). For Zhao, if the serious self-criticisms and even severe self-attacks over the past one and a half centuries were a movement to 'examine China,' then 'rethinking China' has been the most important intellectual movement since the 1990s, and is intellectually more deep-seated as well as scholarly far more profound. Moreover, in today's China there is no shortage of all kinds of Western ideas. What is lacking is China's own overall thinking and holistic thought. The historical implications of 'rethinking China' lie in the efforts to revive China's own capability of thinking, and to rethink China's place in the world. In other words, this is to think about China's road ahead, as well as China's role and responsibility in the world (Zhao, 2005, pp. 6–7).

Zhao argues that China's world view *is* the *tianxia* theory. China's world view of '*tianxia*' is above and beyond the level of the 'state'. While Western thought thinks of conflict, Chinese thought is capable of thinking of harmony. Distinct ideas do exist and they can serve as an important and constructive anchor for the world's future. They cannot be expressed within the Western intellectual framework, and thus they need to be displayed in a new framework and to be developed into a new theory (Zhao, 2005, pp. 15–16). Again, for Zhao, the option is the *tianxia* theory. Especially important in this theory is the principle of 'all-inclusive' (*wuwai*), which can help eliminate a stubborn flaw in Western thought, i.e., the 'enemy assumption' or the 'politics of separation,' developed from the 'pagan awareness' which is based on religious irrationality. On the contrary, *tianxia* is a theory of converting enemy to friend. It advocates conversion (*hua*化), which is a way to attract others rather than to conquer them (Zhao, 2005, p. 33).

For Zhao, *tianxia* is a world system based on the ontology of coexistence. The *tianxia* system may not guarantee that everyone is happy, but can hopefully guarantee peace and security. Its institutional arrangements no longer allow hostile behavior to be a beneficial strategy or have any profit to make. In this sense, the *tianxia* system is a good enough world. As the philosophical foundation of the *tianxia* system, the ontology of coexistence has the following fundamental ideas: first, the intention of existence is continuing to exist, and therefore the meaning of existence lies in the future. Second, the future does not have inevitability but only possibility. Thus, the future issue is to turn a possible world into a reality, so the ontology of being is also a creationology. Third, for human beings, the ontology of being starts from 'facio ergo sum'. Any future unfolds and is determined in the interactive acts between self and others. The *tianxia* system expects a world order of existence based on the principle of coexistence (Zhao, 2015, p. 9).

Zhao's reinterpretation of *tianxia* is stimulating and thought-provoking. Two of his main points can be stressed: one, *tianxia* is a larger and a more desirable unit of analysis for us to look at the world as it goes beyond the state; two, *tianxia* is a philosophy and a worldview that can hopefully lead to the ideal of *tianxia*, one home.

In the world of today, humankind is faced with enormous challenges and problems in different parts of the world, including those concerning conflict and development. The Western model has undergone various frustrations in that regard. Very often, the West has tended to apply elections, as reduced from Western-style democracy, to everywhere in the world, as if it is a panacea. Practice over the past years has suggested this does not work well, and in some cases has even given rise to more problems, such as intensifying ethnic strife. There is an increasing demand in the world for new ways to redress the balance. Against this backdrop, an emerging school of thought argues that the *tianxia* idea may provide an alternative way to think about various kinds of relationships in the world and to forge a new and more constructive way forward. In this sense, *tianxia* theory has the potential to make a difference in tomorrow's intellectual world.

Gongsheng/symbiotic theory

Partly enlightened by research into social symbiosis in the Chinese sociological community over the years, a group of Shanghai-based IR scholars have introduced 'gongsheng/symbiosis' into IR research. Since being established, it has become an autonomous project which has been consolidated and broadened. *Gongsheng*-focused research has been carried out with respect to the traditional interstate system in East Asia, evolution from *guanxi* to *gongsheng*, symbiosis in the international society, and so forth. These efforts have led to a drive for a *gongsheng*/symbiotic theory, and this drive has opened a new avenue for IR theory building in China.

Gongsheng theory is built on differences and diversity rather than sameness between and among things. The fundamental assumptions of the *gongsheng* theory include the following:

First, the nature of the world is pluralism. Plurality is pervasive in all areas of human society. In different parts of the world, there exist multiple civilizations, traditions, cultures, religions, values, habits and customs. It is within a broader environment of plurality that agents – whether individuals or groups – interact. Pluralism is, and will continue to be, the reality of human society. As such, international theory has to be built on this fundamental reality.

Second, there are all kinds of differences between and among things. Just like 'no two snowflakes are alike', difference exists in all areas of human life throughout the world. This difference is an inevitable byproduct of endogenous development, whereby societies prioritize different values given their distinct local histories, traditions and practices. Differences are a given and this is the nature of the world in which we live.

Third, different things can peacefully or even amicably coexist and interact with each other on the basis of equality. They do not necessarily need to clash. Interaction or engagement can and does happen without the need to eliminate differences.

Fourth and finally, different things, through constructive interactions, can together achieve advancement. This sort of constructive interaction does not lead to a result of one swallowing or assimilating the other. Rather, through comparison and mutual learning, they are able to appreciate each other. Acting autonomously allows them to achieve progress and development together. Their respective acts are not forced to be taken and compulsory, but rather a voluntary behavior on the basis of treating each other on an equal footing.

Therefore, the *Gongsheng* theory starts from the very nature of existence of the surviving things in the world. Its ontological foundation is the fundamental fact that the world is plural/multiple in terms of whatever, be they actors, countries, cultures, institutions, religions, civilizations … this is what L.H.M. Ling terms 'Multiple Worlds', which comprise modes of thinking, doing, being, and relating. Multiple Worlds intersect with and reframe the Westphalian World to produce the kind of hybrid, creole, or mélange legacies we have today. These are known, otherwise, as the histories, philosophies, languages, memories, myths, stories, and fables of the human condition (Ling, 2014, p. 13).

In any human society, things depend on one another like a web of all kinds of interrelatedness. As socially existing entities, they are all mutually dependent, and that is the state of *gongsheng*/symbiosis. In a symbiotic situation, there has to be a balance – between big and small, or strong and weak, for example – to ensure a mutually reinforcing existence.

For the *gongsheng* theorists, while the Western thoughts or formulas have their admirable merits, they also have their limitations. In the 21st Century, when the world is faced with a range of vast and daunting problems, the limitations of the Western formulas have been exposed, and they are not able to cope with or resolve the world's problems. Today's liberal international order is porous and problematic, if not in crisis. Multiculturalism is failing. In this disruptive situation, Western thought has to, and also can be, complemented by the ideas that emanate from other parts of the world. *Gongsheng* is such an idea and theory. When properly pursued, *gongsheng* can be a remedy for today's challenging problems, and a pathway leading to a better world. In a *gongsheng* system, agents avoid seeking any form of maximization of power, interest or status. Such maximization acts may lead to the breaking of *gongsheng*. Instead, *gongsheng* allows reasonable interests and satisfactory status. In the *gongsheng* order, each actor has an appropriate place. The places actors are in are equally important as they complement one another regardless of their sizes. Only together do they form a dynamic and robust order in which no one can claim superior cultural or value to others. Therefore, it is a systemic theory that helps handle various relationships for an orderly existence.

In regard to the lingering and protracted issue of war and conflict, the *gongsheng* theory also has a viewpoint. Eliminating war and conflict in a sustainable way has been humankind's common desire and ideal throughout history. For this goal to be attained, people have put forward many proposals or formulas, and one of them, noble and lofty, is to create a 'world government' to govern the globe. 'World government' is a longstanding idea, which originates in past centuries and lingers on into the contemporary era. For many years, people have thought about a transcendent approach to the problem, and they repeatedly came up with the idea of creating a supranational institution in order to maintain perpetual peace. It can be argued that this may be a desirable approach and some progress toward a better world has been made over the years. However, scholars today must rethink the following questions: why haven't global institutions such as the United Nations (UN) achieved the degree of effectiveness that its founders wished for? What is the crux of the problem? Can non-Western intellectual resources complement the existing ideas and help establish a better world order? Ren (2019) argues that Chinese thought, and particularly the *gongsheng*/symbiotic idea, can offer an important intellectual backing. Different from the 'world government' way of thinking, *gongsheng*/symbiosis does not believe that there has to be a supreme authority to guarantee world peace and order. Rather, it holds that this can be achieved through building on the existing sovereignty system. 'Symbiotic peace' simply is peace through symbiotic means. In such a situation, various entities relate with one another and grow together symbiotically. Their robust coexistence and parallel growth does not require them to become the same, but rather to allow and respect the various differences among them. If this could be erected as a principle for global affairs, a different picture of the world might emerge (Ren, 2019).

Conclusion

The movement to build a 'Chinese school' of IR has attracted attention and won supporters in China. To a great extent, there has emerged a consensus in the Chinese IR community that Chinese International Relations scholars should make necessary effort through hard work for China's own theory-building; and the goal can probably be called a Chinese school of IR. This has been fairly widely accepted, explicitly or implicitly, and is now well known. The movement has resulted from an increasing growth of academic self-consciousness of Chinese IR. It also demonstrates the growth of self-confidence among the Chinese scholars in international studies, and highlights their aspirations to 'become producers of knowledge' rather than just 'consumers'.

Taken as a point of departure, the research into and discussions related to building a Chinese school of IR continues to unfold and deepen in China today. IR scholars have debated four key issues: the possibility and necessity of a Chinese school, what its core question should be, the debate of 'scientific vs. humanistic' approaches, as well as how to tap into the broad and profound Chinese intellectual and cultural resources. By and large it is a consensus that such a 'Chinese-style exploration' has to be based on the significant issues that are facing China as a rising power in the world, and to seek solutions through China's own independent research.

For most Chinese IR theorists, in this endeavor the task of highest priority is probably not to seek and build a macro theory, but rather to employ and develop theories at the micro and intermediate levels. A 'Chinese school' or 'Chinese characteristics' in the holistic sense requires the various research organizations and groups to give full play to their respective advantages and to form their own 'schools' or 'characteristics' first. This appears to be a practical means to carry out meaningful research work and to accumulate progress.

In the meantime, it is undoubtedly acknowledged that the objective of building a Chinese school is by no means be easy to accomplish. Rather, it will require persistent commitment, hard work and long-term efforts. Only consistent and painstaking work can eventually yield genuine fruits. This reality indicates a long path ahead.

In the 2010s, different schools of thought or theory started to take shape and they are growing in Chinese IR. The most prominent ones include relational theory, moral realism, *tianxia* theory, and *gongsheng* theorization. This is an encouraging indication of the persistent prosperity of the IR discipline and theory-building within China. The emergence of Chinese IR theories has largely rendered the question 'why is there no non-Western international relations theory?' (Acharya & Buzan, 2010) obsolete. This process is continuing.

Notes

1. The three major nation-wide conferences, among others, were those held in 1987, 1998 and 2004 respectively, all in Shanghai. The resultant products are three edited volumes.

2. For example, in December 2004, a National International Relations Theory Conference was held in Shanghai, and it adopted such a banner as "Creating Chinese Theories, Building a Chinese School." Comparing the three major IR theory conferences, it can be seen that the above-mentioned banner of the 2004 event appeared to be an important step forward.

3. Private conversations.

4. Chen Lemin was a senior research professor and well-known Chinese scholar who used to be Director of the Institute of European Studies at the Chinese Academy of Social Sciences.

5. For the criticisms, see, for example, Zhou Fangyin, "*Tianxia tixi shi zuihao de shijie zhidu ma?*" (Is the Tianxia System the Best World Institution?) *Guoji zhengzhi kexue* (Quarterly Journal of International Politics) No. 14, February 2008. For more balanced discussions, see Xu Jianxin, "*Tianxia tixi yu shijie zhidu,*" (The Tianxia System and World Institution), *Guoji zhengzhi kexue* (Quarterly Journal of International Politics) No. 10, February 2007. Zhao later wrote a response article "*Tianxia tixi de yige jianyao biaoshu*" (A Brief Expression of the Tianxia System) which appeared in *Shijie jingji yu zhengzhi* (World Economics and Politics), No. 10, 2008.

Disclosure statement

No potential conflict of interest was reported by the author.

References

Acharya, A. (2014). Global International Relations (IR) and regional worlds: A new agenda for international studies. *International Studies Quarterly*, *58*, 1–13. doi:10.1111/isqu.12171

Acharya, Amitav and Barry Buzan, eds. (2010). *Non-western international relations theory: Perspectives on and beyond Asia*. London and New York: Routledge.

Callahan, W. A. (2008). Chinese visions of world order: Post-hegemonic or a new hegemony? *International Studies Review*, *10*(4), 749–761. doi:10.1111/j.1468-2486.2008.00830.x

The Ford Foundation. (2003). *International relations studies in China—A review of Ford Foundation past grantmaking and future choices*. Beijing: The Ford Foundation Beijing Office, September 2003.

Kristensen, P. M. (2015). International Relations in China and Europe: The case for international dialogue in a hegemonic discipline. *The Pacific Review, 28* (2), 161–187. doi:10.1080/09512748.2014.948568

Li, B. (2003). *Guoji guanxi lilun yu bentuhua wenti* (International relations theory and the question of indigenization). *World Economics and Politics*, (4).

Liang, S. (1997). *Guoji zhengzhi xue zai zhong guo—zai tan guoji zhengzhi xue lilun de 'zhongguo tese'* (International Politics in China—Re-discussing the 'Chinese characteristics' of Theory of International Politics). *Guoji zhengzhi yanjiu (Studies of International Politics)*, (1).

Liang, S. (2000). *Guoji zhengzhixue lilun (Theory of International Politics)*. Beijing: Peking University Press.

Ling, L. H. M. (2014). *The Dao of world politics: Towards a post-Westphalian, wordlist international relations*. London and New York: Routledge.

Lu, P. (2006). *Chuangjian zhongguo guoji guanxi lilun sizhong tujing de fenxi yu pingjia* (Four approaches to constructing Chinese IR Theories: Analysis and evaluation). *Shijie jingji yu zhengzhi (World Economics and Politics)*, (6)

Mei, R. (2000). *Gai bu gai you guoji zhengzhi lilun de zhongguo xuepai—jian ping meiguo de guoji zhengzhi lilun* (Should there be a Chinese School of Theory of International Politics?). *Guoji zhengzhi yanjiu (Studies of International Politics)*, (1), 63–67.

Nye, J. (1990). Soft power. *Foreign Policy Fall, 80*. doi:10.2307/1148580

Pang, Z. (2003). *kaifang shi de zizhu fazhan: Dui yingguo guoji guanxi lilun de yixiang guancha—sikao zhongguo guoji guanxi lilun de fangxiang* (Open-style Autonomous Development). *Shijie jingji yu zhengzhi (World Economics and Politics)*, 6.

Qin, Y. (2002). *Zong xu' (General preface), See Guoji guanxi lilun qianyan yicong (New directions in the study of world politics)*. Beijing: Peking University Press.

Qin, Y. (2004). *Disanzhong wenhua: Guoji guanxi yanjiu zhong kexue yu renwen de qihe* (The third culture: The convergence of science and humanity in the study of international relations). *World Economics and Politics, 1*, 19–20.

Qin, Y. (2005). *Guoji guanxi lilun de hexin wenti yu zhongguo xuepai de shengcheng* (Core question of IR theory and the formation of a Chinese school) *Chinese Social Science*, (3), 165–176.

Qin, Y. (2006). *Guoji guanxi lilun zhongguo xuepai shengcheng de keneng he biran* (A Chinese School of International Relations Theory: Possibility and inevitability). *World Economics and Politics, 3*.

Qin, Y. (2016). A relational theory of world politics. *International Studies Review, 18*(1), 33–47. doi:10.1093/isr/viv031

Qin, Y. (2018). *A relational theory of world politics*. Cambridge: Cambridge University Press.

Ren, X. (1998). *Guoji wenti yanjiu duanxiang,'* (Some Thoughts on International Studies). *Guoji Guancha (International Review), 4*, 51–53.

Ren, X. (2000). Lilun yu guoji guanxi lilun: yixie sikao,' (Some Thoughts on Theory and International Relations Theory). *Ou Zhou (Europe), 4*, 19–25.

Ren, X. (2003). Xiang yingguo xuepai xuexi,' (Learning from the English School). *Shi jie jing ji yu zheng zhi (World Economics and Politics), 7*, 70–71.

Ren, X. (2004a). *Jiangjiu fangfa, buwei fangfa,'* (Method is important but it is not everything). *World Economics and Politics, 1*, 18.

Ren, X. (2004b). *Guoji guanxi xue buneng meiyou renwen diyun,'* (IR cannot be without a humanistic base) *Guoji zhenghi yanjiu. (Studies of International Politics)*, 4, 145–146.

Ren, X. (2016). The "Chinese School" debate: Personal reflections. In Yongjin Zhang and Teng-chi Chang (Eds.), *Constructing a Chinese school of international relations: Ongoing debates and sociological realities*. London and New York: Routledge.

Ren, X. (2019). Cong shijie zhengfu dao gongsheng heping' (From World Government to gongsheng/Symbiotic Peace). *Guoji Guancha (International Review)*, 1, 36–50.

Shanghai Society of International Relations. (1991). ed. *Guoji guanxi lilun chutan (International Relations Theory: Preliminary Explorations)*, Shanghai: Shanghai Foreign Languages Education Press.

Shi, Y. (2004). *Guoji guanxi lilun yanjiu yu pingpan de ruogan wenti,'* (Some issues concerning the study and review of IR theory. *World Economics and Politics*, 1, 14–15.

Shih, C.-Y., & Huang, C.-C. (2016). Balance of relationship and the Chinese School IR. In Yongjin Zhang and Teng-chi Chang (Eds.), *Constructing a Chinese School of International Relations: Ongoing debates and sociological realities*. London and New York: Routledge.

Shih, C-Y., Huang, C.-c., Yeophantong, P., Bunskoek, R., Ikeda, J., Hwang, Y.-J . . . , Chen, C.-c. (2019). *China and international theory: The balance of relationships*. London and New York: Routledge.

Snidal, D., & Wendt, A. (2009). Why there is *International Theory* now. *International Theory*, 1 (1), 1–14. doi:10.1017/S1752971909000062

Su, C. (2003). *Wenti yu sixiang—zaitan guoji guanli yanjiu zai zhongguo* (Question and Thought—Reconsidering International Relations Research in China). *World Economics and Politics*, 3.

Tickner, Arlene B. and Waever, Ole eds. (2009). *International Relations Scholarship Around the World*. London and New York: Routledge.

Wang, Y. (1995). *Xie zai qianmian (Preface) in Dangdai guoji zhengzhi xilun (An Analysis of Contemporary International Politics)*. Shanghai: Shanghai People's Publishing House.

Wang, Y. (2003). *Zhongguo guoji guanxi lilun: dui chengjiu yu queshi de jidian ganshou* (Theories of international relations in China: Several points of view on achievements and deficiencies). *World Economics and Politics*, 4.

Wang, Z. (2006). *Chengwei zhishi de shengchanzhe* (Becoming a producer of knowledge). *World Economics and Politics*, 3.

Xing, Y. (1983). *tianxia yijia—zhonguoren de tianxia guan (Tianxia One Home—The Chinese Tianxia View)*. In Liu Dai (ed.), *Yongheng de juliu* (pp. 467–468). Taipei: Lianjing chuban shiye gongsi.

Xu, J., & Sun, X. (2016). The Tsinghua Approach and the future direction of Chinese International Relations research. In Yongjin Zhang and Teng-chi Chang (Eds.), *Constructing a Chinese School of International Relations: Ongoing debates and sociological realities*. London and New York: Routledge.

Yan, X. (2004a). *Guoji guanxi yanjiu zhong shiyong kexue fangfa de yiyi* (The Importance of Employing Scientific Method in International Relations Research). *World Economics and Politics*, 1, 16-17.

Yan, X. (2004b). *Kexue fangfa yu guoji guanxi yanjiu* (Scientific method and international relations studies). *Zhongguo shehui kexue (Chinese Social Science)*, 1, 2004.

Yan, X. (2006). *Guoji guanxi lilun shi pushixing de* (International relations theory is universal). *World Economics and Politics, 2,* 1.

Yan, X. (2011). International leadership and norm evolution. *The Chinese Journal of International Politics, 4*(3), 233–264. doi:10.1093/cjip/por013

Yan, X. (2014). daoyi xianshu zhuyi de guoji guanxi lilun (An international relations theory of moral realism). *Guoji wenti yanjiu (International Studies), 5,* 102–128.

Yan, X. (2016). Development of realist theory relies on seeking truth from facts. *Guoji zhengzhi kexue (Quarterly Journal of International Politics, 4,* III-IV.

Yu, Z., Yugang, C., & Changhe, S. (2003). *Ershiyi shiji quanqiu zhengzhi fanshi yanjiu (A study of global political paradigms in the twenty-first century).* Taiwan: Yanshan Press.

Yu, Z. (2005). Preface. In Guo Shuyong (Ed.), *Guoji guanxi: Huhuan zhongguo lilun (International relations: Calling for Chinese theories).* Tianjin: Tianjin People's Publishing House.

Yu, Z., & Yugang, C. (2005). *Quanqiu gongzhi fanshi chutan'* (Global shared governance: A preliminary study). In Guo Shuyong (Ed.), *Guoji guanxi: huhuan zhongguo lilun (International Relations: A Call for Chinese Theories),* (pp. 3-22). Tianjin: Tianjin People's Publishing House.

Zhang, F. (2012). The Tsinghua approach and the inception of Chinese theories of international relations. *The Chinese Journal of International Politics , 5*(1), 73–102. doi:10.1093/cjip/por015

Zhang, Y., & Chang, T.-C. eds. (2016). *Constructing a Chinese school of international relations: Ongoing debates and sociological realities.* London and New York: Routledge.

Zhang, Z. (2005). *Wenti yishi yu xueshu zijue—zhongguo guoji guanxi lilun jianshe de jiben qianti'* (Question awareness and academic self-consciousness—Basic premises for IR theory-building in China). In Guo Shuyong (Ed.), *Guoji guanxi: Huhuan zhongguo lilun (International Relations: A Call for Chinese Theories),* (pp. 181-189). Tianjin: Tianjin People's Publishing House.

Zhao, T. (2005). *Tianxia Tixi: Shijie Zhidu Zhexue Daolun (The Tianxia system: A philosophy for the world institution).* Nanjing: Jiangsu Jiaoyu Chubanshe.

Zhao, T. (2015). Yi tianxia chongxin dingyi zhengzhi gainian: wenti, tiaojian he fangfa (Redefining the concept of the political with tianxia: Its questions, conditions and methodology). *World Economics and Politics, 6,* 4–22.

Zhou, F. (2006). Zhongguo de guoji guanxi fangfalun yanjiu' (IR methodological studies in China). In Wang Yizhou (ed.), *Zhongguo guoji guanxi yanjiu (1995-2005) (IR Studies in China 1995-2005).* Beijing: Peking University Press.

Zi, Z. (2003). *Lilun chuangxin cong yanjiu xin wenti zhong lai* (Theoretical innovation comes from studying new questions). *World Economics and Politics, 3,* 1.

Striving for achievement in a new era: China debates its global role

Ling Wei

ABSTRACT

Since the doctrine of 'keeping a low profile (KLP), attaining some achievement (ASA)' was developed, there has been much attention and study of the KLP, but little discussion of the ASA. However, it is exactly how the ASA has been observed that can well reflect Chinese perception of its global role. In the paper, the ASA is treated as a continuum or a fluid concept with changing values. There have been significant adjustments in the official expression of the ASA doctrine since the 2008 global financial crisis, from the original 'attaining some achievement' to 'proactively attaining achievement' around 2011, 'striving for achievement' in 2013, and 'striving for achievement in a new era' in 2017. Along with these changes, there have been roughly three rounds of debates on the ASA among Chinese scholars. While they generally agree on more proactive diplomacy in attaining achievement, scholars have debated on what achievements to attain and how to attain these achievements. While the ultimate goal is defined officially as Chinese rejuvenation, specific and interim goals of 'striving for achievement' in scholarly debates have targeted mainly China's strategic capability, institutional power and normative power. Chinese scholars have also debated on the general principles, diplomatic style and tactics that China should follow by focusing on three relationships: the relationship between the KLP and the ASA, the Sino-US relationship, and the relationship between China and the international system. The author provides an analytical framework and thorough examination of the development of the ASA doctrine, and presents the scholarly debates along its development path, in the hope that this study may facilitate the understanding of the outside world on how China perceives its global role.

Introduction

For a long time since the end of the Cold War, China's diplomacy has followed the doctrine developed by the late Deng Xiaoping: 'keeping a low profile (*tao guang yang hui,* KLP hereafter), attaining some achievement (*you suo zuo wei,* ASA hereafter)'. However, scholars and policy analysts within and beyond China have so far placed more of their interest in the KLP than the ASA. At the core of their debates is China's strategic intention; that is, whether China is hiding its ambitions for the time being only to challenge the existing international system in the future when it is strong and capable enough to do so (Chen & Wang, 2011; Guan, 2012; Shin, 2011; Xing & Zhang, 2006; Yan, 2014). Such debates have been valuable, but inadequate in understanding how China perceives and performs its global role. A missing part is an in-depth study of the ASA (Tao, 2009, 124) and its policy implications. Given that KLP and the ASA complement each other and make up the relationship for dialectical unity, investigating Chinese scholars' debates on the ASA and the relevance of such debates in Chinese foreign policy making is of significant value in understanding how China perceives its global role.

Substantive debates focused on the ASA only started after the 2008 global financial crisis. The definition of the ASA is strongly correlated with the recognition of China's great power status and its international responsibilities prescribed by this status. The 2008 global financial crisis was a watershed event, which 'magnified and accelerated the ongoing shifts' (Mastanduno, 2014, p. 175) of the world's economic and strategic gravity toward the Pacific and China. Not only did China reach pre-eminent status in international system as it became the world's second largest economy only after the United States (US) and a member of the G20 – a premium platform for global economic and financial governance, it also gained international prestige as it demonstrated to the world an alternative development model (Wang, 2019, p. 56). Two events indicated the first round of serious debates and reconsideration of the ASA. First, the US and China established an economic and strategic dialogue mechanism in 2009 as a 'grand bargain' for a new cooperative framework (Mastanduno, 2014; Wang, 2019), and the core of the bargain was 'power and responsibility' (Wang & Wei, 2009). Thereafter, China's international responsibility has become a constant topic for debates at both home and abroad. Second, the ASA was rephrased in official documents in 2011 for the first time since its formulation.

After the rephrasing, two further rounds of debates on the ASA have taken place, reflecting different interpretations of the ASA in different material and ideational contexts, one in 2013-2014 after the official proposal of the 'Chinese Dream' and the 'Belt and Road Initiative' (BRI), and the other after the 19th National Congress of the Communist Party of China (CPC) and the establishment of the Xi Jinping Thought on Socialism with Chinese Characteristics for a New Era. What drives the debates is China's identity and status-seeking in the international system. As Chinese power continues to grow, the KLP has become increasingly difficult, especially in shouldering due international responsibilities and protecting rapidly expanded Chinese overseas interests. Hence, there is demand for more ASA from both within and outside China. Moreover, as the 'national rejuvenation' narrative prevails and China's historical place is to be reclaimed (Wang, 2012), there is growing self-consciousness in both policy and academic circles to rephrase and redefine the ASA so that it can better match China's rising power status. Especially as China has entered into a 'New Era' and has been faced with fundamental transformation in the international system – unprecedented in the past hundred years (Xinhua, 2018) – the discussions on China's global role and a proper definition of the ASA have become all the more relevant.

Treating the ASA as a continuum of attaining achievements, the author argues that the theme of the debates has evolved from 'attaining some achievement only in some areas, not in others' (*you suo wei, you suo bu wei*), 'attaining some achievement proactively' (*ji ji you suo zuo wei*), to 'striving for achievement' (*fen fa you wei*). The debates have sought to answer three sets of questions in terms of China's diplomacy and global role: how much to achieve, what to achieve and how to achieve. The perspectives and answers to these questions have demonstrated a relatively clear divide in the theoretical orientation of Chinese international relations scholars, and also in strategic and policy preferences between academic institutions and think-tanks. In terms of how much to achieve, different opinions have resulted from different understandings and estimations of Chinese power and the expected international status matching its power. In terms of what to achieve, the debates have mainly focused on China's strategic, institutional and normative power. Scholars have laid emphasis respectively on material, institutional or ideational factors mainly because of their different theoretical dispositions. Finally, as far as 'how to achieve' is concerned, the debates have developed at three interrelated dimensions: the KLP-ASA relationship, major power relations, and China's identity vis-a-vis the international system. For the major power relations, along with heated discussions on the Thucydides trap, most scholars emphasize the importance of maintaining cooperative relations with the US and especially caution against ideological confrontation, although many echo the official discourse of 'bottom-line thinking' (Xinhua, 2019) and the spirit of 'daring to taking resolute actions in critical moments' (People's Daily Editorial, 2013). For China's global role and identification with the international system, a majority view is that China should make its due contribution to introducing incremental reforms to the rules-based international system so that the latter can faithfully reflect the changing power structure of international politics, and improve its representativeness and legitimacy to make up for the deficit of global governance. On the Belt and Road Initiative, besides recognition of its geoeconomic and geopolitical impact and significance in improving global governance, more and more scholars have turned to pragmatic issues in region-specific or country-specific studies.

This paper is a qualitative study with text and discourse analysis. In order to well reflect the richness, diversity and representativeness of the debates, the author includes in the analysis academic articles, policy reports and media articles written and produced by leading Chinese IR scholars, academic institutions and think-tanks from 2009 up to the present. Most of the materials analyzed in the paper are written in Chinese. Given that Chinese scholars publish mainly in Chinese, this paper can help improve the familiarity and understanding of international readers on the academic and policy debates within China, on its global role and the relevance of the debates in China's foreign policy processes.

The following section gives an overview of the three rounds of debates by Chinese scholars on the ASA. To establish what triggered each round of debate, the author seeks to identify the changes in the material and ideational context, and to trace and discuss China's efforts in identity and status-seeking, which has framed the debates on the ASA. In the next three sections, the paper focuses on three respective aspects of the debates. 'How much to achieve' provides an analytical framework by treating the ASA as a continuum. This section reveals Chinese scholars' diverse opinions on the due degree of 'achievement', and the balance between 'attaining achievement in some areas' (*you suo wei*) and 'not attaining achievement in other areas' (*you suo bu wei*) related to a temporal context. The section on 'what to achieve' introduces the key subjects of the debates, summarizes the typical and influential opinions and proposals, and briefly discusses their policy implications and relevance. The section 'how to achieve' reflects Chinese scholars' opinions on the means for 'striving for achievement in a new era'. It concerns a fundamental question of China's identity: how China perceives itself in relation to other major powers and to the existing international system. Finally, the paper concludes with a summary of the key points of the ASA debates, and briefly discusses the significance and contributions of the research.

What triggered the debates: the *shi* and context of the ASA

Contextuality is one of the key elements in Chinese culture that shapes Chinese foreign policy-making. Contextuality means the *shi* (mega-trend) or the overall situation in which decisions are made. Chinese foreign policy and strategy is developed based on the *shi* assumption, which 'emphasizes the importance of the context, the importance of an actor's positioning in the context, and the importance of how people evaluate and judge the mega-trend of the context'. It is believed in China that an actor gains power and prospers when he goes along with the *shi* (Qin, 2011, pp. 47–48). The *shi* assumption can be better understood in distinction from the *xingshi* description that one often comes across in China's official discourse, policy papers and academic discussions. The two terms differ mainly in three aspects. First, the *shi* is a highly abstract notion and category focusing on the mega trend while the *xingshi* is more concrete and descriptive focusing more on what's going on for the time being. Second, the *shi* assumption adopts a holistic approach and particularly emphasizes the positioning of an actor in the overall context, while the *xingshi* description generally adopts a more binary analytical approach, treating the world as the 'external environment'. Third, the *shi* assumption follows a more humanitarian ontological orientation and emphasizes agency of an actor and the eventual co-constitution of the actor and the context, while the *xingshi* assessment is more realistic and objective. Therefore, the *shi* assumption often carries strong strategic implications on how an actor should interact with/within the context or the system for optimal results.

The *shi* assumption and contextuality argument provide a good analytical framework for the development and debates of the ASA because of their strong implication for conscious self-positioning and status-seeking of China in a changing international system. The KLP and the ASA were developed by the late Deng Xiaoping at the end of the Cold War, when China was isolated by the West, undergoing economic sanctions and political condemnation as a result of the Tiananmen incident in 1989. Deng's *shi* assumption mainly includes the following points. First, a world war could be prevented and world peace maintained. Peace and development remained the major themes of the time. Second, the world was moving toward multi-polarization. During this course, power competition would become intense. The development and eventual result of the competition would be shaped and determined by the performance of major powers in economic growth and scientific and technological advancement. Third, China should continue to focus on economic development, which is fundamental to national security. To create a favorable external and internal environment for economic growth, China should keep a low profile in international affairs, never seek leadership or hegemony, and stick firmly to the basic principle of 'reform and opening up' (Deng, 1993). Therefore, a basic assumption of the ASA was that China could achieve the goal of stable economic growth and modernization as long as it focused on its own development instead of seeking confrontation or debate with the US and the West on ideology (Qu, 2001, pp. 15–16). It was in such context that Deng developed the guiding principle for China's diplomacy – 'observe sober-mindedly, secure our position, cope with affairs calmly, keep a low profile, and make some attainment' (*leng jing guan cha, wen zhu zhen jiao, chen zhuo ying fu, tao guang yang hui, you suo zuo wei*) (Qian, 1995, p. 11). Among these 4-character principles, the KLP and the ASA are the core. However, the two didn't actually come together in a single Deng's speech or article (Chen & Wang, 2011, p. 197), but rather were officially summarized in the mid-1990s (Jiang, 2003, p. 202).[1]

Until the mid-2000s, the ASA principle had remained largely unchanged despite China's double-digit annual GDP growth rate since Deng Xiaoping's tour to China's southern provinces in 1992. It was reported that at the annual central conference of diplomatic envoys in 2004, Premier Wen Jiabao emphasized that the principle of the 'KLP, ASA' should be adhered to for at least another hundred years (Wu, 2005). Moreover, the debates on China's 'peaceful rise' (Zheng, 2005) and as a 'responsible stakeholder' (Zoelick, 2005) among Chinese and international scholars and policy makers ended in Chinese official pitch-setting on 'peaceful development' and reiteration of the principles of non-intervention and opposition to power politics and hegemony (Hu, 2007). Such developments provided strong evidence for China's reluctance to revise and go beyond the ASA. The reason for the adherence to the ASA was the shared understanding among policymakers and scholars on the *Shi*. They believed the major themes of the time – peace and development – had remained unchanged, that China should continue to focus on its own economic development, which was the solution to all challenges and problems it faced at home and abroad, and that any deviation from the 'KLP, ASA' principle would cost China dearly (Wu, 2005).

Adjusting the ASA principle was granted serious consideration after the 2008 global financial crisis, as a result of the elevation of China's international status and reconsideration of China's international responsibilities. The *shi* and context for the ASA doctrine had undergone subtle but significant changes. First, as mentioned earlier in the paper, China was foregrounded on the arena of world politics as its material power, institutional power and international prestige were significantly promoted. There was growing demand from the international community for China to shoulder international responsibilities proportionate to its rising power and status, typically demonstrated at the 2009 Copenhagen climate change conference. Second, as Barack Obama was sworn in, the US started to renegotiate a grand bargain with China through the establishment of the economic and security dialogue mechanism. US foreign policy under Obama demonstrated a strong inclination toward neoliberal internationalism, which emphasized the domestic and international responsibilities of sovereign states and great power cooperation in tackling major transnational threats in the 21st century (Jones, Pascual, & Stedman, 2009).

In general, Chinese scholars agreed on three points about China and the international situation. First, the international system was undergoing major changes, where reform needed to be introduced to major international institutions (Ni & Zhao, 2010; Wang, 2010; Wu, 2010); while the second decade of the 21st century would continue to be an era of strategic opportunity for China's development (Wu, 2010; Zheng, 2010). Second, China should manage well and maintain a stable and cooperative relationship with the US (Wu, 2009, 2010). China's rise and status-seeking were not intended to achieve a zero-sum result or to challenge the existing international order (Wang, 2019). Third, while China should remain focused on domestic priorities and refrain from committing to international responsibilities beyond its capabilities, it had to adopt a more proactive diplomacy in managing global insecurity (Wang & Wei, 2009). Disagreements among scholars mainly focused on the speed and extent of change taking place in the international system. Some argued that change was drastic and fundamental, and hence it was urgent for the international community to reform international institutions (Wang, 2010). Others thought that continuity and change were both apparent, and that the reform and adjustment of international institutions should be a long and gradual process (Qin, 2010a; Wu, 2010).

Concerning the ASA, a central issue in this round of the debate was how to maintain a delicate balance between China's domestic development priorities and its international responsibilities increasingly demanded by the international community. And exactly what responsibilities should China undertake? From 2007 to 2009, there was close interaction and consultation between Chinese foreign policy and academic communities on defining the extent of the ASA in undertaking international responsibilities, through domestic and international seminars and policy research projects. China Foreign Affairs University cooperated with the Brookings Institution, introduced their 'managing global insecurity' project to Chinese officials and scholars, and published the Chinese version of the project report *Power and Responsibility* in Beijing simultaneously as the original English version in Washington D.C. in 2009 (Wang & Wei, 2009). Such efforts had a significant impact on shaping the Chinese official perspective of China's power and responsibility. In 2010, the then State Councilor in charge of China's foreign affairs, Mr. Dai Bingguo, published an article in an academic journal, emphasizing that China would on the one hand remain focused on domestic development, and on the other hand play a more proactive role in contributing to global development and undertaking international responsibility proportionate to its economic power (Dai, 2010, p. 7). In 2011, a slight revision was made to the ASA, from 'attaining some achievement' (*you suo zuo wei*) to 'proactively attaining achievement' (*ji ji you wei*), as demonstrated in the White Paper on China' Peaceful Development. In the White Paper, the revised ASA was used specifically to illustrate China's position on living up to international responsibilities, stating that 'China will assume more international responsibility as its comprehensive strength increases' (Information office of the State Council of China, 2011).

The second round of debates took place after the 18th National Congress of the CPC and the official proposal of the Chinese Dream and the Belt and Road Initiative (BRI) in 2012–2013.[2] When making an assessment of the international situation, some emphasized the growth of security and strategic concerns in world politics, the rise of nationalism among middle powers, and uncertainty in major power relations and globalization (Shi, 2013). Some argued for the beginning of a transition of the international structure from unipolarity to multipolarity and the irreversible decline of the relative power of the US, and pointed out that such a transition and significant change was taking place first in the economic realm and in Asia. It was widely believed that a rapidly rising China had become a major player in the transition of international structure and an important contributor to the reshaping of the international order (Cui, 2014; Gao, 2014). Nonetheless, some insisted on the relative stability of the US-led international system based on rules and institutions despite the relative decline of US material power and skepticism toward some political and economic rules and regulations. They predicted that power competition would come with greater intensity and on a larger scale (Feng, 2013). While some went far enough to propose that the year 2013 marked the beginning of a post-US era, which presented both strategic opportunity and challenge for the realization of the Chinese dream (Lin, 2013), others criticized the exaggeration of the rise of Chinese power and status in the international system and the harm it had done to China's external environment, and called for a return to pragmatism and a focus on domestic economic development (Zhang, 2013).

In 2013, as Chinese President Xi Jinping used the term '*fen fa you wei*' (striving for achievement) to call for progressive diplomacy at the Central Conference on Periphery Diplomacy, the principle of the ASA was significantly adjusted. A major area where China's diplomacy was expected to strive for achievement was the Belt and Road Initiative, which was initially called the 'One Belt, One Road' strategy (Caixin Editorial Office, 2015). In general, the BRI was regarded by officials and scholars as a new round of China's opening-up to the outside world, a development opportunity to be shared with countries along the routes, a strategic opportunity to shape the evolving world order toward equitable and balanced development, and a vehicle or channel for China to further commit itself to international responsibilities, and to world peace and development. Some scholars specifically made clear that the BRI could introduce incremental reform and improvements, but not to challenge or overthrow the current international system. Some did argue for the BRI as a vehicle for China's rise to preeminent status, but at the same time emphasized that China's rise should be accomplished within the current international system and not lead to a zero-sum game with the US. Many stressed that the BRI in implementation should follow the principle of 'extensive consultation, joint contribution and shared benefits' [gong shang, gong jian, gong xiang], cautioning against security and fiscal risks, and possible suspicion or even hostility from some parties in the international community. [3]

The most recent round of debates began after the 19th CPC National Congress and the official establishment of the Xi Jinping Thought on Socialism with Chinese Characteristics for a New Era. In his report to the Congress, Xi stressed that the new era should see China moving closer to center stage of the world and making a greater contribution to mankind (Xi, 2017). In mid-2018, Xi Jinping Diplomatic Thought was established, and Xi stated that the world was witnessing a grand transformation unseen in the past one hundred years (Xinhua, 2018). Since then, there have been a lot of discussions about the 'new era' and the 'grand transformation'. As an overarching goal of China's diplomacy in the new era is to build a new type of international relations – meaning taking a new approach to developing state-to-state relations with mutual respect, fairness, justice and win-win cooperation at its core (Zheng, 2018, p. 6) – win-win cooperation should be a defining feature of the new era. Despite disagreements on the specific time frame of the 'past one hundred years' and the 'grandness' of the transformation, scholars in general agreed on significant transformation of international structure in terms of power, institutions, norms and governance, and recognized that China faced both opportunities and unprecedented challenges in seeking appropriate status in the international system.[4] Therefore, 'striving for achievement in a new era' may represent an even more proactive step forward from the ASA.

How much to achieve: a continuum of the ASA

The ASA identifies two relationships of dialectical unity. The first is the relationship between 'attaining achievement in some areas' (you suo wei) and 'not attaining achievement in other areas' (you suo bu wei). And the second is the relationship between the KLP and the ASA. The ASA consists of and actually requires 'attaining achievement in some areas' (you suo wei) and 'not attaining achievement in other areas' (*you suo bu wei*) at the same time. According to Deng Xiaoping, on the one hand, China should stick firmly to its principles and strive for achievement in safeguarding China's sovereignty, regime security and fundamental interests; defending legitimate rights and interests of developing countries; maintaining regional and world stability; and developing a new international political and economic order that is fair and reasonable. On the other, China should not stick its head out, or seek leadership or hegemony (*bu dang tou, bu kang qi, bu cheng ba*) (Deng, 1993, p. 363) – although Deng was not opposed to China playing a role proportionate to its economic weight. The balance between what to do and what not to do is to be maintained based on the judgment of the *shi*. The KLP and the ASA should be treated as an organic whole, a long-term strategy rather than a policy of convenience. Effective implementation of the strategy required a holistic view and accurate judgment of the *shi*, and the right balance between long-term interest and short-term interest, direct interest and indirect interest, and holistic interest and sectional interest.[5] As pointed out by the late Qian Qichen, the then Chinese Foreign Minister, the ASA reflects Deng's distinctive diplomatic style – sticking firm to principles while remaining flexible in tactics (Qian, 1995, p. 16).

Hence, the ASA is actually a fluid concept. It can be regarded as a continuum of 'attaining achievement' (*zuo wei*). Infinitely close to one end of the continuum is 'not to attain any achievement at all' (*bu zuo wei*). And infinitely close to the other end can be 'striving for achievement' (*fen fa you wei*). From one end to the other, there are different degrees of intention and effort in attaining achievement. If we measure the ASA, variation in its value can be represented as follows:

$...$

ASA_0 = not to attain achievement at all (*bu zuo wei*)
ASA_1 = not to attain achievement in certain areas (*you suo bu wei*)
ASA_2 = to attain achievement in some areas, but not in others (*you suo wei, you suo bu wei*)
ASA_3 = to attain achievement in some areas (*you suo wei*)
ASA_4 = to attain achievement proactively (*ji ji you wei*)
ASA_5 = to strive for achievement (*fen fa you wei*)
ASA_n $...$

Various values of the ASA only represent different degrees of intention and effort in making attainment in relative terms. They are not static or structural, but fluid and sometimes mutually complementary or transformative under certain conditions. The flowing value of the ASA is mainly defined by ongoing assessment of the *shi* and mega trend, and then further modified by the goals and means of (not) attaining achievement. Therefore, there should not be absolute or static interpretation or judgment of the ASA. Rather, the ASA is very much process-driven and process-dependent.

Through the discussions on the *shi* and overall context for the ASA, we have found that scholars in general agree on China's diplomacy moving toward the more proactive end of the ASA. This is because China's presence and interest in global affairs has increased as its power and influence have expanded in the last 40 years. From 2008 to 2015, China's share in the global market of Outward Foreign Direct Investment (OFDI) increased from 3.28% to 8.65% (Wang & Zhao, 2017, p. 358). In 2016, China became the second-largest source of OFDI only after the US, with its OFDI surpassing its FDI inflows by 36% (Xinhua, 2017). Moreover, different from many earlier offshore investments – motivated by the search for natural resources – there is 'an overall tendency in China's OFDI of leaning toward high-end industry sectors' (Wang & Zhao, 2017, p. 359). From 2010 to 2018, the number of outbound Chinese tourists increased from 57.4 million to 149.7 million (MCT (Ministry of Culture & Tourism of the People's Republic of China), 2019). Hence, it is only natural and inevitable for China to become increasingly proactive in protecting its interests overseas, and undertaking international responsibilities.

If at the time when the ASA doctrine was initiated, the idea was more about ASA_1 (not to make attainment in certain areas), and then the pendulum swung and tried to maintain a delicate balance between ASA_2 and ASA_3, the flow toward the proactive end of the ASA has been apparent since 2008. After the international financial crisis and China's new status as the second largest global economic power, as the debate continued, the official phrasing of the 'KLP ASA' doctrine evolved into 'continuing to keep a low profile and proactively attaining achievement'. In 2011, in both the White Paper on China's Peaceful Development and the White Paper on China's Diplomacy, 'proactively attaining achievement' (*ji ji you wei*) replaced 'attaining some achievement' (*you suo zuo wei*), reflecting the shift of official position from ASA_3 to ASA_4. In October 2013, at the Central Conference on Periphery Diplomacy, Xi Jinping for the first time used the term '*fen fa you wei*' (striving for achievement) to call for greater efforts in promoting China's periphery diplomacy (Xinhua, 2013), which can be regarded as one strategic step forward from '*ji ji you wei*'. As Chinese Foreign Minister Wang Yi pointed out, a prominent feature of China's diplomacy since the 18th National Congress of the CPC in 2012 has been 'proactively attaining achievement' (*ji ji you wei*), and contributing to world peace and common development with Chinese wisdom (Wang, 2017).

Since 2014, ASA$_5$ (*fen fa you wei*) started to appear in academic articles in the field of China's diplomacy. Using the CNKI database – the largest database for Chinese academic resources – to search for all journal articles with an abstract containing '*fen fa you wei*' (striving for achievement) and '*zhong guo wai jiao*' (China's diplomacy) since 2008, we are able to report the following findings. First, articles meeting such requirements began to appear in 2014, amounting to 41 by June 2019. Second, the peak years were 2015 and 2017, both totaling 12 publications. Third, the contributors of these articles are from more than twenty institutions. The leading institutions in terms of the number of articles are Tsinghua University (5), the Chinese Academy of Social Sciences (4) and Peking University (4). Institutions each contributing two such articles include Fudan University, Guangdong University of Foreign Studies, Nankai University, Party School of the Central Committee of the CPC, and Chinese Institutes of Contemporary International Relations.[6] Given the uninterrupted publication and institutional distribution of the articles, it appears that a shift from ASA$_4$ to ASA$_5$ has occurred and the latter probably has become the new normal template for debates.

What to achieve: strategic, institutional and normative power

The value or due degree of the ASA is often dependent on what kind of achievement is to be attained and how such achievement can be attained. The following analysis will mainly focus on ASA$_5$ (*fen fa you wei*) to find out the means and ends argued by Chinese scholars in seeking China's global status and the relevance of the debates in foreign policy making. While the ultimate goal is defined officially as Chinese rejuvenation, specific and interim goals of ASA$_5$ in scholarly debates have centred mainly on China's strategic capability, institutional power and normative power.

The first focus of the debates is China's strategic capability. Zhou Fangyin argues that since 2013, China has strived for achievement in diplomacy mainly through resisting strategic pressure and defending sovereign and maritime rights and interests on the one hand, while broadening and deepening economic cooperation on the other, and that a long-term challenge and task for China's diplomacy is to narrow the power gap with the US (Zhou, 2017). Zhu Feng also refers to China defending its rights and interests in the South China Sea as a case of 'striving for achievement' (Zhu & Wu, 2018, 34). Shi Yinhong proposes that China establish strategic/military advantage in the western Pacific – the vast ocean area from the Chinese coast to the first island chains – and seek greater economic and diplomatic advantage in Asia and even beyond, and pursue strategic presence or influence in select regions and places (Shi, 2018, p. 30). Yan

Xuetong argues that the turn toward 'striving for achievement' means that the overriding task for China's diplomacy has become building a benign international environment for Chinese rejuvenation instead of mere economic growth. Therefore, China's periphery should be even more clearly identified as the priority region. Since China is a superpower only in East Asia – not yet in the world – it can seek to play a dominant role in the region, which is becoming the center of the world and of vital strategic importance to China. Hence, China should first and foremost make strategic investments in East Asia, where best strategic returns can be expected (Yan, 2017, pp. 5–9). Scholars have also argued about China's policy of not seeking a security alliance. A majority view is that identifying some countries along the BRI routes as strategic nodes is necessary, although China can still officially continue to adhere to the non-alliance principle.

The second focus of the debates is China's institutional power. Ren Xiao points out that China has improved its institutional capability through diplomacy in its home region, especially in agenda-setting. A good example is the Free Trade Area of the Asia Pacific (FTAAP) being set up as the main agenda of the Beijing APEC in 2014 (Ren, 2015, p. 62). Many Chinese scholars propose that China should take advantage of its economic development to provide more international public goods, for instance, in areas of development assistance, infrastructure building and connectivity, and economic governance; and that China should increase its representation and weight in international institutions and play an active role in reforming them for better global governance in the new era (Ren, 2015, p. 63; Zhu & Wu, 2018, p. 35; Liu, 2019, p. 48). Although it is generally agreed that China should shoulder greater international responsibilities as it rises to great power status, some caution that China should not take on responsibilities beyond its capability. The right approach for China to obtain greater institutional power is to seek incremental reform within the international system based on rules and institutions rather than trying to establish something new to replace existing international institutions. The best area for China to develop such institutional capability is regional or global economic governance. Newly established international institutions should complement and partner with existing international institutions rather than replacing them. The Asian Infrastructure Investment Bank, initiated by China, has been a good example and success story so far. But whether such success is sustainable remains to be seen. Although some indeed argue that China should also provide public goods in security in its periphery, they at the same time caution against over-stretch (Yan, 2017, pp. 7–8). In general, the consensus is that 'striving for achievement' requires greater institutional capability and the transformation of China from a beneficiary to a promoter and provider of international institutions for cooperation.

There has been increasing interaction between scholarly debates and policy in building China's institutional capacity. For instance, the AIIB can be regarded as a fruit of long-term track I-track II interaction. As early as the late 2000s, Chinese scholars had proposed setting up a financing institution for infrastructure development in East Asia (Zhu, et al., 2013). Another example regards building China's institutional power through human resources development. For many years, Chinese scholars have repeatedly proposed cultivating talent and sending more Chinese experts and officials to international institutions to enhance China's institutional power. Their specific suggestions mainly included setting up a revolving door mechanism between academic institutions and ministries, supporting Chinese officials and scholars to compete for major positions in international institutions, establishing undergraduate and graduate majors in 'international organization' in institutions of higher learning, and creating and obtaining internship opportunities for Chinese college students in international institutions. In late 2016, the Ministry of Education of China, for the first time, made favorable policies to encourage Chinese college student to seek internship and job opportunities in international institutions (MOE (Ministry of Education of the People's Republic of China), 2016). In April 2017, School of International Organizations was established in Beijing Foreign Studies University, the first of its kind in institutions of higher learning in China (BFSU, 2017).

A third focus of the debates is China's normative power, for which a more popular term in Chinese is *hua yu quan*, referring to the power to develop and diffuse internationally-accepted discourse and internationally-recognized norms based on Chinese values, ideas and theories and to claim the moral high ground in world politics. Since 2013, a series of ideas, concepts, norms and principles for China's diplomacy and international relations have been developed, which have made up the normative base for 'the major-country diplomacy with Chinese characteristics in the new era' established by the 19th National Congress of the CPC in 2017 (Zheng, 2018), and a major component of Xi Jinping Thought on Diplomacy established at the Central Conference on Diplomatic Work in June 2018. The most well-known include 'a community of shared future for mankind' (*renlei mingyun gongtongti*), the principle of 'amity, sincerity, mutual benefit and inclusiveness' (*qin, cheng, hui, rong*) for periphery diplomacy, the philosophy of 'striking a proper balance between friendship and interests' (*zhengque de yiliguan*), sustainable security (*kechixu anquan*), inclusive development (*baorongxing fazhan*), and the principle of 'extensive consultation, joint contribution and shared benefits' for global governance (*gongshang, gongjian, gongxiang de quanqiu zhiliguan*). (Qin & Wei, 2018; Zheng, 2018).

Although these principles and norms have to some extent helped improve China's international image and appeal, Chinese scholars are aware that they are not yet internationalized discourse or universal norms. Therefore, a very important aspect of 'striving for achievement' is for China to play a proactive and even leading role in developing international norms. However, some point out that the emphasis on Chinese characteristics in promoting China's diplomatic principles and practices has actually undermined efforts to build China's normative power. Therefore, a good balance should be kept between Chinese distinctive values and universal values. In other words, on the one hand, China should take advantage of its tradition, culture and values to build normative power; while on the other hand, these cultural and normative elements should have universal appeal and resonate with international audiences (Li, 2018, pp. 88–89). Some argue that China should develop an international vision and be open-minded in international norm-initiation – as China is not only an ancient civilization, but also a modern nation-state with the second largest economy and is moving increasingly closer to the center of the world politics. A good approach to enhance China's normative power might first be doing it selectively in functional areas of strategic importance, where China has a competitive edge, such as in cyber security. Moreover, to play a leading role in developing international norms requires not only the production of internationally appealing ideas, but also the capabilities of agenda-setting and persuasion (Zhang, 2017). Some argue that greater effort should be made in developing international discourse and universal norms to reduce suspicion and worries about China's rise and even frictions between different values, and to build a better discursive and normative international environment for China's rise (Sun, 2019, p. 19).

Another significant effort by Chinese scholars in promoting Chinese normative power is to develop Chinese International Relations (IR) theories. While in general they agree on the necessity of discovering China's core problematic, and introducing Chinese culture, philosophy and practices into IR studies for theory-development, they disagree on whether there should be a 'Chinese' school of IR theories or which theoretic innovations and establishments should be categorized into the 'Chinese' school. The well-established among such studies include Qin Yaqing's relational theory of world politics (Qin, 2018b), Zhao Tingyang's *Tianxia* system (Zhao, 2005), Yan Xuetong's moral realism (Yan, 2018), and a *gongsheng*/symbiotic theory developed by scholars from Shanghai (Ren, 2018). These authors and their studies have contributed to the development of the IR discipline, enhanced Chinese presence and imprint in the knowledge production of global IR, and helped promote China's normative power in framing world politics. However, the 'Chinese-ness' is a double-edged sword. While recognizing their contribution and the significance of local knowledge, IR scholars both within and beyond China have also questioned whether these theories serve China's rejuvenation strategy and policy purpose or whether they can find application in places outside China (Acharya, 2019; Ren, 2020).[7]

How to achieve: flexibility, major power relations and China's identity

While Chinese scholars may in general agree on the transformation of China's diplomacy from 'proactively attaining achievement' toward 'striving for achievement' in a new era, they have debated on the following issues concerning the principle, diplomatic style and tactics that China should follow in trying to attain the desired achievement or to play a global role matching its material power. We may categorize these issues into three sets of relationships: the relationship between the KLP and the ASA, the Sino-US relationship, and the relationship between China and the international system.

First, some scholars do not over-emphasize 'striving for achievement' as they believe in a dialectical unity of the KLP and the ASA. Qin Yaqing argues that *zhongyong* dialectic constitutes a core component of background knowledge on the Chinese, which stresses 'a "both-and" way of thinking', 'interprets the basic state of the relationship between the two polarities as harmonious', and 'always tries to find the appropriate middle where the common ground lies' (Qin, 2018b, p. xvii). Therefore, the relationship between the KLP and the ASA_s (striving for achievement) does not follow the either-or logic or the Hegelian dichotomy. There is no abrupt break between the two, neither going to the extreme ends of the continuum. 'Striving for achievement' is becoming evident only in areas concerning China's core national interests (Qin, 2014, pp. 285–287). Liu Jianfei argues that the KLP should always remain the base for China's diplomatic behavior, while acknowledging the change in the value of the ASA (Liu, 2019, p. 47). Pang Zhongying predicts that tactical flexibility embedded in the oxymoron of the 'KLP ASA' will remain a distinctive feature in China's diplomacy long into the future. For instance, on the one hand, China adheres to the principle of non-intervention; on the other hand, it seeks legitimate and necessary engagement under certain circumstances. While China claims to remain firm on not seeking hegemony, taking the lead in international affairs or building a security alliance, major power diplomacy or the goal of developing a new type of international relations and building a community of shared future for mankind requires China to provide international public goods, including ideational and material goods, where taking the lead becomes inevitable (Pang, 2015, pp. 27–28).

Second, striving for achievement requires carefully handling the Sino-US relationship. It is generally believed that the US will continue to be 'the most important actor in China's overall strategic consideration and design' (Qin, 2014, p. 306) and that Western dominance or the US hegemonic position in the international system remains unchanged (Liu, 2019, p. 47). As there is still a significant gap between China and the US in terms of overall national strength and technological innovation, China should stick firmly to the path of peaceful development, seek cooperative relations with the US and the West, and at the same time manage well the due degree of 'striving for achievement' to demonstrate a peaceful rise to the world (Qin, 2018a, p. 2). In other words, in its interaction with the US, China must strike a balance between the KLP and the ASA, and to strive for achievement in some areas, but not in others. Otherwise, it will encounter more difficulties and barriers during its rise to great power status.

Some scholars caution that China should weaken the element of ideology in dealing with the US. To continue to keep a low profile and avoid ideological confrontation with the US and the West will significantly reduce suspicion about China's strategic intentions, stabilize the major-power relationship, and maintain the basic stability of the international system (Liu, 2019, pp. 47–48). When Xi Jinping proposed that China and the US should establish a new type of major power relationship, defined by 'preventing conflict and confrontation', 'respecting each other' and 'carrying out win-win cooperation', mutual respect meant respecting each other's political system, development approach and core national interests.[8] However, in recent Sino-US competition and conflict in trade and technology, and in the South China Sea and the Indo-Pacific, the element of political system and ideology has appeared more and more prominent. Alert to the rise of the new left (Zhao, 2016) and populism (Liu, 2017), some Chinese scholars hold that the left-right debates are more intense in the field of economics than in politics (Jing, 2018). Some also argue that China will risk deteriorating the external environment and losing the strategic opportunity for its sustainable development if it chooses to strive for achievement in ideology confrontation with the West, or even makes it an overwhelming theme in its interaction with the outside world (Li, 2014; Xiao, 2016).

Finally, striving for achievement should be conducted based on the premise of China's identity vs the international system, or China's global role. Jia Qingguo points out that it is in China's interest to prevent the weakening of the existing international order despite the necessary reform of international institutions for better global governance (Jia, 2015, p. 17). After four decades of reform and opening-up, China has been fully integrated into the international system. Its identity has changed from a revisionist power to a status-quo power and major stakeholder. China's interests have been aligned with the interests of other members of the international system. Therefore, challenging or overthrowing the existing system is not in China's interest (Jia, 2015, p. 16). Shi Yinhong holds that striving for achievement in a new era requires both broadening and deepening China's participation in global economic and political governance (Shi, 2018, p.30). Yan Xuetong argues that China should continue to promote social and economic development at home and continue to improve domestic governance to build capacity for a leading role in global governance (Yan, 2017, pp. 10–11). Liu Jianfei maintains that China can and ought to shoulder responsibilities proportionate to a major power with systemic influence, proactively participate in the reform of the global governance system, take the initiative in building a benign international environment and seeking strategic opportunity for its own continuous development, and stay committed to orienting the international order toward greater justice and fairness (Liu, 2019, p. 48). Hence, despite the demand for reform of international institutions and greater Chinese capability for domestic and global governance, deeper integration and full socialization of China into the current international system is in general supported by Chinese scholars.

Conclusion

The paper tries to ascertain the Chinese perception of China's global role through examining the scholarly debates on the ASA. Since the late Deng Xiaoping developed the doctrine of the KLP and the ASA, there has been much attention and study of the KLP, but little discussion of the ASA. However, it is exactly how the ASA has been observed that can well reflect Chinese perception of its global role, mainly including what achievements China intends to attain in the international system and how China is going to attain these achievements. The author lays out two logical frames for analysis of the scholarly debates on the ASA. One is temporal, where three different material and ideational contexts are identified for the discussion. The other is conceptual, where the ASA is treated as a continuum or a fluid concept with changing values. Infinitely close to one end of the continuum is 'not to attain any achievement at all' (*bu zuo wei*), while close to the other end is 'striving for achievement' (*fen fa you wei*). From one end to the other, there are different degrees of intention and efforts in attaining achievement. The flowing value of the ASA is mainly defined by ongoing assessment of the mega trend, and then further modified by the goals and means of (not) attaining achievement. The ASA is very much process-driven and process-dependent. After the 2008 global financial crisis, there have been significant adjustments in the official expression of the ASA doctrine from the original 'attaining some achievement' to 'proactively attaining achievement' around 2011, 'striving for achievement' in 2013, and 'striving for achievement in a new era' in 2017.

Along with these changes, there have been roughly three rounds of debates on the ASA among Chinese scholars. While they generally agree on more proactive diplomacy in attaining achievement, scholars have debated on what achievements to attain and how to attain these achievements as China rises to great power status and becomes stronger (*qiang qi lai*). While the ultimate goal is as defined officially as Chinese rejuvenation, specific and interim goals of 'striving for achievement' in scholarly debates have targeted mainly at China's strategic capability, institutional power and normative power. A majority view is that China should further prioritize East Asia in its strategic investment and identify some countries as strategic nodes in promoting the BRI. Moreover, 'striving for achievement' requires greater institutional capability and the transformation of China from a beneficiary to a promoter and provider of international institutions. In addition, more and more Chinese scholars propose that China should strive for achievement in '*hua yu quan*', the power to develop and diffuse internationally-accepted discourse and internationally-recognized norms based on Chinese values, ideas and theories and to claim the moral high ground in world politics; although some have reminded that these Chinese ideas should have universal appeal and resonate with international audiences.

Chinese scholars have also debated the general principles, diplomatic style and tactics that China should follow in striving for achievement in a new era or trying to play a role matching its material power. The discussions have developed around three sets of relationships: the relationship between the KLP and the ASA, the Sino-US relationship, and the relationship between China and the international system. Scholars in general have cautioned against the over-emphasis on 'striving for achievement' and ideological confrontation with the US and the West. They have remained alert to the rise of the new left and populism, and suggested continuity of a more balanced ASA doctrine, a cooperative relationship with the US and deeper integration of China into the international system.

The paper may have made intellectual contributions in three aspects. First, it sets up an analytical framework of the ASA, examines its dialectical unity and conceptual fluidity in a thorough manner, and hence provides a very useful conceptual tool for understanding the 'what-to-do' and 'what-not-to-do' thinking in China's diplomacy. Second, it traces the development and evolution of the ASA principle since the 2008 global financial crisis, and makes clear the continuity and change in China's diplomacy and the contexts of such developments. Therefore, it may have helped with the predictability of China's international behavior and global role in the future. Third, the paper collects and analyzes the views of Chinese scholars from a variety of theoretical orientations and official affiliations in the past decade, and presents the interaction of the international/domestic background, official policies and scholarly opinions. Hence, it may have provided some insight into how debates have gone on within China and how relevant they have been to China's international behavior and global role. Although it is hard to prove any cause-effect hypothesis, there have been at least some connections between academic debates and official policies and principles found in this study.

Notes

1. For the summarized doctrine, see relevant talks given by Deng Xiaoping recorded in *Selected Works of Deng Xiaoping, III*, pp. 321, 354, 363.

2. Chinese Institutes of Contemporary International Relations hosted a conference on 'International Situation and Changes in Major Power Relations' in Beijing in April 2013, where over 30 scholars from leading Chinese IR institutions were invited to present their views. A summary of the presentations of major speakers were published in a special section of Issue No.4 of the *Xiandai Guoji Guanxi [Contemporary International Relations]*, which is a good representation of the debates then.

3. See articles written by Lin Yifu, Jin Liqun, Wu Jianmin, Zhang Yunling, Gao Bo, Ge Jianxiong, etc. in Caixin Editorial Office (2015). The book collects dozens of articles written by government officials and scholars from prominent universities, institutions and think-tanks on the BRI by 2015. See also Qin and Wei (2018).

4. From late 2018 to early 2019, discussions on the 'new era' and the 'grand transformation' appeared in journals like *Shijie Zhishi (World Affairs), Xiandai Guoji Guanxi (Contemporary International Relations), Yatai Anquan yu Haiyang Yanjiu (Asia Pacific Security and Maritime Studies)*, etc.

5. The official interpretation of Deng's judgment of the *Shi* and his doctrine of the KLP comes from *Deng Xiaoping Waijiao Sixiang Xuexi Gangyao [A Study Guide to Deng Xiaoping Diplomatic Thought]*. (2000).Beijing: World Affairs Press. This book was written and edited by a writing group organized by the *Zhongyang Waiban* (Office of the Leading Group for the Diplomatic Work of the Central Committee of the Communist Party of China).

6. Search through cnki.net on 20 June 2019. The distribution of articles by year is 2019 (3), 2018 (5), 2017 (12), 2016 (5), 2015 (12), 2014(4).

7. A thorough discussion about the Chinese IRT was conducted at an international conference on 'Global IR and Non-Western IR Theory' held by China Foreign Affairs University in Beijing on 24 April 2018, where all the authors quoted here were present. See also Ren (2020).

8. For Chinese scholars' debates on new type of major power relations, see also Zeng and Breslin (2016).

Disclosure statement

No potential conflict of interest was reported by the author.

References

Acharya, A. (2019). From heaven to earth: "Cultural Idealism" and "Moral Realism" as Chinese contributions to global international relations. *Chinese Journal of International Politics. 12*(4), 467–494. doi:10.1093/cjip/poz014.

BFSU (Beijing Foreign Studies University). (2017). Beijing waiguoyu daxue beiwaixueyuan, guojizuzhi xeuyuan chengli dahui juxing [The founding ceremony for the BFSU School of Beiwai and the BFSU School of International Organizations was held]. April 9. Retrieved from https://news.bfsu.edu.cn/archives/260871.

Caixin Editorial Office. (2015). Ed. *'Yidai Yilu'* Yinling Zhongguo ['One Belt, One Road' Guiding China]. Beijing: Zhongguo Wenshi Chubanshe [Chinese Literature and History Publishing House].

Chen, D., & Wang, J. (2011). Lying low no more? China's new thinking on the tao guang yang hui strategy. *China: An International Journal, 9*(2), 195–216. doi:10.1142/S0219747211000136

Cui, L. (2014). Guoji geju zhuanbian yu zhongguo waijiao zhuanxing [Changing international situation and the transformation of China's diplomacy]. *Guoji Guanxi Yanjiu [Journal of International Relations], 4*, 3–11.

Dai, B. (2010). Jianchi zou heping fazhan daolu [Stick firmly to the path of peaceful development]. *Dangdai Shijie [Contemporary World], 12*, 4–8.

Deng, X. (1993). *Deng Xiaoping Wenxuan (Disanjuan). [*Selected Works of Deng Xiaoping, III]. Beijing: People's Publishing House.

Deng Xiaoping Waijiao Sixiang Xuexi Gangyao [A study guide to Deng Xiaoping diplomatic thought]. (2000). Beijing: World Affairs Press.

Feng, Y. (2013). Dabianjuxia de daguo zhanlue jingzheng [Strategic competition among major powers in the grand transformation]. *Xiandai Guoji Guanxi [Contemporary International Relations], 4*, 10–12.

Gao, Z. (2014). Xingxingshixia guoji zhanlue sanda qushi [Three major trends of international strategy under the new circumstances]. *Qianxian [Frontiers], 5*, 3–38.

Guan, Q. (2012). Zhongguo yiran xuyao tao guang yang hui. [China Still Needs to Keep a Low Profile]. *Xueshu Qianyan [Frontiers], 9*, 63–72.

Hu, J. (2007). Gaoju zhongguo tese shehuizhuyi weida qizhi, wei duoqu quanmian jianshe xiaokang shehui xinshengli er fentou—zai zhongguo gongchandang dishiqici quanguo daibiao dahuishang de baogao [Hold High the Great Banner of Socialism with Chinese Characteristics and Strive for New Victories in Building a Moderately Prosperous Society in all Respects—Report to the Seventeenth National Congress of the Communist Party of China]. Oct. 15. Retrieved from http://www.chinadaily.com.cn/hqzg/2007-10/31/content_6220592.htm.

Information office of the State Council of China. (2011). China's peaceful development. Beijing, 6 Sept. Retrieved from http://www.gov.cn/english/official/2011-09/06/content_1941354.htm.

Jia, Q. (2015). Xinshiqi huhuan xinlinian, xinzuofa: dui woguo waijiao de jidian sikao [A new era calls for new ideas and new approaches: Reflections on China's diplomacy]. *Xiandai Guoji Guanxi [Contemporary International Relations], 2*, 1–17.

Jiang, Z. (2003). *Jiang Zemin Wenxuan (Dierjuan). [*Selected Works of Jiang Zemin, II]. Beijing: People's Publishing House.

Jing, T. (2018). Zhongguo xinzuopai sichao de chengyin yu shanbian luelun [A brief discussion on the formation and transformation of China's new left thinking]. *Xiandai Zhexue [Modern Philosophy], 5*, 55–62.

Jones, B., Pascual, C., & Stedman, S. J. (2009). *Power and responsibility: Building international order in an era of transnational threats*. Washington D.C.: Brookings Institution Press.

Li, Q. (2014). Lun xinzuopai dui zhongguo tese shehuizhuyi daolu zixin de weixie yu huajie lujing [How to meet threats posed by new-left thoughts to self-confidence in the path to socialism with Chinese characteristics]. *Nanjing shida xuebao (shehui kexueban) [Journal of Nanjing Normal University (Social Sciences)]*, 4, 19–26.

Li, Z. (2018). Zhongguo "fen fa you wei" waijiao de genyuan, xingzhi yu tiaozhan [A strategic autonomy perspective on China's diplomatic activism: Causes, nature, and challenges]. *Guoji Zhanwang [International Perspective]*, 2, 70–90.

Lin, L. (2013). 2013 guoji zhanlue xingshi pinggu [An assessment of the 2013 international strategic situation]. *Xiandai Guoji Guanxi [Contemporary International Relations]*, 12, 9–19.

Liu, J. (2019). Xinshidai zhongguo waijiao ji xuyao taoguangyanghui yeyao fenfayouwei [China's diplomacy in the new era requires both keeping-a-low-profile and striving-for-achievement]. *Zhongguo Dangzheng Ganbu Luntan [Chinese Cadres Tribune]*, 1, 46–48.

Liu, X. (2017). Dangqian zhongguo wangluo mincuizhuyi sichao de yanjintaishi jiqi zhili [The ongoing internet populism in China, its development trend and management]. *Tansuo [Probe]*, 4, 48–56.

Mastanduno, M. (2014). Order and change in world politics: The financial crisis and the breakdown of the Us–China grand bargain. In G. John Ikenberry (Ed.), *Power, order and change in world politics*. Cambridge: Cambridge University Press.

MCT (Ministry of Culture and Tourism of the People's Republic of China). (2019). Zhonghua renmin gongheguo wenhua he lvyoubu 2018nian wenhua he lvyou fazhan tongji gongbao [The 2018 statistics report on culture and tourism development by the Ministry of Culture and Tourism of the People's Republic of China]. Beijing. 30 May. Retrieved from http://zwgk.mct.gov.cn/auto255/201905/t20190530_844003.html?keywords=.

MOE (Ministry of Education of the People's Republic of China). (2016). Jiaoyubu guanyu zuohao 2017jie quanguo putong haodengxuexiao biyesheng jiuyechuangye gongzuo de tongzhi [The MOE Notification on the Employment and Business Development of the 2017 Graduates from Institutions of Higher Learning]. Nov. 25. Retrieved from http://www.moe.gov.cn/srcsite/A15/s3265/201612/t20161205_290871.html.

Ni, S., & Zhao, S. (2010). Guoji xingshi de bianhua yu shijie zhixu de chongjian [The change of International situation and the reconstruction of world order]. *Jilin Daxue Shehui Kexue Xuebao [Jilin University Journal Social Sciences Edition]*, 50(1), 17–25.

Pang, Z. (2015). Guoneiwai dou xuyao zhongguo gengjia yousuozuowei. *Lingdao Wencui*, 10(2), 25–28.

People's Daily Editorial. (2013). Guanjian shike ganyu liangjian (Daring to take resolute actions in critical moments). *Renmin Ribao [People's Daily]*, 2 Sept. Retrieved from http://opinion.people.com.cn/n/2013/0902/c1003-22768027.html.

Qian, Q. (1995). Shenru xuexi Deng Xiaoping waijiao sixiang, jinyibu zuohao xinshiqi waijiao gongguo [Carry out in-depth study of Deng Xiaoping diplomatic thought, press ahead with diplomatic work in the new era]. Speech delivered at the opening ceremony of a seminar on Deng Xiaoping diplomatic thought of the Chinese Foreign Ministry, 12 Dec. In *Deng Xiaoping Waijiao Sixiang Xuexi Gangyao [A Study Guide to Deng Xiaoping Diplomatic Thought]* (pp. 7–16). Beijing: World Affairs Press.

Qin, Y. (2010a). Guoji tixi de yanxu yu biange [Continuity and change of the inter-national system]. *Waijiao Pinglun [Foreign Affairs Review]*, *1*, 1–13.

Qin, Y. (2010b). Shijie geju, guoji zhidu yu quanqiu zhixu [World situation, inter-national insitutions and global order]. *Xiandai Guoji Guanxi [Contemporary International Relations]*, Special issue for the 30th anniversary of the China Institutes of Contemporary International Relations (CICIR), 10–17.

Qin, Y. (2011). Chinese culture and its implications for foreign policy-making. *China International Studies*, September/October, *5*, 45–65.

Qin, Y. (2014). Continuity through change: Background knowledge and China's inter-national strategy. *Chinese Journal of International Politics*, *7*(3), 285–314.

Qin, Y. (2018a). Shijiuda Baogao' yu zhongguo waijiao de xinshidai [Xi Jinping's Report at 19th CPC National Congress and the new era of China's diplomacy]. *Yatai Anquan yu Haiyang Yanjiu [Asia Pacific Security and Maritime Studies]*, *3*, 1–4.

Qin, Y. (2018b). *A relational theory of world politics*. Cambridge: Cambridge University Press.

Qin, Y., & Wei, L. (2018). Xinxing quanqiuzhili guan yu 'yidaiyilu' hezuoshijian [Global governance and the Belt and Road Initiative: Innovative ideas and international practices]. *Waijiao Pinglun [Foreign Affairs Review]*, *2*, 1–14.

Qu, X. (2001). Jianchi "taoguangyanghui yousuozuowei" de waijiao zhanlue [Stick to the diplomatic strategy of "keeping a low profile and making some attainment"]. *Zhongguo Renmin Daxue Xuebao [Journal of Renmin University of China]*, *5*, 13–17.

Ren, X. (2015). Sanda fenghui yu zhongguo waijiao xinquxiang [Three summits and the new orientation of China's diplomacy]. *Shijie Zhishi [World Affairs]*, *1*, 62–63.

Ren, X. (2018). A gongsheng/symbiotic theory of international relations. Paper pre-sented at the conference on 'Global IR and Non-Western IR Theory,' Beijing, China, 25 Apr. 2018.

Ren, X. (2020). Debating a Chinese school of international relations. *The Pacific Review*, This issue.

Shi, Y. (2013). Quanqiu zhengzhi xingshi he guoji geju toushi [Global political situ-ation and an analysis of the international structure]. *Xiandai Guoji Guanxi [Contemporary International Relations]*, *4*, 1–3.

Shi, Y. (2018). Deng Xiaoping zhihou de zhongguo: tansuo guochengzhong de guo-jia duiwai zhanlue [China after Deng Xiaoping: The search process for foreign strategy]. *Meiguo Yanjiu [the Chinese Journal of American Studies]*, *32*(3), 9–31.

Shin, K. (2011). The development of the debate over "hiding one's talents and biding one's time" (taoguan yanghui). *Asia-Pacific Review*, *18*(2), 14–36.

Sun, J. (2019). Zhongguo guoji huayuquan de suzao yu tisheng lujing [China's Approach to Shape and Improve Its International Discursive Power]. *Shijie Jingji yu Zhengzhi [World Economics and Politics]*, *3*, 19–43.

Tao, J. (2009). Meiguo xueshujie guanyu Deng Xiaoping "ershiba zi waijiao fangzhen" yanjiu shuping [A review of American scholars' study of Deng Xiaoping's "28-char-acter diplomatic doctrine]. *Zhonggong Dangshi Yanjiu [CPC History Studies]*, *11*, 118–124.

Wang, G. (2012). China's historical place reclaimed. *Australian Journal of International Affairs*, *66*(4), 486–492. doi:10.1080/10357718.2012.692533

Wang, Y. (2017). Dang de shibada yila zhongguo wajiao de xinchengjiu xinjingyan. [New achievements and experience in China's diplomacy since the 18th national congress of the CPC]. *Dangjian Yanjiu [Journal of CPC Capacity Building Studies]*, *6*, 23–26.

Wang, Y., & Wei, L. (2009). Fuzeren zhuquan, daguo hezuo yu guoji zhixu—ping *Quanli yu Zeren: Goujian Kuaguo Weixie Shidai de Guoji Zhixu* [Responsible sovereign, major power cooperation and international order—A review of *Power and Responsibility: Building International Order in an Era of Transnational Threats*]. *Waijiao Pinglun [Foreign Affairs Review]*, *2*, 147–152.

Wang, Y., & Zhao, L. (2017). Outward Foreign Direct Investment from China: Recent Trend and Development. *The Chinese Economy*, *50*(5), 356–365. doi:10.1080/10971475.2017.1345274

Wang, Z. (2010). Lishxing bianju tuxian xitongxing tiaozheng jinpo [Historic change highlights the urgency for systematic adjustment]. *Xiandai Guoji Guanxi [Contemporary International Relations]*, *1*, 1–19.

Wang, W. Z. (2019). Destined for misperception? Status dilemma and the early origin of US-China antagonism. *Journal of Chinese Political Science*, *24*(1), 49–65. doi:10.1007/s11366-018-09596-6

Wu, J. (2005). Bawo shidai tedian, zou heping fazhan daolu [Grasp the features of the era and follow the road of peaceful development]. *Waijiao Pinglun [Foreign Affairs Review]*, *10*, 6–12.

Wu, J. (2009). 2009 nian guoji xingshi sidakandian [Four major noteworthy points in international situation in 2009]. *Shijie Zhishi [World Affairs, 4*, 40–41.

Wu, X. (2010). Guoji xingshi jubianxia zhongguo de guoji quxiang [China's international orientation in the drastic change of the international situation]. *Guoji Wenti Yanjiu [China International Studies]*, *1*, 21–26.

Xi, J. (2017). Secure a decisive victory in building a moderately prosperous society in all respects and strive for the great success of socialism with Chinese characteristics for a new era. Report delivered at the 19th National Congress of the Communist Party of China. Beijing, 18 Oct. Retrieved from http://www.xinhuanet.com/english/download/Xi_Jinping's_report_at_19th_CPC_National_Congress.pdf.

Xiao, G. (2016). Jingti jizuopai de jizuohua weixian [Be alert to the danger of extremist tendency of the extreme left]. Renmin Luntan [People's Tribune], Jan. 1, 48–49.

Xing, Y., & Zhang, Y. (2006). Tao guang yang hui zhanlue zai sikao [Rethinking "keeping a low profile" strategy]. *Guoji guancha [International Observation]*, *6*, 13–19.

Xinhua. (2013). Xi Jinping zai zhoubian waijiao gongzuo zuotanhuishang fabiao zhongyao jianghua [Xi Jinping delivered an important speech at the Central Conference on Periphery Diplomacy]. Beijing. 25 Oct. Retrieved from http://news.xinhuanet.com/politics/2013-10/25/c_117878897.htm.

Xinhua. (2017). China becomes world's second-largest source of outward FDI: Report. Beijing. 8 June. Retrieved from http://www.xinhuanet.com/english/2017-06/08/c_136350164.htm.

Xinhua. (2018). Xi Jinping chuxi zhongyang waishi gongzuo huiyi bing jianghua [Xi Jinping attended central conference on work relating to foreign affairs and gave a talk]. Beijing, 23 June. Retrieved from http://www.81.cn/jmywyl/2018-06/23/content_8069393.htm.

Xinhua. (2019). Xi Jinping zai shengbuji zhuyao lingdao ganbu jianchi dixiansiwei zhuoli fangfan huajie zhongdafengxian zhuanti yantaoban kaibanshi shang fabiao zhongyao jianghua [Xi Jinping delivers an important speech at the opening session of the seminar on sticking to bottom-line thinking and striving to mitigate major risks participated by provincial and ministerial leaders]. Beijing, 21 Jan. Retrieved from http://www.gov.cn/xinwen/2019-01/21/content_5359898.htm.

Yan, X. (2014). From keeping a low profile to striving for achievement. *The Chinese Journal of International Politics, 7*(2), 153–184. doi:10.1093/cjip/pou027

Yan, X. (2017). Waijiao zhuanxing, liyi paixu yu daguo jueqi [Diplomatic transformation, interest ranking and rise of a major power]. *Zhanlue Juece Yanjiu [Journal of Strategy and Decision-Making], 3*, 4–11.

Yan, X. (2018). *Leadership and the Rise of Great Powers*. Princeton: Princeton University Press.

Zeng, J., & Breslin, S. (2016). China's 'new type of Great Power relations': A G2 with Chinese characteristics? *International Affairs, 92* (4), 773–794. doi:10.1111/1468-2346.12656

Zhang, R. (2013). Guoji geju bianhua yu zhongguo dingwei [Changes in international situation and China's positioning]. *Xiandai Guoji Guanxi [Contemporary International Relations], 4*, 20–22.

Zhang, Z. (2017). Zengqiang zhongguo zai guoji guize zhidingzhong de huayuquan [Enhance China's discursive power in the institutionalization of international norms]. Renmin Ribao [People's Daily], 17 Feb.

Zhao, F. (2016). Xin zuopai wuda fazhan qushi [Five development trends of the new left]. Renmin Luntan [People's Tribune], Jan. 1, 44–47.

Zhao, T. (2005). *Tianxia tixi: Shijie zhidu zhexue daolun [The Tianxia System: A Philosophy for the World Institution]*. Nanjing: Jiangsu Jiaoyu Chubanshe [Jiangsu Education Publishing House].

Zheng, B. (2005). China's "peaceful rise" to great power status. *Foreign Affairs, 84*(5), 18–24.

Zheng, B. (2010). Jixu zhuazhu he yonghao woguo fazhan de zhongyao zhanlue jiyuqi [Continue to seize and utilize the era of strategic opportunity for China's development]. *Dangjian Yanjiu [Journal of CPC Capacity Building Studies], 11*, 22–25.

Zheng, Z. (2018). Major-country diplomacy with Chinese characteristics in the new era. China International Studies, May/June, 5–14.

Zhou, F. (2017). Fenfayouwei de shouyi yu chengben [Benefits and costs of Striving-for-achievement]. *Zhanlue Juece Yanjiu [Journal of Strategy and Decision-Making], 3*, 56–68.

Zhu, C., et al. (2013). Dongya jichusheshi hulianhutong rongzi: wenti yu duice [East Asian infrastructure connectivity financing: Problems and policy recommendations]. *Guoji Jingji Hezuo [International Economic Cooperation], 10*, 24–29.

Zoelick, R. (2005). Whither China? From Membership to Responsibility: Remarks to the National Committee on US-China Relations. 21 Sept. Retrieved from https://www.ncuscr.org/sites/default/files/migration/Zoellick_remarks_notes06_winter_spring.pdf.

Chinese conception of the world order in a turbulent Trump era

Zhimin Chen and Xueying Zhang

ABSTRACT
The arrival of the Trump administration in the United States has sent shock-waves through the global system, triggering widespread rethinking of the current world order and its future direction. This happens at a time when China is starting to embrace a more proactive role in shaping the world order, based on its growing national strength and global influence. During the last seven decades, China has transformed itself from a 'revolutionary order-challenger' to a 'reformist order-shaper'. In the post-Cold War hybrid world order, China has gradually developed its view regarding the positive components of the world order which should be maintained, the deficient aspects of the world order to be reformed, and a vision of shared future to be promoted. Facing the challenge of the Trump era, Chinese scholars are debating future scenarios for the world order and how China could position itself and contribute to a more resilient international system. Though worst-case scenarios are considered, cautious optimism is maintained.

Introduction

The world is in an era of profound change, and the world order as we knew it, even in the recent past, is approaching a crossroads. Mega-trends have been transforming the world over the decades since the end of Cold War, and global power has substantially diffused away from the traditional power center of the West toward the global South. Rapid technological advancements are empowering some people and countries while marginalizing others; governance challenges are on the rise in all countries, even in the developed North; while the proliferation of regional and global problems calls for more effective multilateral solutions. Yet, it is the policy choices of governments that are leading the world towards unchartered territory. In particular, the United States (US) – the leading state in the current era – has significantly altered its view of the world and hence its policies, risking a more disorderly world.

Since the founding of the People's Republic of China, China has witnessed at least three distinct periods in terms of its role in the world order. From 1949 to 1978, China had positioned itself as a 'revolutionary order-challenger'. Professor Qin Yaqing, from the Foreign Affairs University of China and his colleagues, described China during that time period as a 'revolutionary state' and 'a challenger to the hegemons in a hegemonic system', with a 'strong struggle mentality' (Qin et al., 2009, p. 85). As the most outspoken ideological advocate for anti-imperialism and anti-capitalism, for a long time, China had been denied membership of the United Nations (UN). Even after China regained its membership in the UN and its Security Council in 1971, China still perceived that the global system and its institutions were unjustifiably dominated by the US and the Soviet Union, and maintained its challenger role both within and outside of global institutions.

The reform and opening-up policy pioneered by Deng Xiaoping turned China from a revolutionary state into a new developmental state. As economic development became the central task for China, and as the Western world developed strong interests to tap China's immense internal market, China started to embrace the world as a 'practical order-participator'. China developed a foreign policy predominantly to foster a peaceful international environment and deepen economic cooperation with the developed world. Since then, China has benefited greatly from its integration into the globalization process and its participation in regional and global institutions. It has achieved unprecedented economic growth, becoming the second largest economy considering nominal GDP in 2010. Not all developing countries succeeded in the same way within the same world order, and many even failed. The efforts of people and governments make a tremendous difference in their endeavors to develop their countries – Chinese people and Chinese governments made many correct decisions in the past four decades. At the same time, the world order, even with its flaws that China has long complained about, has generally been conducive to China's development.

Since the 18th National Congress of the Chinese Communist Party in 2012, under the leadership of President Xi Jinping, a new narrative has been developed regarding internal development in China and China's relations with the world. Internally, as Xi proclaimed in his report to the 19th National Congress of the CPC, China has in the previous two periods 'stood up, grown rich', and now 'is becoming strong', therefore, socialism with Chinese characteristics is 'entering a new era' (Xi, 2017a, p. 9). Externally,

China has started to pursue 'major country diplomacy with Chinese characteristics'. With its Belt and Road Initiative (BRI) from 2013, its championing of the development of 'a community with a shared future for mankind', and its role in encouraging the evolution of the global governance system, China has seen 'a further rise' in its 'international influence, ability to inspire, and power to shape' (Xi, 2017a, p. 6). Therefore, we can argue that China is becoming more proactively 'a reformist order-shaper'.

However, with global trends and the major shift in American policy under the Trump administration reconfiguring the world order, how is the Chinese conception of the world order evolving? And is it undergoing a major transformation? As the second largest economy in the world – still growing at a pace much faster than the developed North – any significant revision of the Chinese view of the world order will not only redefine the way China engages with the world, but also have a systemic impact on the future evolution of the world order.

This article attempts to understand how China's scholarly and policy community have viewed the world order in the past, and particularly how they view it in this turbulent moment. This paper proceeds to analyze the challenges facing the world from Chinese perspectives, and also offers Chinese assessments about the future of the world order.

The hybrid nature of the world order

Often, terms such as 'world order', 'international order' and 'global order' are used interchangeably in academia and policy discourse. But differences do stand out. In Oran Young's definition, 'international orders are broad framework arrangements governing the activities of all (or almost all) the members of international society over a wide range of specific issues' (Young, 1989, p. 13). Cai Tuo, a professor from China University of Political Science and Law, describes the international order as 'the characteristics, norms, patterns and systems formed by state actors in international interactions' (Cai, 2014, p. 15). Hedley Bull defines the world order as a much broader concept which includes 'not only order among states but also order on a domestic scale, as well as order within a wider world political system of which the states system is only part' (Bull, 2002, p. 21).

There is a clear preference in Chinese discourse for using the term 'international order'. Two reasons might explain this. The first is the shift from class-based analysis of world politics, of classical Marxism in the pre-reform era, to the state-centric view after China embraced reform and opening-up. A new focus was placed on China's modernization through international cooperation, rather than ideological struggles between socialism and capitalism. The second reason is that since Chinese scholarship

THE FREQUENCY OF USING THE TERM
'INTERNATIONAL ORDER' 'WORLD
ORDER' 'GLOBAL ORDER' AS PAPER
TITLE IN CHINA ACADEMIC JORUNALS
FULL-TEXT DATABASE 2010-2018

	2010	2011	2012	2013	2014	2015	2016	2017	2018
international order	19	19	23	29	40	51	55	40	44
world order	22	13	18	30	19	45	52	45	30
global order	3	2	2	3	3	12	8	1	5

Figure 1. Frequency of use of term 'international order', 'world order', 'global order' as paper title in CNKI database, 2010-2018.

started to build up its new focus on international studies, scholars have mostly encountered and interacted with the American state-centric scholarship of international politics.

Nevertheless, in the early-21st Century, we also saw a trend of growing usage of the term 'world order' in Chinese academic writings. Looking from the Chinese experience, scholars believed there was a need to stress the importance of including domestic order within a country as a crucial component of the world order, since any disorder within states could generate negative externalities, and destabilize the world order. Therefore, a stable order within states is the foundation to the world order (Chen, 2016a, pp. 152–163). Cai Tuo argued that the concept of 'international order' does not capture the totality and commonality of a new global system, therefore needs to be replaced by the concept of 'world order' or 'global order' (Cai, 2014, pp. 15–17). While official Chinese discourse still sticks to the concept of 'international order', the increasing attention given to global governance and the promotion of the idea of a shared future for mankind, yields to a growing embracement of the spirit and substance of the 'world order' concept. Therefore, this article will integrate the discourses on world order and international order to discuss the Chinese perception of world order (Figure 1 and Table 1).

With the above clarifications in mind, to the authors of this article, the world order of today is a hybrid one, with the uneasy coexistence of a sovereignty-based world order enshrined in the UN Charter and the American-

Table 1. Countries with largest quota share in the IMF since 1948.

Country	1948	1959	1966	1970	1978	1980	1983	1992	1999	2011	2010 reforms
Quota Share (Percent to Total)											
United States	32.5	28.4	24.3	23.1	21.2	21.2	20.2	18.8	17.7	17.7	17.4
Japan		3.4	3.4	4.1	4.2	4.2	4.8	5.8	6.3	6.6	6.5
China, P.R.: Mainland						3	2.7	2.4	2.2	4	6.4
Germany		5.4	5.7	5.5	5.4	5.4	6.1	5.8	6.2	6.1	5.6
United Kingdom	15.4	13.4	11.5	9.7	7.4	7.4	7	5.2	5.1	4.5	4.2
France	6.2	5.4	4.6	5.2	4.9	4.8	5.1	5.2	5.1	4.5	4.2
Italy	2.1	1.9	2.9	3.5	3.1	3.1	3.3	3.2	3.4	3.3	3.2
India	4.7	4.1	3.5	3.2	2.9	2.9	2.5	2.2	2.4	2.7	
Russia								3.1	2.8	2.5	2.7
Brazil	1.8	1	1.7	1.5	1.7	1.7	1.7	1.5	1.4	1.8	2.3
Canada	3.5	3.8	3.5	3.8	3.4	3.4	3.3	3.1	3	2.7	2.3
Saudi Arabia		0.1	0.4	0.3	1.5	1.7	3.6	2.3	3.3	2.9	2.1
Spain		0.7	1.2	1.4	1.4	1.4	1.5	1.4	1.5	1.7	2
Mexico	1.1	1.2	1.3	1.3	1.4	1.3	1.3	1.2	1.2	1.5	1.9
Netherlands	3.3	2.8	2.5	2.4	2.4	2.4	2.6	2.4	2.5	2.2	1.8
Korea, Republic of		0.1	0.1	0.2	0.4	0.4	0.5	0.6	0.8	1.4	1.8
Australia	2.4	2.1	2.4	2.3	2	2	1.8	1.7	1.5	1.4	1.4
Belgium	2.7	2.3	2	2.2	2.2	2.2	2.4	2.2	2.2	1.9	1.3
Switzerland								1.7	1.6	1.5	1.2

Source: IMF Working Paper, emerging powers and global governance: whither the IMF? WP/15/219.

led new liberal order. Tang Shiping, from Fudan University, argues that every order rests upon a mixture of power, institution, and norm, thus defining order should not base on 'ideal types' such as power-based or rule-based. Tang contends that 'there have been and will be international order(s), rather than a single international order' (Tang, 2019, p. 120).

Ikenberry believed that in the post-Cold War era, the American-led hierarchical international order has been a prevailing international order, even if he identified two of the five dimensions of an international order were sovereign independence and sovereign equality (Ikenberry, 2009, p. 78). Chinese scholars have encountered difficulty on many fronts to endorse the perception of world order only in the form of liberal international order. Tang questioned the liberal nature of the liberal international order, contending that if the order is imposed on others it could not be liberal, and that the liberal part of the order is only partial; prominently in the area of trade (Tang, 2019, p. 120). Some scholars saw deviation between the US' hegemon status and the liberal international order it wanted to offer the world. Qin Yaqing argued that it is questionable to regard the post-Cold War order as equivalent to the US-led liberal hegemonic order. Apart from American leadership, the post-Cold War order also rests upon three areas of consensus regarding order in international society: the consensus on multilateralism, the consensus on international cooperation and the consensus on institutional governance (Qin, 2017, p. 6). Jia Qingguo from Peking University stressed that the so-called liberal international order is not ideal for all. Due to its inherent structural defects, the liberal international order failed to alleviate but on the contrary triggered endless wars. With unbalanced advances in globalization and technology, the disparity between rich and poor economies has not retrenched (Jia, 2019, p. 55).

Chinese scholars strongly view the foundation of the world order as the Charter of the UN, and the principles and norms that the charter embodies. Yu Keping, a prominent intellectual and then vice-director of the Central Compilation and Translation Bureau argued that, even as the ongoing globalization process has diversified the political power of the nation-state to many other stakeholders and actors, 'the nation-state remains the most important political community of mankind to date', and 'defending its territorial integrity remains the country's most important political function' (Yu, 2004, p. 18). Li Qiang, a professor at Peking University, observed that regardless of the various criticisms directed at the principle of the sovereign state, it is undeniable that, 'sovereign states remain the basic unit which can combine political power and responsibility, and reflect the principle of democratic rule' (Li, 2001, p. 21). In official discourse, sovereign equality is regarded as 'the most important norm governing state-to-state relations over the past centuries and the cardinal principle observed by the UN and all other international organizations' (Xi, 2017b).

While China is one of the staunchest advocates, defenders and proponents of the sovereignty principle, that does not imply it has maintained a dogmatic view of sovereignty. As Fudan University professor Pan Zhongqi observes, 'unlike the previous approach to protect sovereignty by the use of force, China seems more flexible than before in seeking peaceful settlement on international disputes through diplomatic means' (Pan, 2010, p. 9). As Dong He and Yuan Zhengqing from the Chinese Academy of Social Sciences (CASS) note, the evolution of the Chinese conception of the international order can be understood as an accommodating process between domestic realities and the external environment (Dong & Yuan, 2016). Liu Zhiyun, a professor from Xiamen University, argues that we should develop a scientific criterion to define national sovereignty in the era of globalization. As long as a concrete arrangement of national sovereignty is conducive to the development of the productive force, to the strengthening of a country's comprehensive national power and to the enhancement of the people's living standard, that arrangement shall be the best defense of national sovereignty in the context of globalization. (Liu, 2003, p. 25) Therefore, to cope with this hybrid world order, a number of balancing acts are displayed in Chinese diplomatic discourses and practices.

First, in a sovereignty-based UN order, sovereignty means that China should and can protect its territorial integrity and maintain its own choice of political system, and its ability to choose its own development path. In one of the early definitions of China's core interests, the 2011 White Paper on China's Peaceful Development identified six core interests which included 'state sovereignty, national security, territorial integrity and national reunification, China's political system established by the Constitution and overall social stability, and the basic safeguards for ensuring sustainable economic and social development' (Information Office of the State Council of China 2011). Cai Liang emphasizes the Chinese view of sovereignty also implies that sovereign states should be independent in choosing their own political regimes, and the values underpinning them should also be self-reliant. Countries should avoid letting 'superior civilizations replace the others even if they are at variance' (Cai, 2018, p. 35). Not only is China making stronger efforts to protect its sovereignty, it has also stepped up its activism in defending the principles of sovereignty and non-interference around the world. Chen Zheng, from Shanghai Jiaotong University, explains that some Western interventions in the name of humanitarian intervention or the 'responsibility to protect' principle have created turmoil and chaos in some regions (Chen, 2018, p. 11). As Li Tingkang observed, although China's abstention allowed the UN Security Council to pass a resolution authorizing international military intervention in the Libya conflict in 2011, China was later critical of the intervention led by Western powers which deviated from the actions authorized by the Security Council. Therefore, 'to prevent the repeat of the Libya tragedy in Syria', China has vetoed multiple UN Security Council resolutions which might trigger similar Western military intervention in the Syrian conflict (Li, 2019, p. 125).

Second, China should embrace economic globalization, accepting the necessary rules and norms that protect the world's open trading system. Initially, China was reluctant to adopt liberal reforms at home in order to join liberal economic institutions such as the General Agreement on Trade and Tariffs (GATT); later succeeded by the World Trade Organization (WTO). However, China gradually realized the necessity to accept global rules and regimes that promote more liberal trade and investment, seeing this as the only way to participate in economic globalization and achieve mutually beneficial forms of economic cooperation. Therefore, out of China's own economic interests and the perceived general interests of the world, China made tremendous efforts to reform its own economic system and pushed for economic liberalization by seeking to join the global economic institutions which were created under the American-led liberal order. This indicates that China acknowledges that part of the liberal international order is legitimate, and should be preserved. Da Wei argues that even if China does not embrace the concept of the 'liberal international order', China is exercising a leading role, in supporting and defending the reasonable institutional arrangements within the existing international system (Da, 2018, p. 90). Qin Yaqing also stresses the importance to preserve the multilateral institutions which serve as a key component of the existing world order (Qin, 2017, p. 5). Strict WTO rules and the supranational dispute settlement mechanism within the WTO does regulate members' trade and economic practices – which is in contradiction to the absolute sovereignty concept – but China accepts the WTO and has displayed a solid record of compliance. From 2004–2018, 41 complaints were brought against China related to 27 issues. Of those, '5 are still pending, 12 were litigated all the way through, and 10 were resolved through some kind of settlement, or not pursued after the measure was modified' (CATO, 2018). In addition to that, empirical research conducted by Chinese scholars also demonstrates a relatively good compliance record of China (Zhang & Li, 2013).

Beyond economic rules and norms, China has also demonstrated its willingness to participate in and accept global institutions in other areas. For example, as Xia Liping observed, Beijing has shown gradual improvement in support for the rules and norms of the global nonproliferation regime (Xia, 2008, p. 2). As Chinese foreign minister Wang Yi stressed, China's firm support for the international order and system not only centres around the UN Charter, but also around 'the rules-based multilateral system of free trade, and the Paris Agreement and international climate action' (Wang, 2018).

Thirdly, China – as well as other developing countries – should be allowed to participate in the rule-making process commensurate with their economic power and influence. Acknowledging the importance of international rules and institutions aside, China generally sees itself and other developing countries as being in a disadvantageous position in the rule-making processes of the liberal order, particularly at a time of a major power shift in favor of developing world. In December 2014, President Xi directed officials to 'have more Chinese voices and inject more Chinese elements in the formulation of international rules' in order to 'maintain and expand our country's developmental interests' (Xi, 2014). With its increasing economic influence, Zhou Fangyin argues that China should embrace a new strategy of 'striving for achievement' *(fenfa youwei)* by revising certain international rules (Zhou, 2016, p. 46). For Zhao Minghao, 'institutional balancing' *(zhidu zhiheng)* has turned out to be a new feature in China's competition with the US for international prestige (Zhao, 2019, p. 17). In that competition and in institutional balancing, the core contest is about the provision of public goods (Li, 2016, p. 54).

Fourthly, while supranational governance – in which a country gives up its veto power – may be necessary in the area of trade, China strongly champions the bottom-up approach to negotiate global rules, norms and the distribution of national responsibilities, allowing countries to be the basic decisive actors in global rule-making. Based on the concept of internet sovereignty, the Chinese version of global cyber-space governance demonstrates an open Chinese desire to contest the existing multi-stakeholder model of internet governance promoted by the US (Zeng, 2017, p. 443). At the UN, China has led efforts to include the term 'multilateral' instead of 'multi-stakeholder' in a key 2015 document presented at the Ten Year Review of the World Summit on the Information Society, which acknowledges governments' leading role in cyber issues. The document also 'grants authority to UN bodies in which China exerts significant influence' (Levin, 2015). This intergovernmental approach toward international cooperation is also reflected in China's involvement in climate change regime-building, particularly in establishing the 'nationally determined contributions (NDCs)' as the basic mechanism to decide the obligations from individual states, rather than following the top-down approach of quantified emission limitation favored by the West. At the same time, countries should make greater effort to align their own interests with the general common interests of the world and other countries, in order for their domestic development to contribute to the further enhancement of development in other countries and in the world at large. If all countries worked in that direction, China envisages a desired future world order as 'a Community of Shared Future for Mankind'.

The rise of the rest and the call for order reform

The rise of the Rest is a defining feature in the eyes of Chinese observers of the new unfolding world order. Looking at the rapid growth rate of the non-Western countries, particularly the two most populous countries, China and India, the shifting balance of overall economic size in terms of purchase power parity between the global North and global South, and their collective growing influences in the world thereafter, Chinese observers believe that the unipolar world of the early period of the post-Cold War era is coming to an end, and is being replaced by a multi-polar world. The West, including the US, are perceived as being in relative decline, even if they are not in absolute terms. While the US is still the leading state, many in China realize that in a multi-polar world, China – with the second largest economy – has become the second largest power. Yang Jiemian, from the Shanghai Institute of International Studies (SIIS), states that as the world today 'is undergoing profound changes unseen in a century' *(bainian weiyou zhi da bianju)*, the multi-polarization process is approaching a tipping point, moving from quantitative change to qualitative change. The political and economic power of the non-Western world has risen significantly, and is rapidly extending to other areas, such as science and technology, culture, education and public opinion (Yang, 2019, p. 2). Wang Xiangsui, from Beihang University, argues that the rapid rise of emerging markets in developing countries has produced a more balanced global power configuration, which is deepening the multi-polarization process. At the same time the rise of the global South also indicates that modern Western capitalism might not be the only or the dominant system for development. The emergence of a viable Chinese development model highlights the multi-polarization process in another aspect (Wang, 2019, pp. 29–31).

Nevertheless, different views deviating from that mainstream do exist, and come from well-known researchers. For example professor Hu Angang, from Tsinghua University, published a co-authored article proclaiming that China's comprehensive national power would surpass the United States in 2020 in all nine categories, and will be 1.75 times that of American power (Hu et al., 2017). This view is widely disputed in China as representing a misleading exaggeration of Chinese power. Long Yongtu, former chief negotiator of China's accession to the WTO, emphasizes that China should acknowledge the continuing power gap with the US, and thus maintain a sense of urgency for further development (Long, 2018). Professor Yan Xuetong, from Tsinghua University, presents an alternative view to the multi-polarizing discourse. He believes that even by 2023 China's power will not fully catch up with the US in terms of national comprehensive power, but argues that China will become the only other power reaching a similar level of power and influence to the US, thus the world may enter a so-called new 'bi-polar system' (Yan, 2015). These two views share the widespread sense of China's growing power within the multi-polarization discourse, yet their inflated assessment of Chinese power does not draw too many followers in the academic and policy communities.

In a world moving toward multipolarity, Chinese observers strongly believe that the rules and norms of the global system need reforming to a certain degree. Clearly, Western countries maintain a central position in decision-making, agenda-setting and perception-shaping in global governance and its related institutions (Wu & Bing, 2018, p. 6). Many of the operating rules and norms in the liberal order have been shaped by the West, particularly the US, and are in favor of Western interests and values. The majority of developing countries are therefore in a disadvantaged environment where unfairness often occurs, placing them in a difficult situation to decide whether to accept certain rules or not (Wu, 2016, p. 26). As we discussed in the previous section, China was a selective order-participant in the post-Cold war liberal order; some rules and norms of this order were accepted by China, such as free trade arrangements promoted by the WTO, as well as many of the World Bank loan practices. Peacekeeping in the UN is another example whereby China has transitioned from a strong opponent to a proactive participant. The narrative of sustainable development was initially perceived as a Western attempt to slow the development of developing countries, but later was fully embraced by China in its own pursuit of scientific and green development.

Having said that, China does see major differences in the political values promoted by Western countries and the use of military and non-military coercion to advance these values. Niu Xinchun, a senior researcher from Chinese Institute for Contemporary International Relations (CICIR), describes how China has successfully 'utilized its political and economic statecraft' to 'integrate deeply into the international economic system'; but notes that 'the political integration is still limited, if not declined'. He argues that the ideology underpinning the liberal international order is poorly suited for China to exert its global political influence (Niu, 2013, pp. 3–5). Liu Jianfei, a senior fellow from National Academy of Governance, sees the international order as a basis for the US hegemony. Accordingly, he attributes the core of disagreement to the issue of leadership, with points of divergence centred on contestation on ideologies. He contends that the existing liberal international order is at odds with the domestic order led by the Chinese Communist Party within China, constituting an important structural contradiction which fuels divergence at the global systemic level (Liu, 2016, p. 14). In such a world of diversified values and cultures, for the Chinese, to manage this value divergence, it is of utmost importance that countries can strengthen dialogue, appreciate the merits of each other and learn from each other, rather than impose onto each other.

Second, key global institutions created to support the functioning of the current world order are now outdated in terms of representativeness. While China is satisfied with its privileged position in the UN Security Council, Chinese observers are quick to point out how the decision-making mechanisms of other major international organizations have lost touch with reality. Zhang Qianming claims the outdated system – which fails to reflect the reality of the shifting global economic landscape – leads to the severe questioning of the effectiveness and legitimacy of the major international institutions (Zhang, 2013, p. 11). Cai Liang argues the representativeness and inclusiveness of current world order is limited; hence the deficient global governance institutions are far from satisfying the growing demands of the international community (Cai, 2018, pp. 25–26). The most widely invoked examples of this under-representation problem include: the monopoly of leading positions in the World Bank and the International Monetary Fund (IMF) occupied by US and European nationals, and the growing mismatch between China's economic weight and China's quota shares and voting rights in the World Bank and IMF. Although the quota reform of 2010 was finally implemented in 2016 after a long delay, Chinese voting weight in the IMF only increased to 6.4%; less than half its GDP weight in the world economy in nominal terms (Figure 2 and Table 1).

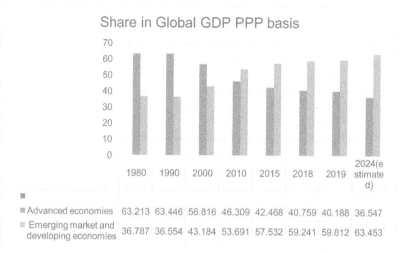

Figure 2. Share in Global GDP PPP basis, source: data from World Economic Outlook Database, IMF 2019.

Third, there is the issue of under-supply of public goods. Faced with mounting regional and global challenges, the mechanisms and resources to cope with such challenges are inadequate. Chinese scholars are particularly concerned that the major past suppliers of international public goods have displayed a reduced willingness to contribute. Renmin University professor Pang Zhongying raised the issue of 'international leadership deficit', speaking of a lack of 'strong, effective and correct international leadership in multilateralism' and consequently many failures in finding multilateral solutions (Pang Zhongying 2010, pp. 4–18). Tsinghua University professor Sun Xuefeng argues that, key to the US' benign hegemony is its ability to provide indispensable public goods for other states. Yet over the long term the US' dominant role is set to decline and its willingness to provide international public goods will become uncertain (Sun, 2015, pp. 83–90). Even if Western countries still provide aid, it is increasingly tied to political conditions to support efforts to expand their security networks and promote democracy and human rights. The arrival of the Trump government further exacerbates this problem.

Forth, the self-serving national policies of Western countries has often negatively influenced the Rest. Cai Liang, a research fellow from the Shanghai Institute for International Studies (SIIS), argues that Western interventions in the global South are more often in line with Western domestic needs and national interests, and have not produced positive results in many countries (Cai, 2018, p. 28). For example, Western military intervention in Libya in 2011 resulted in a quick military victory and achieved its regime change objective. However, the US and its European allies did not have a post-conflict plan or long-term commitment strategy for Libya. They disengaged quickly, leaving Libya in chaos. Zhou Qi and Shen Peng from CASS have also criticized the US' Middle East strategy for its objective to impose upon the region a particular democratic belief system, aiming to fulfill its own national interests rather than for the interests of the Libyan people (Zhou & Shen, 2012, p. 24).

There are strong calls from China that these aspects of world order should be reformed. Yet instead of radically overhauling the order, gradual reform has been the prevailing view in China. Su Changhe suggested a gradual and incremental reform approach to the current order (Su, 2009, p. 30). Xue Li, a senior fellow from CASS, also argued that building a future order in a peaceful environment is bound to be a gradual process. A new equilibrium will be created and the process will last until whenever 'the order advocated by China has been steadily set up, and the soft and hard power of China has been accepted by the current international order' (Xue Li, 2019).

The emergence of the G20 was welcomed in China as a positive development to build more inclusive mechanisms for global governance. The rising importance of emerging economies within the global economy since the 1990s has gradually become better reflected within the current global governance architecture. In the area of climate governance, during the 2009 Copenhagen climate conference, the West still intended to impose a solution upon emerging economies and blamed the latter for the failure of talks. During the 2016 Paris climate conference, views and contributions from emerging economies were taken more seriously and through collective efforts, the Paris Agreement was concluded. These cases indicated to the Chinese that a gradual reform approach would likely be slow, but may not be impossible.

At the same time, the slow process of institutional reform has raised serious concerns in China. After the immediate US economic crisis was managed with assistance from G20 members, the G20-pushed IMF voting rights reform of 2010 was blocked in the US congress for five years, indicating to the global South that the old powers were reluctant to share decision-making with the newcomers. These concerns prompted the developing countries to make additional efforts to build new institutions of their own. For Xu Xiujun, a senior fellow at CASS, to reshape the international economic order China could look to undertake three types of actions: modifying institutional reform, constructive institutional supplement, and innovative institutional replacement; which might lead to respectively three different scenarios: an embedded order in which China participates, a competitive order that China promotes, or an inclusive order that China might lead (Xu, 2015, pp. 91–98). Chen, (2016b) argued that if reforming the existing international institutions could be seen as a product of China's 'reform from within' strategy, then creating new institutions or networks outside of the existing international institutions could be labeled as constituting a 'reform from outside' strategy, which includes as least four sub-strategies:

1. The creation of 'plurilateral regional orders' composed of neighboring countries. These orders may emerge in areas where the existing order is weak or absent, with the purpose of promoting autonomous regional co-operation and stability, such as the Shanghai Cooperation Organization (SCO).
2. The creation of 'plurilateral embedded orders', where like-minded countries create new international arrangements to provide additional governance resources, such as the Chiang Mai Initiative Multilateralization (CMIM). However, these institutions are designed explicitly to complement the existing order, as most of the CMIM loan decisions are be tied to IMF decisions.
3. The creation of 'plurilateral parallel orders', with new institutions outside the existing order created by like-minded countries, such as the Shanghai-based New Development Bank (NDB) and the Beijing-based Asian Infrastructure Investment Bank (AIIB). These arrangements bring in additional governance resources and capacities and operate independently, but have overlapping functions with existing mainstream institutions. Observing recent developments related to the two new banks, we can also see some differences between them; notably that the AIIB has a greater willingness to work with existing development financing institutions such as the World Bank.
4. The creation of China-initiated 'bilateral networks', mostly through China's 'Belt and Road Initiative (BRI)', which stands for the continental Silk Road Economic Belt initiative and the Maritime Silk Road Initiative, announced by China in 2013. Since then, the BRI has attracted more than 100 individual countries around the world, many groups of countries, and regional and international organizations to work with China in promoting connectivity and bilateral co-operation.

Facing up to the Trump-era challenges

Donald Trump's surprise victory in the October 2016 US presidential election marked a departure from expected US foreign policy, posing systemic challenges to the world. The first challenge is the nature of the Trump foreign policy revolution, marked by its unprecedented combination of unilateralism and nationalism. President George Bush junior's unilateral foreign policy constituted a first major turnaround after a decade of new liberal foreign policy under presidents George Bush senior and Bill Clinton, but this unilateralism was only in the military aspect, taking the US into more military interventions than before. In essence, it was still a globalist foreign policy, though more unilateral rather than multilateral, as previously. The administration of Barack Obama restored the new liberal foreign policy. Li Kaisheng, from the Shanghai Academy of Social Science (SASS), observed that the Obama government was tasked with making the post-financial crisis international order more effective in dealing with various global challenges on the one hand, while 'renewing American leadership in the world' on the other (Li, 2017, pp. 89–92). However, by adopting an 'American First' doctrine, the Trump administration places the US' narrow national interests unprecedentedly above global engagement and responsibilities, representing the largest isolationist turn in contemporary US foreign policy. Yan Xuetong argues that 'under Trump, the country has broken with this tradition, questioning the value of free trade and embracing a virulent, no-holds-barred nationalism' (Yan, 2019a, p. 41). Furthermore, Trump foreign policy has pushed its unilateralism into a new extreme, particularly through its unilateral and coercive use of economic sanctions in the advancement of the US' narrow interests.

The second challenge from the Trump government is its relegation of US support for many core aspects of the liberal order that the US helped to create and has benefitted from for decades. After the end of the Second World War, the US played a central role in establishing a new set of institutions, rules, principles and arrangements, including the UN, World Bank and global trading and climate regimes which most members of the international community accepted and joined. The US also played a leading role in building many important regional and bilateral arrangements. Since Trump's election, the US has withdrawn from the Paris agreement and a number of international treaties and institutions, and has demanded major changes to the WTO. In 2018 alone, it pulled out of the Intermediate-Range Nuclear Forces Treaty – the nuclear deal with Iran – and withdrew from the UN Human Rights Council. The US under Trump has also made efforts to change the North American Free Trade Agreement (NAFTA), negated the Trans-Pacific Partnership (TPP), launched a series of non-WTO-compatible tariff wars against key trading partners, and was even antagonistic to its traditional Western allies. In sum, even if Trump has talked of a free trade agreement with the EU, the US has still become the major disruptive force in the free trade system that it created, by restoring frequent tariff coercion in all directions. If the provision of economic public goods and military alliance is the moral foundation of the US liberal international order (Sun, 2018, pp. 32–33), then Trump foreign policy is posing a major threat the continuation of that order. Yuan Zheng from CICIR argues that Trump's pri-oritization of domestic considerations over international will eventually result in the decay of Western political regimes, as well as eroding the glo-bal governance system (Yuan, 2019, p. 26).

The third challenge comes from the Trump government's emerging strategy and tactics toward China. Most Chinese observers failed to predict the election of Trump in 2016. Some Chinese observers regarded Trump's anti-China rhetoric during the election campaign as vote-winning tactics, which would likely not be implemented after he moved into the White House. Wang Yizhou in 2016 argued that the US and China were inter-dependent, and that common challenges such as climate change, counter-terrorism, and nuclear-proliferation called for two countries to cooperate rather than confront each other. Thus, no matter which president gained power, or which party he or she came from, it would not negatively impact US-China relations (Wang, 2016). Some scholars pointed out that a Trump win over Hilary Clinton might be positive for US-China relations, as Trump promised to withdraw from TPP negotiations. Mei Xinyu, from the Chinese Academy of International Trade and Economic Cooperation, commented that Trump's decision to withdraw from the TPP might be good news for Beijing, ease the strategic pressure on China from the US and Japan (Mei, 2017). The Obama administration, with Hillary Clinton as secretary of state, had developed a 'pivot to Asia' strategy in 2010, which aimed to strengthen and enlarge the US' alliance system in the Asia-Pacific region backed by the proposed TPP trade pact.

However, as Trump stepped up pressure on China in order to deliver his campaign promises, Chinese observers started to ponder that Trump might be the most dangerous American leader for China. Yang Qijing, from Renmin University, warned that Trump might exploit every policy to help sustain US hegemony until the next election (Yang, 2016). Varying views about Trump's real intentions have been developed. Some argue that the Trump administration is determined to see China as the real rival to US pre-dominance in the world, and that the US would take convoluted measures to contain or even overturn a rising China, to a faltering China (Zhang, 2019; Yu, 2019). The Trump administration's first National Security Strategy report clearly defined China as a strategic rival on a global scale and claimed that China sought to 'displace the US in the Indo-Pacific region, expand the reach of its state-driven economic model and reorder the region in its favor' (The White House, 2017). The then policy planning chief of the State Department Kiron Skinner described a new 'clash of civiliza-tions' and regarded China as an ideological rival (Skinner, 2019). The Trump government's full-scale trade war against China and its decision to block key supplies to a number of China's main high-tech companies, serves as further proof that the US is using its power to disrupt China's rise. Others, including Da Wei from the University of International Relations, still view Trump as a transactional deal-maker, and see his maneuvers as tactics to renegotiate the terms of the US-China economic relationship (Da, 2017, p. 81). More importantly, leaving aside the different understandings in China about the nature of Trump's China policy, his willingness to maximally exploit the US' relatively better position within a deep economic mutual interdependence, and to extract Chinese concessions by threatening to decouple the two economies through additional tariffs and trade blockades, has alarmed the Chinese side that the nature and foundation of the US-China relationship may now be experiencing a critical shake-up. Former vice Foreign Minister Fu Ying cautions that the divergences between the US and China are clearly becoming enlarged, especially due to signals in the Trump era that the US is starting to emphasize competition over cooperation (Fu, 2018).

Many Chinese scholars are very concerned about the major economic and technological decoupling underway between the US and China. China's past economic success has owed a great deal to its integration within the world economy, and in particular to the US economy. Decoupling with China's No. 1 trading partner, and biggest source of trade surplus, would be seen as major setback for China, and is not a choice that most Chinese would like to embrace. Therefore, many still hope that in the end, China will further open up its market for the access of foreign companies, strengthen its protection of intellectual property, and make efforts to reduce its trade surplus with the US, so that a major decoupling can be avoided. At the same time, seeing what Trump has done in terms of raising tariffs on the massive volume of Chinese exports to the US, and US attempts to paralyze Chinese high-tech companies, resisting excessive US demands and defying US bullying is becoming the mainstream view in China; even if it might lead to further escalation of trade conflict, risking a semi-decoupling or even a total decoupling in the future. From Chen Qingqing's perspective, the US' technological embargo against Huawei reflects Washington's dangerous Cold War mentality that will lead to further US-China decoupling, which is also casting a shadow over stalled trade negotiations between two countries and will hurt the eco-system of the global tech industry (Chen, 2019). One commentary, from the official Xinhua News Agency, states that:

> 'China never wants to fight a trade war, but will fight one whenever it is necessary. As China defends its development rights and core interests, it is also fighting for trade multilateralism with the World Trade Organization at its core and a fair environment for global development, demonstrating a strong ability to control risks and a sense of responsibility as a major country' (Xinhua, 2019).

The escalation of current trade conflicts between the US and China presents a dilemma for both countries: to work toward a mutually acceptable solution, or to embrace at least a partial decoupling or even potentially a total decoupling. On January 15, 2020, the two sides signed a "phase one" trade deal which reduced tensions over trade, the high level of competition between the two countries will not simply disappear. So, the Trump challenges and the consequences for US-China relations are posing big questions for other countries and especially for China: whether, and how, the Rest of the world can sustain the central components of the existing world order which are still endorsed by them? What kind of future world order is unfolding? And, whether China can continue to stick to its role of a 'reformist order-shaper', or needs to prepare for a new confrontational Cold War?

Scenarios of future world orders

The future of the world order appears more uncertain than just a few years ago. As we discussed in the previous section, the Trump administration has negated many aspects of the longtime American pursuit of a US-led liberal order. That order is already under challenge from the outside, but now the US itself appears to be withdrawing its support to sustain that order. Given this context, what other options are still in sight?

During the Obama administration, in the West, even if there were people in the US still championing American preeminence, scholars such as Ikenberry already saw that with the relative decline of the US and entire Western world, the West needed to forge a close coalition to ensure its continued predominance in the world, through the norms and institutions the that the West collectively created and maintained. A Western-led liberal order could be more viable than a US-led one. Obviously, this is not an option that China would endorse. Zhao Chen finds that the efforts to negotiate a Trans-Atlantic Trade and Investment Partnership (TTIP) reflected the collective will of the West to collaborate in a time of 'weakened West', to set new trade standards for the world through the building of an 'economic NATO'. Such a development is certainly not in the interests of developing countries (Zhao, 2016). To build a Western-led liberal order, it faces the problem of alienating developing countries and forcing them to build alternative institutions outside of existing institutions; and it will also likely encounter a problem of sustainability when emerging countries become the leading economic powers in over the next two decades (Chen, 2013). What the Chinese envisage, is a world of further multi-polarization with the Rest rising inevitably to obtain a more meaningful decision-making position in the global system. The hierarchical nature of the order should be mitigated.

The arrival of the Trump administration has further undermined the possibility of such a future world order. On the one hand, the Trump administration has created a wider value gap with the US' Western allies, and advocates many policies which are opposite to the liberal values shared by its Western allies. It withdrew from the Paris Agreement and the Iranian nuclear deal – two agreements the EU deemed central to core European interests. On the other hand, the Trump administration also does not treat its Western allies as equal partners. The Trump administration has raised demands in an already-stalled TTIP negotiation, imposed or threatened to tariffs on European exports to the US, and forced its European NATO allies to increase military spending to a target 2% of GDP. As Zhao Huaipu, a professor from China Foreign Affairs University, pointed out, in the eyes of Trump, 'relations between the United States and the Europe is just a transactional relationship between the protector and the protected' (Zhao, 2019, p. 5). Obviously, Trump does not want to share global leadership with Europe.

Nevertheless, it is equally true that a US-led unilateral order has a lower chance of being accepted in the world than a US-led or Western-led liberal multilateral order. Chinese observers have come to an understanding that the Trump administration favors bilateral negotiation, disdains multilateral trade mechanisms, has adopting an approach of retreating in order to advance, and intends to pursue unilateralism to shape a new international economic order (Yuan, 2019). They point out the US' remaining areas of hegemonic power over the world, such as extraterritorial hegemony (Jiang, 2019), technological hegemony (Wang, 2019) and financial hegemony (Zhang, 2018). Despite these advantages, it is increasingly strange that the Trump administration still believes a US-led unilateral order could replace a US-led or Western-led liberal multilateral order to ensure even more solid US leadership in the world. As Wu Xinbo argues, the Trump administration has acquired a 'syndrome of hegemonic decline'. The US' economic and foreign policy under Trump is harming its economic power and international standing, and is accelerating the process of US decline (Wu, 2018). A PEW poll released on 1 October 2018 shows that, across 25 nations polled, a median of only 27% of respondents had confidence in Trump to do the right thing in world affairs; 70% lack confidence in him. In the same poll, 70% said the US only looks after its own interests in world affairs; ignoring the interests of other nations. (Wike et al., 2018)

If a future world order, in the era of Trump, could not be a collective Western-led order, a US-led unilateral order, or a US-led liberal order, then how have Chinese scholars discussed and conceptualized an alternative future model of the world order?

There are a number of academic endeavors in China to theorize the future world order. From the authors' view, in the academic community, the *Gongsheng/symbiosis* view of the world is more attuned to the mainstream discourse in China. Yang Jiemian, from SIIS, contends that along with China's gradual transformation from a global power to a global great power, the construction of its theories of foreign policy moved to the second phase of peaceful symbiosis from the first phase of peaceful coexistence starting from 1950s, and is now on its way to a third phase: harmonious symbiosis (Yang, 2013, p. 4). The *Gongsheng/symbiosis* view refers to an order in which countries – regardless of their sizes, strengths, cultures, civilizations and values – can equally coexist and mutually benefit each other, avoiding 'zero-sum' antagonism. In the *Gongsheng/symbiotic* system, countries have interlinked interests, rights and responsibilities (Su, 2016, p. 9). The *Gongsheng* school values the differences between state actors and sees diversity as the stimulator for social development. For Ren (2019, p. 48), *Gongsheng*, as an international relations theory, provides an alternative approach because it argues that global governance can be conducted through a sovereignty-based system, rather than requiring a supranational structure.

The modern reinvention of the *Tianxia* (All under the heaven, or the world) view constitutes another Chinese imagination of world order. The *Tianxia* view in Ancient China envisages a family-state-*Tianxi*a structure, with *Tianxia* as a family of states and people all under the heaven, following a set of rule and rituals. Zhao Tingyang, a philosopher from the Chinese Academy of Social Science (CASS), first reintroduced the academic *Tianxia* debate. In his reinvention, the *Tianxia* vision of world order departs from a state-centered paradigm, and regards *Tianxia* as the most important analytical unit (Zhao, 2014, p. 141). Zhao sees the UN as an international institution, not a world institution. Governing the world demands a world institution, which should be one with the 'highest political power' in a multi-layered political system (Zhao, 2005, pp. 150–151). However, in Zhao Tingyang's institutional imagination of *Tianxia*, — a powerful world institution is a jump too far from the reality of international politics. For Wang Qingxin, a world government would be very difficult to establish. If one is ever established, it would not solve the problems of instability and majority tyranny. A *Tianxia* world government would face the further problem of persuading the rest of the world to accept a world government based on Confucius culture (Wang, 2016, p. 98). Despite these controversies, the *Tianxia* concept has inspired discussion of 'new *Tianxiaism*' articulated by Xu Jilin, and 'new cosmopolitanism' advanced by Liu Qing, both professors from East China Normal University. Both aim to reintroduce to the modern world elements of the Tianxia tradition, such as the norms of inclusiveness, harmony in diversity, and seeking common points while reserving differences. They also want to remove the China-centric component of the *Tianxia* tradition, aiming to build a new universal consensus through civilizational dialogue so as to overcome the conflict-prone nationalism of the modern world. To distinguish from the hierarchical *Tianxia* tradition, Xu Jilin's 'new Tianxiais' emphasizes 'de-hierarchicalization' (Xu, 2015), and Liu Qing just moves further by using the 'cosmopolitanism' instead of '*Tianxiaism*' (Liu, 2015).

Moral realism, articulated mainly by Yan Xuetong and scholars based in Tsinghua University, attempts to develop a worldview with China at center stage. Moral realism regards morality as of equal importance to policy-making as power, capability, and interest. When a rising state's political leadership based on moral attraction surpasses that of the dominant state, the power disparity between the two states is reversed, rendering the rising state the new dominant state (Yan, 2019b). He argues that 'the level of morality of the hegemon is related to the degree of stability of the international system and the length of time of its endurance' (Yan, 2011, p. 65). Applying pre-Qin thoughts into international relations theories, Yan believes that, a rising China should set its aim to become a country of 'humane authority (*wangquan*)' and 'a moral world superpower', which implies that 'China will establish a fairer and safer international order' (Yan, 2015, pp. 215–216). Before China can reach that goal, China would face a world of bipolarity, in which, opposed in their strategic interests but evenly matched in their power, China and the US will be unable to challenge each other directly and settle the struggle for supremacy definitively. The world may 'expect recurring tensions and fierce competition, yes, but not a descent into global chaos' (Yan, 2019b).This moral realism does not depart too far in its emphasis on China's moral attraction with the official Chinese discourse of a desired world order; it also helps scholars direct more of their research on the important role of China in the shaping of the future world order. However, moral realism attempts to build a China-led benign hierarchical world order, which is not in line with the reality of modern world of sovereign states and with the trend of power diffusion in the world.

There is a more clearly articulated official conception of the world/international order, in the notion of 'a Community of Shared Future for Mankind': a vision based on sovereign states and the multi-polarizing balance of power, but supportive of necessary multilateral and bilateral mechanisms to promote the level of cooperation required in a globalized world. It is not an order to replace the existing one, but an improvement of the current order. In a major speech by President Xi Jinping at the UN office in Geneva on 18 January 2017, he presented five aspects of such a future world: countries stay committed to building a world of lasting peace through dialogue and consultation; build a world of common security for all through joint efforts; build a world of common prosperity through win-win cooperation; build an open and inclusive world through exchanges and mutual learning; and make the world clean and beautiful by pursuing green and low-carbon development (Xi, 2017b). Zhang Wenmu commented that, through 'a Community of Shared Future for Mankind', China presents a 'China solution' for global governance which meets the needs of human-kind by embracing ancient oriental wisdoms. (Zhang, 2017, p. 24) Gao Cheng from CASS emphasizes the idea of 'contributing together and bene-fiting together' within 'a Community of Shared Future for Mankind', allow-ing China's development model to serve as a template and inspiration to countries encountering similar development challenges, in order to help them achieve long-term political stability and prosperity (Gao, 2016, p. 104).

Overall, Chinese scholars are cautiously optimistic that this is a future world order to be promoted. First of all, Chinese in general believe that US dominance in the world is not sustainable. A recent survey conducted in China showed that a majority of Chinese citizens (57.7%) who participated in the survey believed that China will eventually surpass the US in terms of overall development (Huazhong keji daxue guojia chuanbo zhanlue yan-jiuyuan (Huazhong University of Science & Technology National Communication Strategy Institute), 2019). A future China might not be a new dominating power, but the US will surely lose its dominating position (Zhang, 2019). Therefore, any hegemonic world order will not be viable in the future.

Secondly, a globalized world demands cooperation among states and other global actors. Even if globalization has its many flaws, it remains one of the mega-trends in the world. Globalization is already an 'objective real-ity of the contemporary world' and could not 'be altered by the subjective will of some people' (Qin, 2017). The mounting number of global issues has also enlarged the wide gap between the necessity of global governance and current global governance capacity, creating a fundamental problem which requires the adjustment of the international order (Fu & Fu, 2017).

Thirdly, in the wider global South, and even in most Western countries, China would still find many like-minded partners in terms of developing economic partnerships, and governance partnerships to address large-scale regional and global challenges, such as regional security, nuclear prolifer-ation, climate change and sustainable development,. Countries in the European Union are mostly NATO allies and key supporters of the past US-led liberal international order. While European states share some concerns of the Trump administration regarding policy towards China, they are also bewildered by rising US unilateralism and are willing to work with China on many key bilateral and global agendas. Chinese observers are following the

EU's new foreign direct investment review mechanism, which has a fairly explicit aim to restrict Chinese direct investment in EU countries (Zhang, 2019) They are also paying close attention to the EU's collaboration with the US and Japan in pushing WTO reforms which would restrict state subsidies and curb the role of state-owned companies in national economies (Xu & Zhang, 2019). Nevertheless, these differences do not overshadow the broader shared understanding and support between European states and China on the key aspects of a desired future world order. Both sides champion multi-lateralism (Michalski & Pan, 2017), while a number of key European countries have joined the China-initiated 'AIIB' (Pang, 2015). In a recent Joint Statement from the 21st EU-China Summit, leaders on both sides stressed that the EU and China 'reaffirm their resolve to work together for peace, prosperity and sustainable development and their commitment to multilat-eralism, and respect for international law and for fundamental norms govern-ing international relations, with the UN at its core' (European Council, 2019). This European example showcases that the rest of the world is unlikely to fol-low the template of the Trump government, or embrace similar forms of nar-row nationalism and isolationism in economic and foreign policy.

Conclusion

After becoming the world's second largest economy in 2010, China embarked on a road of 'major country diplomacy with Chinese characteris-tics', and discussions thereafter about world/international order proliferated. If Zhao Tingyang's *Tianxia* view and its variations represent an idealist cosmopolitan imagination of a world order, and moral realism presents a realist China-centric conception, then sitting in the middle is the official vision of 'a community of shared future' and the mainstream view centred on a desired cooperative world based on sovereign states. This official and mainstream vision does not aim to overthrow the existing world order by promoting an entirely different one. It is mainly calling for an improvement of the current order. To achieve this, Chinese observers share a general con-sensus that the world needs to preserve the UN and many aspects of the liberal order including open trade, climate governance and sustainable development. Chinese observers have strong reservations in relation to the hegemonic side of the liberal international order, whether in the form of unilateral US leadership or collective Western leadership. They also have a problem with the heavy-handed promotion of liberal political values and norms, above respect for the principle of sovereignty. Therefore, the main-stream view in China demands some reforms of the existing arrangements, to increase the representativeness of developing countries in the current major multilateral institutions, making them compatible with an increasingly post-hegemonic new power balance reality. Chinese scholars also call for reforms to allow developing countries to better participate in multilateral rule-making processes, so that these rules and norms fall more closely in line with their interests and aspirations. They also see an additional need to further enhance capacity to conduct effective global governance, and support China as a new supplier of material and ideational resources. As Qin Yaqing observed, such a loosely-organized but multilateral order based on sovereignty may be less efficient, yet it is a relatively democratic and inclusive order, and it might be a practical order for the 21st century (Qin, 2014, p. 15).

This Chinese view of a desired world order encounters a turbulent world in the era of the Trump administration. Within countries, even the developed world is starting to feel the governance challenges associated with the rise of anti-establishment populism and anti-globalization nationalism. Among the countries, an open trading system, which has been the foundation for the globalization process, is under attack from countries that helped to build it in the first place. The problem of the global leadership deficit is exacerbated by the Trump administration, while the problem of inadequate leadership and poor decision-making in the past, notably the disastrous intervention in Libya, has not been mitigated.

Nevertheless, there is still a sense of a cautious optimism among Chinese observers over the future world order; although some are still deeply worried at the unprecedented level of trade and high-tech warfare between China and the US, and harbor concerns about a decoupling of the strong bilateral economic relationship which served a great deal to aid China's rapid modernization over the past four decades. As China itself becomes a systemically important player in the global system, any instability between China and the leading Western state could also create destabilizing effects in Asia and beyond.

As the US' growing unilateralism under Trump has alienated many countries, there is a perceived wider common interest in the world working together to sustain the key elements of the existing world order, through mutual commitment and implementing necessary reforms. With or without the US, countries are striving to move forward the Paris agreement and sustain the Iranian nuclear deal. These cases demonstrate that, if others can work together, the US is not as indispensable as it was in the past. Having said that, to make this task easier, China and the US must find a way to forge a new stable relationship between them. Without that, the future world order will be plagued by an intensifying US-China rivalry.

Disclosure statement

No potential conflict of interest was reported by the author(s).

References

Da, W. (2017). Telangpu zhengfu "meiguo youxian" waijiao zhengce: chubu guancha yu fenxi [Trump's "American First" Foreign Policy: preliminary observation and analysis]. *Zhongguo guoji zhanlue pinglun [China International Strategic Review]*, 12, 79–90.

Bull, H. (2002). *The anarchical society: A study of order in world politics* (3rd ed.). New York, NY: Palgrave Macmillan.

Cai, L. (2018). Shixi guoji zhixu de zhuanxing yu zhongguo quanqiu zhili guan de shuli [Analyzing the transformation of the international order and China's construction of its global governance outlook]. *Guoji Guanxi Yanjiu [International Relations Review]*, 2, 25–38.

Cai, T. (2014). Quanqiu zhuyi shijiao xia de guoji zhixu [The world order under the globalism perspective]. *Xiandai Guoji Guanxi [Contemporary International Relations]*, 7, 15–17.

CATO. (2018, November 15). Discipling China's trade practices at the WTO: How WTO complaints can help make China more market-oriented. Retrieved from https://www.cato.org/publications/policy-analysis/disciplining-chinas-trade-practices-wto-how-wto-complaints-can-help

Chen, Q. (2019, May 16). Huawei ban reflects "Cold War mentality". *Global Times*. Retrieved from http://www.globaltimes.cn/content/1150289.shtml

Chen, Z. (2013). Duoji shijie de zhili moshi [Governance models of a multipolar world]. *Shijie jingji yu zhengzhi [World Economics and Politics]*, 10, 4–23.

Chen, Z. (2016a). Guojia zhili yu shijie zhixu jiangou (State governance, global governance and the reconstruction of the world order). *Zhongguo Shehui Kexue (Chinese Social Science)*, 6, 152–163. doi:10.1080/02529203.2016.1241500

Chen, Z. (2016b). China, the European Union and the fragile world order. *Journal of Common Market Studies*, 54(4), 775–792. doi:10.1111/jcms.12383

Chen, Z. (2018). Shiheng de ziyou guoji zhixu yu zhuquan de fugui [The unbalanced international order and the back of sovereignty], *Guoji zhengzhi kexue [Quarterly Journal of International Politics]*, 3(1), 1–24.

Da, W. (2018). "Ziyou guoji zhixu" de qianlu yu zhongguo de zhanlue jiyu qi [The future of "liberal international order" and China's period of strategic opportunity], *Quanqiu zhixu [Global order]*, 1, 90–106.

Dong, H., & Yuan, Z. (2016). Zhongguo Guoji Zhixuguan: Xingcheng yu neihe [China's view of international order: the formation and cores]. *Jiaoxue yu yanjiu [Teaching and Research]*, 7, 45–51.

European Council. (2019, April 9). EU-China Summit Joint Statement. Retrieved from https://www.consilium.europa.eu/media/39020/euchina-joint-statement-9april2019.pdf

Fu, M., & Fu, Y. (2017). Bianhua de shijie, buqueding de shidai: dangqian guoji zhixu yanbian de qushi [The changing world and uncertain times, the current trend of the evolution of the international order]. *Renmin luntan xueshu qianyan [Frontiers· People's Forum]*, 4, 6–11.

Fu, Y. (2018, July 19). Guoji zhixu weilai de fangxiang (The future of international order). *Global Times*. Retrieved from http://opinion.huanqiu.com/hqpl/2018-07/12522414.html?agt=15438

Gao, C. (2016). Zhongguo jueqi yu xin guoji zhixu guan de jiangou(China's rise and the construction of a new outlook on world order). *Wenhua zonghe (Beijing Cultural Review)*, 10, 100–104.

Hu, A., Gao, Y., Zheng, Y., & Wang, H. (2017). Daguo xinshuai yu zhongguo jiyu: guojia zonghe shili pinggu [Rise of fall of great powers and the opportunities for China: an evaluation of comprehensive national power]. *Jingji daokan [Economic Herald]*, 3, 14–25.

Huazhong keji daxue guojia chuanbo zhanlue yanjiuyuan (Huazhong University of Science and Technology National Communication Strategy Institute). (2019). Zhongmei liangguo gongzhongde shijieguan yu guojia yinxiang yanjiu baogao 2017-18 (Research Report on the world view and national impression of the public in China and the United States 2017-18). *Renmin luntan xueshu qianyan [Frontiers·People's Forum]*, 5, 4–7.

Ikenberry, J. (2009). Liberal Internationalism 3.0: America and the Dilemmas of Liberal World Order. *Perspectives on Politics*, 7(1), 71–87. doi:10.1017/S1537592709090112

Information Office of the State Council of China. (2011, September 11). The White Paper, China's Peaceful Development. Ministry of Foreign Affairs of the People's Republic of China. Retrieved from https://www.fmprc.gov.cn/web/zyxw/t855789.shtml

Jia, Q. (2019). Guojizhixu zhibian yu zhongguo zuowei [The changing world order and Chinese contributions]. *Zhongyang shehui zhuyi xueyuan xuebao [Journal of the Central Institute of Socialism]*, 4, 53–60.

Jiang, S. (2019). Diguo de sifa changbi: meiguo jingji baquan de falv zhicheng [The empire's long-arm jurisdiction: United States' legal support for its economic hegemony]. *Wenhua zonghe [Beijing Cultural Review]*, 8, 84–93.

Levin, D. (2015, December 16). At U.N., China tries to influence fight over internet control. *New York Times*. Retrieved from www.nytimes.com/2015/12/17/technology/china-wins-battle-with-un-over-word-in-internet-control-document.html

Li, K. (2017). Rongna zhongguo jueqi: shijie zhixu shijiao xiade meiguo zeren jiqi zhanlue xuanze [Accommodating China's rise: world order and the responsibility and strategic option of the US]. *Shijie jingji yu zhengzhi [World Economy and Politics]*, 11, 89–107.

Li, Q. (2001). Quanqiuhua, zhuquanguojia yu shijie zhengzhi zhixu [Globalization, sovereign state and world political order]. *Zhanlue yu guanli [Strategy and Management]*, 2,13–24.

Li, T. (2019). Zhongguo zai lianheguo anlihui de toupiao bianhua yanjiu [Research on China's voting changes in the UN Security Council]. *Guoji zhengzhi yanjiu [The Journal of International Studies]*, 2, 115–142.

Li, W. (2016). Guoji zhixu zhuanxing yu xianshi zhidu zhuyi lilun de shengcheng [The transformation of international order and the birth of realistic institutionalism]. *Waijiao pinglun [Diplomatic Review]*, 1, 31–59.

Liu, J. (2016). Zhongmei xinxing daguo guanxi zhong de guoji zhixu boyi [The game on international order under the new model of major country relations between China and the United States]. *Meiguo yanjiu [American Studies]*, 5, 9–18.

Liu, Q. (2015). Xun qiu gongjian de pubianxing: cong tianxia lixiang dao xin shijie zhuyi [Seeking the universality of co-construction: from the ideal of Tianxia to the neo-cosmopolitanism]. In X. Jilin & L. Qinq (Eds.), *Zhishi fenzi luncong [Forum of intellectuals]* (Vol. 13, pp. 54–63), Shanghai: Shanghai renmin chubanshe.

Liu, Z. (2003). Guojia zhuquan de tezheng fenxi yu quanqiuhua beijingxia zhuquan lilun de chuangxin [An analysis of sovereignty and its theoretical innovation against the background of globalization]. *Shijie jingji yu zhengzhi [World Economy and Politics]*, 7, 20–25.

Long, Y. (2018, February 22). Zhongmei jingji shili haiyou henda chaju, yaoyou jinpogan weijigan [Major gap still exists in China-US economic strengths, we should have the sense of urgency]. Retrieved from http://news.ifeng.com/a/20180222/56169331_0.shtml

Mei, X. (2017, February 5). Does Trump present a New Year gift to china by withdrawing from TPP? *Xinhua*. Retrieved from http://www.xinhuanet.com/fortune/2017-02/05/c_1120413168.html

Michalski, A., & Pan, Z. (2017). Role dynamics in a structured relationship: the EU-China strategic partnership. *Journal of Common Market Studies*, 55(3), 611–627. doi:10.1111/jcms.12505

Niu, X. (2013). Zhongguo waijiao xuyao zhanlue zhuanxin [China's Diplomacy Requires a Strategic Transformation]. *Xian guoji guanxi [Contemporary International Relations]*, 1, 1–8.

Pan, Z. (2010). Cong "suishi" dao "moushi" youguan zhongguo jinyibu heping fazhan de zhanlue sikao [China's new strategy for peaceful development: from tide-surfing to tide-making]. *Shijie jingji yu zhengzhi [World Economy and Politics]*, 2, 4–18.

Pang, Z. (2010). Xiaoguo buzhang de duobian zhuyi he guoji lingdao chizi [Ineffective multilateralism and the leadership deficit: China's leadership responsibility in international collective actions]. *Shijie jingji yu zhengzhi [World Economy and Politics]*,6, 4–18.

Pang, Z. (2015). Quanqiu zhili zhuanxing zhong de zhongou zhanlue huoban guanxi [EU-China strategic partnership in the transformation of global governance]. *Dangdai shijie [Comtemporary World]*, 7, 30–33.

Qin, Y. (2014). Guoji tixi, guoji zhixu yu guojia de zhanlue xuanze [International system, world order and nation-states' strategic choices]. *Xiandai guoji guanxi [Contemporary International Relations]*, 7, 13–15.

Qin, Y. (2017). Shijie zhixu chuyi [Discussion on the world order]. *Shijie jingji yu zhengzhi [World Economics and Politics]*, 6, 4–13.

Qin, Y., Zhu, L., Wang, Y., Wei, L., Gao, F., Sun, J., Gao, S., Jing, X., & Yu, H. (2009). *Guoji tixi yu zhongguo waijiao [International system and china's diplomacy]*, Beijing: World Affairs Press.

Ren, X. (2019). Cong shijie zhengfu dao "gongsheng heping" [From world government to "gongsheng peace"]. *Guoji guancha [International Review]*, 1, 36–50.

Skinner, K. (2019, May 18). Clash of civilization or crisis of civilization? *Asia Times*. Retrieved from https://www.asiatimes.com/2019/05/article/clash-of-civilizations-or-crisis-of-civilization/

Su, C. (2009). Zhongguo moshi yu shijie zhixu [China model and the world order]. *Waijiao pinglun [Diplomatic Review]*, 4, 21–31.

Su, C. (2016). Cong guanxi dao gongsheng: zhongguo daguo waijiao lilun de wenhua he zhidu chanshi [From Guanxi through Gongsheng: a cultural and institutional interpretation: China's diplomatic theory]. *Shijie jingji yu zhengzhi [World Economy and Politics]*, 1, 5–25.

Sun, R. (2018). Meiguo tongmeng yu guoji zhixu biange: yi fendan fudan weili [The US alliance and the reform of international order: with the case study of sharing burdens]. *Guoji zhengzhi kexue [Quarterly Journal of International Politics]*, 2, 1–35.

Sun, X. (2015). Dengji shijiao xiade meiguo danji tixi zouxiang [The future of the unipolar world: From a social structure perspective]. *Waijiao pinglun [Diplomatic Review]*, 2, 80–103.

Tang, S. (2019). The future of international order(s). *Washington Quarterly*, 41(4), 117–131. doi:10.1080/0163660X.2018.1557499

The White House. (2017, December 18). National security strategic of the United States of America. Retrieved from https://www.whitehouse.gov/wp-content/uploads/2017/12/NSS-Final-12-18-2017-0905.pdf

Wang, J. (2019). Zhishi chanquan baohu yu meiguo de jishu baquan [Intellectual property protection and U.S. technological hegemony]. *Guoji zhanwang [Global Review]*, 4, 115–134.

Wang, Q. (2016). Rujia wangdao sixiang, tianxia zhuyi yu xiandai guoji zhixu de weilai [Confucian wang dao concept, all-under-heaven system, and the future of international order]. *Waijiao pinglun [Diplomatic Review]*, 3, 73–99.

Wang, X. (2019). Shijie duojihua fazhan yu zhongguo de yingdui zhice [The development of a multi-polarity world and China's responses]. *Jingji daokan [Economic Herald]*, 6, 29–31.

Wang, Y. (2016, February 22). Trump came into power wouldn't challenge the fundamentals of Sino-US relations. *Pangu Think Tank*. Retrieved from http://www.sohu.com/a/122315257_343251

Wang, Y. (2018, December 11). Speech by H.E. Wang Yi State Councilor and Minister of Foreign Affairs at the opening of symposium on the international situation and China's foreign relations in 2018. Ministry of Foreign Affairs of the People's Republic of China. Retrieved from https://www.fmprc.gov.cn/mfa_eng/wjdt_665385/zyjh_665391/t1621221.shtml

Wike, R., Stokes, B., Poushter, J., Fetterolf, J., & Devlin, K. (2018, October 1). Trump's international ratings remain low, especially among key allies most still want U.S. as top global power, but see China on the rise. *Pew Research Center*. Retrieved from https://www.pewresearch.org/global/2018/10/01/trumps-international-ratings-remain-low-especially-among-key-allies/

Wu, X. (2018, November 2). Huashengdun de mangdong jiaju meiguo baquan shuai-luo [Blindness in Washington exacerbates the decline of US hegemony]. *Huanqiu shibao [Global Times]*. Retrieved from https://opinion.huanqiu.com/article/9CaKrnKekmL

Wu, Z. & Bing, L. (2018). Quanqiu zhili huayuquan tisheng de zhongguo shijiao [Promoting the discursive power in global governance from China's perspective]. *Shijie jingji yu zhengzhi [World Economy and Politics]*, 9, 4–21.

Wu, Z. (2016). Quanqiu zhili dui guojia zhili de yingxiang [The impact of global governance on state governance]. *Zhongguo shehui kexue [China Social Science]*, 6, 22–28.

Xi, J. (2014, December 6). Zhonggong zhongyang zhengzhiju jiu jiakuai ziyou maoyi qu jianshe jinxing jiti xuexi [Xi Jinping stresses need to accelerate Free Trade Zone Strategy, speaks at the 19th collective study session of the CCP Political Bureau]. The State Council of the People's Republic of China. Retrieved from http://www.gov.cn/xinwen/2014-12/06/content_2787582.htm

Xi, J. (2017a, October 18). Secure a decisive victory in building a moderately prosperous society in all respects and strive for the great success of socialism with Chinese characteristics for a new era, Delivered at the 19th National Congress of the Communist Party of China. Xinhua. Retrieved from http://www.xinhuanet.com/english/download/Xi_Jinping's_report_at_19th_CPC_National_Congress.pdf

Xi, J. (2017b, January 18). Work together to build a community of shared future for mankind, Speech by H.E. Xi Jinping, President of the People's Republic of China at the United Nations Office at Geneva. Xinhua. Retrieved from http://www.xinhua-net.com//english/2017-01/19/c_135994707.htm

Xia, L. (2008). *Nuclear nonproliferation from a Chinese perspective* (Vol. 8, pp. 1–9). FES Briefing Paper.

Xinhua. (2019, August 19). Commentary: China's fight against U.S. bullying bears global significance. *EnPeople*. Retrieved from http://en.people.cn/n3/2019/0819/c90000-9607064.html

Xu, H., & Zhang, Q. (2019). Meiouri dui WTO gaige de hexin suqiu yu zhongguo duice [The core demands of US, Europe and Japan for WTO reform and China's countermeasures]. *Guoji maoyi [Intertrade]*, 2, 18–23.

Xu, J. (2015). Xin tianxia zhuyi yu zhongguo de neiwai zhixu [New Tianxiaism and China's internal and external orders]. In J. Xu & Q Liu (Eds.), *Zhishi fenzi luncong (Forum of Interlectualls)* (Vol. 13, pp. 3–25). Shanghai: Shanghai renmin chubanshe.

Xu, X. (2015). Jinrong weiji hou de shijie jingji zhixu: shili jiegou, guize tixi yu zhili linian [The world economic order in the post-financial crisis era: economic power, international rules, and governance philosophy]. *Shijie jingji yu zhengzhi [World Economy and Politics]*. 5, 82–101.

Xue, L. (2019, February 12). What kind of Future order should China pursue? *Chinausfocus*. Retrieved from https://www.chinausfocus.com/foreign-policy/what-kind-of-future-order-should-china-pursue

Yan, X. (2011). *Ancient Chinese thought, modern Chinese power*. Princeton, NJ: Princeton University Press.

Yan, X. (2015). *Shijie quanli de zhuanyi: zhengzhi lingdao yu zhanlue jingzheng [World power's transition: Political leadership and strategic competition]*. Beijing: Peking University Press.

Yan, X. (2019a). The age of uneasy peace: Chinese power in a divided world. *Foreign Affairs*, Jan./Feb., 40–46.

Yan, X. (2019b). *Leadership and the rise of great power*, Princeton, NJ: Princeton University Press.

Yang, J. (2013). Zhongguo zouxiang quanqiu qiangguo de waijiao lilun zhunbei: jieduanxing shiming he jiangouxing zhongdian [On the theories of foreign policy for China's ongoing transformation into a global great power: their mission and focus]. *Shijie jingji yu zhengzhi [World Economy and Politics]*, 5, 4–14.

Yang, J. (2019). Dangqian guoji dageju de bianhua, yingxiang he qushi [The change, influence, and trend of current world system]. *Xiandai guoji guanxi [Contemporary International Relations]*, 3, 1–6.

Yang, Q. (2016, December 7). China might face great challenges when welcomes Trump comes into power. *Chawang*. Retrieved from http://www.cwzg.cn/politics/201612/32862.html

Young, O. (1989). *International cooperation: Building regimes for natural resources and the environment*, Ithaca, NY: Cornell University Press.

Yu, H. (2019). Meiguo baquan de yanjing luijing yu zhongmeiguanxi de weilai zoushi [The evolution path of American hegemony and the future trend of Sino-US relations]. *Lilun yu gaige [Theory and Reform]*, 3, 70–78.

Yu, K. (2004). Lun quanqiuhua yu guojia zhuquan [Discussing globalization and sovereignty]. *Makesi zhuyi yu xianshi [Marxism and the reality]*, 1, 4–21.

Yuan, Z. (2019). Meiguo danbian zhuyi chongji guoji zhixu [US's unilateralism has eroding the international order]. *Renmin luntan (People's Forum)*, 1, 24–27.

Zeng, J. (2017). China's solution to global cyber governance: unpacking the domestic discourse of internet sovereignty. *Politics and Policy*, 45(3), 432–464. doi:10.1111/polp.12202

Zhang, F. (2018). Quanqiu jinrong zhili tixi de yanjin: meiguo baquan yu zhongguo fangan [Evolution of global financial governance system: US hegemony and Chinese approach]. *Guoji guanxi yanjiu [The Journal of International Studies]*, 39(4), 9–36.

Zhang, Q. (2013). Cong guoji hefaxing shijiao kan xinxing daguo qunti jueqi dui guoji zhixu zhuanxing de yingxiang [A study on the impact of the rise of emerging powers on the transformation of international order: an international legitimacy perspective]. *Zhejiang daxue xuebao:renwen shehui kexueban [Journal of Zhejiang University (Humanities and Social Sciences)]*, 43(1), 5–17.

Zhang, W. (2017). Yidai yilu yu shijie zhili de zhongguo fangan [The belt and road initiative and China's proposal for global governance]. *Shijie jingji yu zhengzhi [World Economics and Politics]*, 8, 4–25.

Zhang, W. (2019). Xin shidai de zhongmei bianju yu shijie qiantu [The Sino-US Change in the New Era and the future of the world]. *Taipingyang xuebao [Pacific Journal]*, 27(4), 1–12.

Zhang, X. (2019, May 16). In the uneasy trade triangle with the US, China and Europe can address security concerns and deepen their partnership. *South China Morning Post*. Retrieved from https://www.scmp.com/comment/insight-opinion/article/3010272/uneasy-trade-triangle-us-china-and-europe-can-address

Zhang, X., & Li, X. (2013). The Politics of Compliance with Adverse WTO Dispute Settlement Rulings in China. *Journal of Contemporary China*, 23(85),143–160. doi: 10.1080/10670564.2013.809986

Zhang, Y. (2019). Zhongmei hui xianru bainian chongtu ma? (Will China and the United States fall into "the looming 100-year US-China conflict?). *Dongya pinglun [East Asia Review]*, 1, 1–3.

Zhao, C. (2016). Zouxiang "maoyi xinshijie" de meiou guanxi:" kua daxiyang maoyi yu touzi huoban guanxi xieding" de zhengzhi jingjixue fenxi [A political economy analysis of the Transatlantic Trade and Investment Partnership Agreement]. *Meiguo yanjiu [American Studies]*, 5, 50–66.

Zhao, H. (2019). Telangpu zhizhenghou meiou tongmeng guanxi de xinbianhua jiqi yingxiang [US-EU relationship after Trump came into power: new changes and its implications]. *Dangdai shijie [Comtemporary World]*, 3, 4–10.

Zhao, M. (2019). Is a new cold war inevitable? Chinese perspectives of US-China competition. *The Chinese Journal of International Politics*, *12*(3), 371–394. doi:10. 1093/cjip/poz010

Zhao, T. (2005), *Tianxia tixi: shijie zhidu zhexue daolun [The Tianxia system: a philosophy for the world institution]*. Nanjing: Jiangsu Jiaoyu Chubanshe.

Zhao, T. (2014). The "China Dream" in question. *Economic and Political Studies*, 2(1), 127–142. doi:10.1080/20954816.2014.11673854

Zhou, F. (2016). Guoji zhixu bianhua yuanli yu fenfa youwei celue [The reasons for the change in international order and China's strive for achievement strategy]. *Guoji zhengzhi kexue [Quarterly Journal of International Politics]*, 1, 33–59.

Zhou, Q. & Shen, P. (2012). Meiguo de zhongdong zhanlue cong weichi wending bianwei tuijin minzhuhua [The US's Middle East Strategy- from peace keeper to democracy advocator]. *Dangdai shijie [Contemporary World]*, 2, 24–27.

Chinese perception of China's engagement in multilateralism and global governance

Hongsong Liu

ABSTRACT

With China's reintegration into the international system its involvement in multilateral initiatives, interactions with international institutions, and participation in global governance have become integral parts of Chinese foreign policy. Chinese scholars have conducted a great deal of research on these topics. The first stage of Chinese scholars' research centered on China's multilateral diplomacy and the interaction between China and international institutions, while the second stage focused on China's participation in global governance. Although some scholars have made substantial achievements, in general, most of the research only interprets the ideas and policies related to global governance proposed by the Chinese government, and has not explained China's strategies and actions in global governance. Furthermore, Chinese scholars provide little analysis on the dynamics of China's participation in different issue areas. Many scholars have articulated a series of policy recommendations, but no specific measures have been suggested.

Introduction

For a long time after its establishment, the People's Republic of China had not fully integrated into the global governance system, consisting of international institutions in various issue areas. In the international environment of confrontation between East and West, China was wary of and even resistant to the international institutions dominated by Western countries at that time, and therefore only participated in some multilateral diplomatic activities between socialist countries or developing countries. In the 1950s and 1960s, China regarded the United Nations (UN) as the United States' (US) tool to implement aggressive policies throughout the world, and a place for political deals between the US and the Soviet Union. The international economic institutions such as the International Monetary Fund (IMF) and the World Bank, under the Bretton Woods system, were perceived as a form of imperialism.

China's restoration of its legitimate seat in the UN in 1971 was the starting point for China's reintegration into the global governance system. The reform and opening-up period marked a turning point in China's attitude toward international institutions. China's accession to the World Trade Organization (WTO) in 2001was a sign of China's full integration into the global governance system, and a starting point for China's deeper participation in the building and rule-making of international institutions. The substantial increase in China's relative economic power after the global financial crisis of 2008 then provided China with an historic opportunity to play a leading role in the global governance system. China thus has become more actively involved and is now a major actor in global governance.

Within this context, Chinese scholars have carried out a great deal of research on China's multilateralism practice, the interaction between China and international institutions, and China's participation in global governance. Multilateralism refers to cooperation or coordination that is regulated through common rules and norms within the multilateral form (Ruggie, 1992). Accordingly, multilateralism practice involves multilateral diplomacy, compliance with multilateral rules and interaction with multilateral institutions, which constitute the institutional framework of global governance. As such, Chinese scholars' research on these issues represents their perception of China's engagement in multilateralism and global governance.

This paper aims to assess and draw conclusions on Chinese scholars' research on China's participation in international institutions and global governance. Research by Chinese scholars on these issues can be divided into two phases: the first focused on China's multilateral diplomacy and the interaction between China and international institutions; while the second centered on China's participation in global governance. The rest of this paper proceeds in four sections. The first section presents reviews and comments on research during the first phase. The second section looks at the research on China's participation in global governance in the second phase. The third section assesses the existing research on China's participation in global governance. The fourth section is the conclusion.

The rise of research on the interaction between China and international institutions

The earliest papers on China's multilateralism practice that can be found on *Zhongguo zhiwang* (China National Knowledge Infrastructure, or CNKI) were published in 1998. In the article *'1949-1989 nian Xin Zhongguo Duobian Waijiao de Shijian jiqi Tedian'* (The Practice and Characteristics of New China's Multilateral Diplomacy from 1949 to 1989), Tang Wei divided China's multilateral diplomacy during this time into two stages: the period of behaving as an outsider to the UN system (1949–1971), and the period of expanded participation based on UN diplomacy (1971–1989). Tang analyzed the instability of China's multilateral foreign policy, the limited nature of Chinese participation in multilateral diplomacy, and the dependence of multilateral diplomacy on bilateral diplomacy (Tang, 1998). Wang Yizhou pointed out that, in the changing international environment and given China's domestic progress, China's understanding of its national interests has deepened; and thus it has accepted some of the international rules, but still remains cautious about those in the fields of arms control and human rights. In terms of international rules, China cannot adopt a simplistic and excessively rigid approach (Wang, 1998).

Wang Yizhou actively promoted the study of the relations between China and international institutions. At the invitation of Wang Yizhou, American scholar Alastair Iain Johnston published a paper entitled *'Zhongguo Canyu Guoji Tizhi de Ruogan Sikao'* (Some Thoughts on China's Participation in the International institutions) in the journal *Shijie Jingji Yu Zhenghzi* (World Economics and Politics) in 1999, expounding that China's participation in international organizations was close to that of developed countries, and that China's behavior in the international system had changed significantly (Johnston, 1999). In 2001, Wang also invited some scholars to publish a series of papers on the interaction between China and international institutions in the fields of arms control, the environment, human rights and economy in the journal *Shijie Jingji Yu Zhenghzi* (World Economics and Politics). These papers were included in the book *Mohe Zhong de Jiangou: Zhongguo yu Guoji Zuzhi Guanxi de Duoshijiao Toushi* (Construction in Run-in: A Multi-perspective analysis on the Relationship between China and International Organizations), edited by Wang Yizhou (Wang, 2003). Meanwhile, Wang Yizhou wrote an article emphasizing that multilateral diplomacy consists an integral part of great power diplomacy, and helps to safeguard China's national interests more effectively (Wang, 2001). The article called on Chinese scholars to 'objectively clarify the nature of the relationship between China and different international organizations, the process of engagement, the existing obstacles, and the prospect of China's role, while fully absorbing the research already available, and to, on this basis, present truly innovative ideas and influential views' (Wang, 2002).

The research agenda proposed by Wang Yizhou attracted the attention of many Chinese scholars. Around 2000, there were multiple academic achievements related to the analysis of representative cases of China's integration into international institutions in Chinese diplomatic history, the interaction between China and international regimes after the Cold War, the strategic innovation of China's participation in international regimes after China's accession to the WTO, China's multilateral diplomatic strategy, the change of China's understanding of multilateral diplomacy, the characteristics of China's multilateral diplomacy at the turn of the century, and China's participation in the establishment of the Shanghai Cooperation Organization (SCO) (Guo, 1999; Qiao, 2001; Chu, 2001; Zheng & Sun, 2001; Jiang, 2003; Wang, 2004). In general, research during this period involved some cases of interaction between China and international institutions in specific issue areas but lacked in-depth case study analysis and theoretical discussion. Moreover, most scholars have not conducted continuous research on these topics, and the academic accumulation of such work is limited as a result.

Following Wang Yizhou, Su Changhe also contributed to the study of the relations between China and international institutions. He took the lead in proposing research on the influence of international institutions on China (Su, 2002). In a series of papers, he explained in detail the dramatic changes in China's diplomatic thoughts and behavior, and the impact that participation in international institutions had exerted influence on China's domestic economy, politics and diplomacy; against the evolving background where China was playing an increasingly important role in international institutions and international norms, and where China's domestic economy and politics were in a state of transition (Su, 2005; Su, 2006; Su 2007). Under the active promotion of Wang Yizhou, Chinese scholars conducted research on the following topics:

Explaining China's turn to multilateralism

Men Honghua sought to explain the relationships between China and international institutions using three variables: pressure, perception and international image. He argued that the needs of domestic development and progress (domestic pressure), international pressure, perception of national interests and international image were the major driving forces for China's participation in international institutions (Men, 2005). Xie Liyan described the difficult course of China's turn toward multilateralism and attributed it to the constraints of domestic culture, the international landscape, and leaders' personalities and ideas (Xie, 2009). Fang Changping pointed out that after the Cold War, China adopted the strategy of multilateralism in order to safeguard its national interests, and to create an international institution – the SCO – represented by the new security concept (Fang, 2004).

Yu Jianjun examined the ideational reasons for this change in China's attitude toward international institutions with a constructivist approach. He argued that China's participation in international institutions was a process of perception and acceptance of international norms after the transformation of China's role in the global arena (Yu, 2009). These studies analyzed the reasons for China's turn to multilateralism from different angles, but did not frame a theoretical approach to explain the causal relationship, nor did they test the hypothesis put forward in their works by conducting case studies. In this regard, Wang Yizhou pointed out that such research lacks theoretical innovation, and so far, there was no theoretical monograph on the relations between China and international institutions (Wang, 2002). Wang Xuedong's work is an exception. With the international institution as the independent variable, the demand for national reputation as the mediating variable, and participation in the international system as the dependent variable, he constructed a theoretical framework to explain China's active participation in international institutions after the Cold War. He argued that the reputation of a rising power could convey its intention of maintaining the status quo, so as to avoid balancing from other states. After the Cold War, the aim of China's active participation was to enhance its reputation in order to ease structural pressures and avoid joint balancing from the US and other countries (Wang, 2007). Chen Hanxi criticized elements of Wang Xuedong's theory and contended that the latter did not realize that China's reputation was only a legal-moral reputation, rather than a political reputation (prestige), and critiqued that there was no empirical test for the causal relationship between changes in structural pressure and China's level of participation in international institutions (Chen, 2008). Responding to Chen Hanxi's criticism, Wang held that although China's reputation gained through participation in international institutions is a legal-moral reputation, such a reputation could help China convey its intentions to maintain the status quo, thus avoiding suspicions and balancing from other countries (Wang, 2009). However, Wang's statement still lacks an explanation of how participation in international institutions in non-security areas, such as human rights, can help China accumulate legal-moral reputation in the security field.

The impact of international institutions on China

Since Su Changhe proposed research on how international institutions influence China, some scholars have conducted research on the impacts on China's domestic politics and governance. Cong Riyun believed that in the face of the UN and in the era of global governance, China faces challenges in its own government's system and behavior, the development of domestic civil society and the cultivation of citizenship. The participation in international institutions such as the UN and WTO provides China with external motivation for reform (Cong, 2005). From the perspective of compliance, Bo Yan discussed the impacts of the international environmental regimes on China's environmental governance. Taking China's implementation of the London Amendment to the Montreal Protocol on Substances that Deplete the Ozone Layer as an example, Bo analyzed China's changes in environmental behavior (Bo, 2005). Through in-depth interviews and questionnaire surveys, Yu Hongyuan examined the impact of international climate change institutions on China's climate diplomacy decision-making and related coordination mechanisms. He pointed out that international climate change institutions influenced the operating environment of climate diplomacy decision-making, and prompted China to establish a counter coordination department or system (Yu, 2008). Wang Ronghua and Chen Hanxi examined the impacts on the legislation of the Chinese Red Cross under the theoretical framework of the relations between states and international society. They argued that the reason why the Chinese government accepted the basic norms of the International Red Cross Movement in the 1990s was because China shifted from a revolutionary state to a status quo state, thus increasingly recognizing the international norms generally accepted within international society (Wang & Chen, 2007). Zhu Xufeng and Wang Haiyuan studied the role of the UN Development Program (UNDP) in the formulation of China's micro-credit policy. The scholars held that international organizations played the role of information disseminators, policy testers and policy advisors. The UNDP first adopted a grassroots pilot approach to demonstrate to central and local policymakers the feasibility and effectiveness of different models of micro-credit in various parts of China. After achieving initial results, the UNDP progressively communicated with poverty alleviation institutions, within China's central and local governments, to promote micro-credit throughout China (Zhu & Wang, 2012). Taking the UN, the International Labor Organization (ILO) and World Bank as examples, Liu Dongmei examined the impacts of international regimes on China's social security system and legal reforms. She pointed out that different international organizations have resorted to different ways to promote the world's common development and the framework of common actions, and that they organize policy dialogues, propose recommendations, publish research reports and provide technical assistance (Liu, 2011).

On the 10th anniversary of China's accession to the WTO, Tian Ye analyzed the effect of China's accession to the WTO on the reform of state-owned enterprises. He argued that the rigid constraints of WTO rules harden the budget constraints of state-owned enterprises in a direct or indirect manner, thus making them increasingly competitive in profitability in the market (Tian, 2011). Tian also adopted the state autonomy framework to explain China's pursuit of state autonomy. China drew on international labor standards set by the ILO to promote domestic labor legislation (Tian & Lin, 2009). Moreover, from the perspective of international policy diffusion, Tian discussed how collective bargaining, an international labor standard, was introduced into China's multiple labor laws (Tian, 2014). The abovementioned research included case studies, based on empirical research, on the impact of international institutions in specific areas of China's foreign policy decision-making and economic and social governance. Wang Ronghua and Chen Hanxi utilized the archives and interviews of the Chinese Red Cross. However, these case studies have not achieved adequate process tracing, and therefore do not provide sufficient empirical support for the hypothesis in relation to understanding the specific ways and mechanisms of influence.

Peaceful rise/peaceful development, harmonious world concept and China's multilateral diplomacy

In Wei Ming's article, he pointed out that, in the international situation in the new era, in order to achieve China's sustainable development and build a harmonious world, China should continue to adhere to and continuously expand its multilateral diplomacy, further improve the form of and expand the scale of multilateral diplomacy, and give full play to it (Wei, 2007). Pang Sen, then vice president and director of the United Nations Association of China, reviewed the development of China's multilateral diplomacy since the implementation of the reform and opening-up policy in 1978, and summarized China's contributions to safeguarding world peace and promoting the development of the world economy as a responsible great power (Pang, 2008). Zhang Ji and Wang Hongbin pointed out that China, as a peacefully rising world power, should not only fully participate in international institutions, but also safeguard national sovereignty and interests within the existing international institutional framework, and strive to play a greater constructive role in it (Zhang & Wang, 2005). Chen Dongxiao argued that, in the multilateral diplomatic process of participating in the reform of the international (governance) system, China is facing growing pressure to play a leading role and assume international responsibility. Thus, China needs to constantly adapt to its changing national identity in multilateral diplomacy, to strengthen multilateral mechanisms in the strategic planning and layout of coordinating international institutions in various regions and issue areas, and to enrich the concept of a harmonious world in multilateral diplomacy (Chen, 2009). Song Xiuju and Ma Ludong elaborated on the nature of a harmonious international (governance) system and on its close connection with a harmonious world. They believed that the strategic focus of promoting a harmonious world should be to build a harmonious international (governance) system (Song & Ma, 2013). These articles took the concept of peaceful rise, peaceful development, and harmonious world as the key words, expounding the significance of carrying out multilateral diplomacy and constructing international institutions. This was in line with the peaceful development strategy and concept of harmonious world proposed by the Chinese government during the Hu Jintao era.

Chinese scholars' understanding of China's participation in global governance

As early as the beginning of the 21st Century, Chinese scholars started to pay attention to China's participation in global governance. In 2004, Cai Tuo noticed that global governance in the form of cross-border cooperation reflected China's rising global awareness and concern for global values. During governance, global awareness and global values were fostered and better recognized (Cai, 2004). However, this issue did not gain wider attention from Chinese scholars until the dramatic change of China's role in global governance. Some studies summarized the characteristics of China's participation in global governance; for instance, Yang Na summarized four characteristics of China's participation in global governance since the reform and opening-up. China was first estranged from the global governance system, before opting to take part in it and later becoming a leading figure. Meanwhile, China's participation expanded from economics to a full range of issue areas. The path of participation shifted from the mere observance of international rules to the promotion of innovation (Yang, 2018). Cao Yabin summarized the characteristics of China's participation in global governance in the fields of security, economy, society and the environment in the 21st Century (Cao, 2015). In addition, Chinese scholars carried out research on issues such as the 'Belt and Road Initiative' (BRI) and global governance, Chinese solutions for global governance, China's global governance strategy, China's participation in global economic governance, and China's participation in new areas of global governance.

Belt and road initiative and global governance

On the implications of the BRI for China's participation in global governance, Sun Jinsong pointed out that the BRI is one of the means of the construction of the 'Community of Shared Future for Mankind'. It is also an important measure for China to actively take part in global governance under the current international order and is a manifestation of China's wisdom (Sun, 2019). Xu Deyou believes that the implementation of the BRI provides an economic basis for China's voice on rules of global governance, builds a new 'friend circle' (a social media platform for sharing) for China, and contributes to Chinse solutions and wisdom on global economic governance (Xu, 2018).

By tracing the international background of China's participation in global governance, some Chinese scholars proposed that China should promote global governance progressively under the BRI, that is, first to smoothly pass the adjustment phase of the economic cycle, then explore internationally recognized global governance solutions, and finally advance inter-regional connectivity to achieve the ultimate goal of the 'Community of Shared Future for Mankind' (Hu, 2017). From the perspective of constructivism, Liu Xuelian and Sang Pu pointed out that the continuous deepening of the BRI will strengthen the construction of collective identities amongst the countries along the Belt and Road, and could have a demonstration effect on third parties, thus further disseminating and implementing the concept of China's global governance centred on 'communication, co-construction and sharing' (Liu & Sang, 2018). He Zhipeng believes that the BRI is a crucial opportunity for China to contribute to the international (governance) system. China should form a new model of 'adaptative management' under the BRI in accordance with a gradual and progressive approach (He, 2016). Furthermore, the implementation of the BRI shows that, in the field of international legal system, China has changed its traditional passive response thinking and instead pursued a more proactive mode of thinking, which means that China will adhere to the practice of 'crossing the river by feeling the stones' shaped during the reform and opening-up, which is a 'non-systematic' manner of exploration (He, 2017). With regard to the impact of the BRI on global governance, it is considered that this initiative implements the global governance values advocated by China: respect for the culture and political systems of other countries, equality and justice, mutual benefit, and coordinated and win-win development, which will advance the development of global governance as a whole (Ma, 2018). Also, it is believed that the BRI is Chinese wisdom and a solution to promote the transformation of the global governance system and the development of regional economic cooperation. The BRI is based on the principles of joint discussion, co-construction and sharing. Through the path of connecting development strategies, it promotes regional economic cooperation by optimizing resource allocation to achieve common development and prosperity (Liu & Zhang, 2017).

Chinese solutions for global governance

What is China's solution for global governance? Chinese scholars have proposed four viewpoints. The first is that building the 'Community of Shared

Future for Mankind' is the solution. China's leading national power, changes in its role in international institutions, its adherence to the path of peaceful development, an excellent traditional culture, Marxist intellectual resources, and a willingness to contribute have made the 'Community of Shared Future for Mankind' the predominant proposal by China (Ren, 2018). This solution is a crucial part of the socialist ideology with Chinese characteristics in the new era (Hao and Zhou 2018) and a transcendence of modernity (Wu, 2017). For example, Wang Yi pointed out that the fundamental goal and core task of building the 'Community of Shared Future for Mankind' is to construct a world of lasting peace, universal security, common prosperity, openness, tolerance, cleanliness and beauty (Wang, 2018). Qiao Yuqiang argued that the concept of 'Community of Shared Future for Mankind' is China's global governance idea based on the common interests of all people around the world and international justice. It is China's solution to the challenges in global governance against the background of the failing traditional global governance system, and frequent conflicts since the financial crisis of the late-2000s and early-2010s (Qiao, 2018). Geng Bujian and Shen Dandan also believe that this concept is a solution able to solve urgent global problems. So as to put this solution into practice, China must strive to take ecological collectivism as the value basis for the 'Community of Shared Future for Mankind', which emphasizes the overall and long-term dual harmony of 'human and nature' and 'human and society' (Geng & Shen, 2019).

The second perspective is that China's path, and the practical experience accumulated in the reform and opening-up, is China's solution for global governance. For instance, Chen Fengying argued that in addition to building a 'Community of Shared Future for Mankind', the Chinese road itself is also a solution for global governance. China's path provides a new choice for countries who want to accelerate their development and at the same time maintain their independence, thus contributing to solving collective problems that all countries are faced with (Chen, 2017). Bao Jianyun pointed out that China's reform and opening-up can provide a reference and idea resource for global governance reform, and an experience reference for the construction of risk control mechanisms. It can also serve as a reference of openness and development for developing and emerging countries, and underdeveloped regions (Bao, 2018).

The third viewpoint is that Chinese solutions for global governance are China's specific and concrete solutions, governance methods and paths for various global issues. For example, Wang Qiuyi believes that China's solution comes in the form of concrete plans put forward by China, in terms of global economic cooperation, the construction of peaceful major power relations and the resolution of regional hotspot issues – including via the BRI, the dual-track approach to promote a final resolution of the South

China Sea issue, the two-track approach to resolve the North Korea nuclear issue, and the three-phase measure to deal with the Rohingya crisis in Myanmar (Wang, 2018). Shen Yamei argues that Chinese solutions include proposals related to the construction of a global governance theory system, complementing and improving global governance mechanisms, reforming global governance rules and supporting the expansion of the voice of developing countries. The 'Community of Shared Future for Mankind' is the core of the global governance theory system proposed by China, and is only one aspect of China's solution (Shen, 2017). In addition, Li Dan also argued that China's solution includes five dimensions: governing body, pattern, platform, path and goal. In regards to the governing body, China emphasizes equal participation and opposes hegemony. In terms of pattern, China attaches great significance to cooperation based on institutional rules. Regarding the platform, China advocates adopting both new and old mechanisms, while making incremental improvements. Concerning the path, China emphasizes increasing the representation and voice of developing countries. As for the goal, China promotes the 'Community of Shared Future for Mankind' and advocates inclusive and win-win forms of economic globalization (Li, 2018).

The fourth view divides Chinese solutions into five types: the first is to supplement, modify, and improve the current system; the second is to transform China's domestic governance solution into a global solution; the third is to propose alternatives given that existing solutions are proving ineffective; the fourth is to reach a compromise between existing experiences or models; and the fifth is to propose new approaches for new and emerging global issues (Pang, 2018).

China's global governance strategy

Regarding the strategy that China should adopt in global governance, Chinese scholars proposed several points as follows: to promote institutional discourse power, to advance global governance system reform, to lead the global governance system reform with Chinese solutions, and to integrate national and global governance.

Strengthen institutional discourse power

Institutional discourse power construction is an important way for China to promote global governance transformation and establish a new global governance order. Su Changhe pointed out that the current institutional capacity and discourse power should be centered on the rules of international relations with the cooperation and win-win principles at the core, along with the BRI interconnectivity rules and the harmonious and symbiotic

'Community of Shared Future for Mankind' (Su, 2016). Wang Mingguo believes that China's institutional discourse power in global governance is still relatively weak and faces several challenges. China still needs to continue to promote international institutional reform, actively build a new system, enhance its capacity to promote its own international system, and improve the capacity of the supply of international public goods so as to strengthen its institutional discourse power (Wang, 2017).

Advance the transformation of the global governance system

Chinese scholars believe that China should play a greater role in promoting the transformation of global governance. It is necessary to gradually transfer 'China under global governance' into 'China's global governance'. Furthermore, China can steadily propose macro-concepts and initiatives related to global governance based on its own strength and actual needs, and gradually advocate and implement them. At the same time, as a responsible great power while advocating new governance mechanisms, China should consider how to integrate existing mechanisms and enhance their fairness and effectiveness (Bi & Niu, 2016). China not only needs to continue to join existing international institutions and participate in global governance, but must also increase global public goods investment and actively look to transform the global governance system (Zhu, 2018). Current global governance ideas and model preferences that countries hold diverge and compete fiercely. In view of this, the core goal of China's global governance strategy should be to seize the opportunity of changes in global governance, to promote the positive interaction between China and the world, and to become an advocator, designer, shaper and leader within the global governance system (Men, 2017).

Regarding China's strategy for the transformation of the global governance system, Chen Zhimin argues that China is incapable of completely transforming the Western-led global governance system, and that China should adopt an overall strategy of incremental improvement (Chen, 2014). Wang Honggang points out that China should comprehensively understand the characteristics and development trends of the global governance system, rationally determine strategic objectives, actively participate in global governance on the basis of adequate preparation, promote the reform of the global governance system and make full use of external resources for the goal of national rejuvenation. China should strive to realize the mutual promotion of China's own rejuvenation and the evolution of the global governance system (Wang, 2017). Chen Weiguang points out that, confronted with the undesirable situation caused by the de-globalization of developed countries, China should promote the transformation of global governance from the aspects of ideas, platforms and approaches (Chen,

2017). Niu Jusheng and Liu Min believe that China's triple identity – as the socialist country, the largest developing country, and the country close to the center of the world – determines China's unique global governance strategy which aims to achieve the 'Community of Shared Future for Mankind' through transforming the existing global governance system and establishing a new fair and just order. It is the way of progress, of change, and of national rejuvenation (Niu & Liu, 2019). They also point out that China should adhere to the value orientation of the 'Community of Shared Future for Mankind' while leading the global governance. China must firmly adhere to the values of responsibility, openness and tolerance and to the principles of joint discussion, co-construction and sharing (Niu & Liu, 2019). In addition, Wang Xinying contends that China should promote the institutional innovation of the global governance system and place great importance on the role of new institutions and platforms formulated through the BRI. Moreover, China should also raise its capacity related to agenda-setting in global governance and ensure that new problems and challenges in global governance are characterized as common concerns to the international community. Further, China should strengthen its capability in relation to resource integration and international coordination, while the unique advantages of the UN, G20 and other institutions and platforms in global governance should be brought into play (Wang, 2019).

In terms of specific strategies, Zhang Yong points out that major-country consensus, soft law governance, practice orientation, cross-institutional interaction and new inter-regional governance have become the new trends of global governance. China should promote Sino-US coordinated governance mechanisms, seek to actively expand low-agenda governance, act as a cross-institutional coordinator, create a network of integrated neighborhood governance structures and promote joint governance concerning both soft and hard laws (Zhang, 2017). Scholars such as He Fan et al divide the international rules related to global governance into three categories. First is current major international mechanisms and rules. Second are those that are undergoing or will undergo great changes. The third are new rules that may in the future become of systemic importance. Based on the abovementioned several types, They put forward several principles that China should follow: interest accrual, interest inclusion and shared responsibility (He, Feng, & Xu, 2013).

Lead the global governance system reform with Chinese solutions
Some scholars believe that China should promote the reform of the global governance system with Chinese solutions. For instance, Chen Fengying points out that China should strive to contribute Chinese wisdom toward improving global governance. China should also lead the transformation of

the system with Chinese solutions toward the increase of discourse power of emerging markets and developing countries. China can thus ultimately build a rational, fair and equitable new architecture for effective global governance (Chen, 2016). Ren Haiping and Xu Chaoyou emphasize that China should comprehensively look to build a cooperative and win-win form of international relations into global governance, applicable to handling relations with major powers, neighboring countries and developing countries. China should also actively participate in the resolution of global hot issues, propose more Chinese solutions, actively initiate the development of rule-making and promote the transformation and improvement of the global governance system (Ren & Xu, 2017). Hu Jian also points out that China should actively participate in the establishment of international institutions, actively lead regional governance, and prepare for an international power shift. At the same time, he emphasizes that China should accelerate internal institutional innovation, and achieve coordination between internal and external institutions (Hu, 2015).

Integrate national and global governance

There are also Chinese scholars who stress that China's global governance strategy should focus on the integration of national and global governance structures and on the coordination of internal and external politics (Su, 2011). Concerning the interaction between national and global governance, national governance restricts the degree of a state's global governance participation and the realization of the state's discourse power in global governance rulemaking (Liu & Yao, 2016). Chen Zhimin points out that as a fast-growing developing country, it is necessary for China to form and implement a proactive national governance strategy alongside a global governance participation strategy. China should make its own efforts for the overall goal of good governance (Chen, 2016). Some Chinese scholars also point out that, in addition to improving the supply capacity of international public goods and strengthening the capabilities of international agenda-setting and political mobilization, China must also modernize its national governance structures and lay the base for global governance (Liu, 2017). China needs to strengthen national governance and promote the modernization of its national governance system and capacity: only in this way can China more effectively participate in global governance (Lu, 2015). In the process of participating in global governance, China must ensure a central role for the Communist Party of China – as the leading ruling party – to contribute more new ideas, solutions and practices that accelerate both domestic and global development (Wang & Liu, 2019).

China's participation in global economic governance

After the global financial crisis in 2008, Western countries were besieged by economic difficulties. In response to this crisis, Western developed countries decided to engage in dialogue with emerging market economies, such as China, on equal footing, and upgraded the G20 mechanism from the finance ministers and central bank governors' meeting to the leaders' summit. After the G20 was upgraded from the ministerial meeting mechanism to the summit mechanism, it quickly became a very important platform for China to improve its discurse power in global economic governance. With the G20 platform, China increased its share and voting rights in the World Bank and the IMF, and joined two global financial institutions – the Financial Stability Board and the Global Tax Forum – that had turned down China in the past. China's voice in institutions such as the Basel Committee, and the International Organization of Securities Commissions, has also increased significantly post-crisis. Therefore, the G20, as the core mechanism of global economic governance, attracted the attention of many Chinese scholars. Using the conceptual framework of political opportunities, Liu Hongsong analyzed China's utilization of favorable political opportunities to successfully shape the G20 agenda on the issues of international financial regulatory reform and international institutional reform. The Chinese initiatives and solutions are reflected in the guiding principles of global economic governance based on the G20's political consensus (Liu, 2016). Zhang Shirong points out that following the global economic downturn, Chinese solutions proposed at the G20 Hangzhou Summit took into account the concerns of all parties, reflected the responsibility of a great power and demonstrated China's leading role in global economic governance (Zhang, 2017). Zhang Haibing believes that the G20 has enabled China to move from the periphery of global economic governance to the center. China's participation has also enhanced the legitimacy and influence of the G20 in global economic governance. Meanwhile, China has demonstrated the leadership and strength of a great power through the G20 (Zhang, 2017).

More Chinese scholars focused on China's strategic choices for participation. Some Chinese scholars believe that the global economic governance system established after the Second World War can no longer fully meet the needs of countries around the world for international public goods. In order to adapt to the changes in global economic governance, China not only needs to advance the governance network at the regional and global levels, but also constantly strengthen internal mechanisms and capacity building (Huang, 2016). As a participant, promoter and beneficiary of globalization, China should strive to curb the trend of de-globalization, persist in deepening opening-up processes, and advocate the establishment of a cooperative and win-win governance mechanism to promote the improvement of the global economic governance system. In this process, China should focus on creating a stable and open environment, strive to improve the supply capacity of international public goods, accelerate financial reforms and innovation, and enhance its position and voice in the global monetary and financial system (Chen & Zhang, 2017). Sheng Bin and Gao Jiang explain that, against the background of profound changes in the international economic structure, China has actively participated in the practice of the new global economic rules via the G20, APEC, regional trade agreements, the BRI and new financial institutions. Global economic governance reform led by China should adhere to the development orientation, build mutually beneficial and win-win partnerships, explore diversified mechanisms and maintain flexibility. In the short term, China is focusing on trade-related infrastructure construction, investment, e-commerce, and Small and Medium-Sized Enterprises (SMEs) (Sheng & Gao, 2018). For global financial governance, Sheng Bin and Ma Bin also propose that China should actively advance the 'stock' reform of global financial governance, and also the 'incremental' reform. Moreover, China should advocate a development-oriented global financial governance concept (Sheng & Ma, 2018). In terms of global trade governance, He Min, after assessing China's contribution in this field, proposed several policy recommendations: China should advocate WTO and RCEP negotiations, participate in global trade governance through the G20 mechanism, and promote domestic economic reforms (He 2017). Yang Pan and Dong Jiang'ai analyzed the challenges that China's regional integration development is faced with. They believe that the domestic economic base needs to be consolidated. They also propose continuing to enhance discursive power in global economic governance, creating new cooperation mechanisms, and building a comprehensive domestic economic governance network through existing mechanisms such as the G20 (Yang & Dong, 2018). Regarding how to improve China's voice in global economic governance, Liu Yong and Zhang Yi suggest that China should use the concept of a 'Community of Shared Future for Mankind' to shape common values for global economic governance, improve the institutional systems within the BRICS New Development Bank (NDB) and the Asian Infrastructure Investment Bank (AIIB), and enrich public goods in the global sphere through the BRI (Liu & Zhang, 2018).

With regard to current challenges confronting global economic governance, some Chinese scholars have pointed out that the escalation of US trade protection against China has made the international economic environment more complicated. In the face of this particular challenge, China needs to maintain a strategic focus on persisting with reform and opening-up, maintaining the present order of globalization and promoting global economic inclusiveness (Yu, 2018). Since President Trump took office, the interest of the US in global economic governance has declined dramatically, and China's role in global economic governance has been questioned. The divergence between China and the US in global economic governance has begun to increase. China needs to face up to the concerns of the Trump administration and more effectively handle relations with the US on the major issues in global economic governance (Song, 2018). Global economic governance is not only confronted with the crisis of failing value consensus and the severe impact of unilateralism. Another challenge is that competition for global trade rulemaking power is fierce. In this context, China should actively promote the transformation of the global economic governance system in a more just, rational and effective manner and play a leading role in relation to values, while being a co-constructor of international institutions, contributor of global solutions and participant in collective action (Lu, 2019).

China's participation in new areas of global governance

Analyzing China's interests in the international seabed, Liu Fangming and Liu Dahai proposed recommendations that China should strive to participate in the rulemaking of international seabed governance, improve relevant domestic legislation, research on seabed related planning, develop key technical capabilities and strengthen international cooperation (Liu & Liu, 2017). Based on field research, Wang Wen and Yao Le analyzed the challenges facing China in Antarctic governance in the new era. They pointed out that China urgently needs to reconsider the status of Antarctic governance in its overall strategy and continuously enhance its ability to participate in this area. China should contribute its wisdom and solutions to maintaining the Antarctic Treaty system and resolve problems related to the region (Wang & Yao, 2018).

Regarding the global governance of cyberspace, Tan Youzhi points out that China is a rising country in the increasingly competitive cyberspace sphere. In order to better maintain, realize and expand China's national interests, it is necessary to explore the China's path of participating in the global governance of cyberspace in three aspects: ideas, systems and technologies (Tan, 2013). Liu Zhenye and Yang Tianyu argue that China must develop a long-term network investment strategy, seize the commanding points of global Internet technology and its application, and vigorously improve its internet technology, internet industry and market share. China should also promote cooperative governance through a variety of bilateral and multilateral channels (Liu & Yang, 2016). Wang Gaoyang examined sovereignty-based Chinese solutions, concluding that China's cyberspace governance practices could provide new rules and ideas for the governance of cyberspace on a global level (Wang, 2018).

In addition, Chinese scholars are concerned about how China should participate in global intellectual property and space environmental governance. Xu Yuan analyzed China's role in the global governance of intellectual property rights, and believes that in that field, China's best choice is an active coordinator; not a follower of the US or a leader of developing countries (Xu, 2018). Han Wanqu and Jia Meichao propose that the Chinese solution to deal with space environmental governance should adhere to the principles of peaceful development and equal sharing. They suggest it should involve establishing a multi-center and cross-domain space governance system, building a platform to coordinate the supply of international public goods in the space environment, and the constructing a space governance system based on the concept of the community of shared future for space (Han & Jia, 2018).

Assessing research on China's participation in global governance

Although many Chinese scholars have conducted research on China's participation in global governance and obtained useful results, these studies have multiple shortcomings. Some of these problems have not been thoroughly studied, and are manifested in the following five aspects.

First, most Chinese scholars only interpreted the ideas and polices of global governance concepts and policies proposed by the Chinese government, instead of China's strategies and actual actions. Under the leadership of Hu Jintao, research mainly focused on how participation in global governance could contribute to China's peaceful development and the construction of a harmonious world. During the Xi Jinping period, studies centered on the interpretation of policy discourses such as the principles of 'Community of Shared Future for Mankind': joint discussion, co-construction and sharing. Other focuses of research have included Chinese solutions and the BRI. Only a few scholars have explored the conditions under which China can successfully shape the G20 agenda (Liu, 2016).

Second, Chinese scholars have conducted research on various issues related to China's participation in global governance. Different views have emerged on issues such as Chinese solutions for global governance, but there is little debate, and no scholars have summarized and compared different opinions. In fact, the four perspectives on Chinese solutions for global governance proposed by Chinese scholars are not mutually exclusive. The 'Community of Shared Future for Mankind' is the guiding principle of the Chinese solution. The Chinese practices applied to global governance are characterized by specific governance approaches and paths for various issues. Some of these approaches and paths serve as supplements, improvements, substitutions, or compromises in relation to the existing mechanisms. The governance experiences and concepts developed by China in its long-term economic construction and reform provide the practical basis for Chinese solutions.

Third, Chinese scholars have not theoretically expounded the dynamics of China's participation in global governance in various areas or explained how China can promote global governance reform, or how Chinese solutions should be incorporated into the global agenda. Although China has attached unprecedented significance to participation in global governance, China's emphasis and proactiveness varies in accordance with different periods in different issue areas. Chinese scholars have not provided any explanation for this phenomenon. Furthermore, China actively strives to enhance its institutional discurse power in global economic governance and has proposed reform initiatives in order to increase the representation of emerging market economies and developing countries in the IMF. However, the IMF quota reform proposal was not implemented, long after being approved by the G20 member states, until the US Congress passed the proposal at the end of 2015, to make it effective. What strategy did China adopt and through what mechanism did this particular strategy prompt the US to accept the proposal? This question remains unanswered and no Chinese scholar has provided a possible answer. What's more, many Chinese scholars believe that China's domestic governance experience can provide a model reference for global governance mechanisms, and that it represents the practical basis for China's global governance. However, few Chinese scholars have focused on how the domestic governance experience in specific areas should be introduced into the global agenda, and what factors might influence the outcome of such actions. Du Yang explored how China can integrate domestic experiences in poverty reduction into the global agenda, promote reforms and adjustments of relevant governance mechanisms, and thus provide highly referential ideas and methods for other developing countries (Du, 2011). However, this study did not delve into the reasons why the Chinese solution based on domestic poverty reduction governance experiences surpassed other programs, nor did it explain what factors helped China introduce the experience into relevant global governance mechanisms.

Fourth, Chinese scholars brought forward a series of policy recommendations on how China should participate in global governance, but did not give any specific policy measures; nor have they conducted an in-depth analysis of the effectiveness and feasibility of these policies or strategies. Many scholars held the point that China should enhance its institutional discourse power and promote the reform of global governance system. Yet they did not analyze under what circumstances can the appeal for institutional discourse power be accepted by the established order, and what specific power resources China can resort to in order to have its claims accepted. Furthermore, scholars suggested that China should improve its ability to set agendas. However, they have not assessed specific elements related to this capability or proposed any practical measures.

Fifth, Chinese scholars have paid relatively more attention to the role of the BRI in global governance. They believe that China should rely on the BRI to provide international public goods and promote global governance reform. However, few scholars have carried out empirical research on the specific construction projects implemented in countries along the Belt and Road. Thus, these scholars failed to clarify the problems and challenges during the implementation phase, which makes the opinions and policy recommendations put forward by these scholars lack empirical evidence-based support.

Conclusion

As China reintegrated into the international system and its economic strength grew dramatically, China's role in global governance first shifted from an outsider to a participant, and then to a contributor. In recent years, China has attached unprecedented significance to its participation in global governance. China actively advocates the gradual reform of existing international institutions, proposes governance solutions, initiates reform proposals in global governance institutions such as the G20, leads the establishment of new international institutions such as the BRICS NDB and the AIIB, and actively promotes the BRI.

These changes prompted many Chinese scholars to conduct research on China's multilateral diplomacy, China's participation in international institutions and global governance, and their impact on China in return. Although many studies are already published, in general, most lack empirical evidence-based support and in-depth analysis, and focus too heavily on the policy discourses proposed by the Chinese government and the global governance strategies China should adopt. Many failed to put forward evidence-based arguments and specific feasible policies based on sufficient investigation into China's role in global governance, in various issue areas.

Disclosure statement

No potential conflict of interest was reported by the authors.

References

Bao, J. Y. (2018). Lun quanqiu zhili tixi biange de zhongguo fangan: laizi zhongguo gaige kaifang de gongxian' [Chinese solutions for the reform of the global governance system: Contributions from China's reform and opening-up]. *Guojia zhili [National Governance]*, (3), 37–44.

Bi, H. D., & Niu, W. G. (2016). Quanqiu zhili zhuanxing yu zhongguo zeren' [Global governance transformation and China's responsibility]. *Shijie jingji yu zhengzhi luntan [Forum of World Economics and Politics]*, (4), 125–140.

Bo, Y. (2005). Zhongguo yu guoji huanjing jizhi: cong guoji lüyue jiaodu jinxing de fenxi' [China and the International Environmental Regimes: Analysis from the perspective of international compliance]. *Shijie jingji yu zhengzhi [World Economics and Politics]*, (4), 23–28.

Cai, T. (2004). Quanqiu zhili de zhongguo shijiao yu shijian' [China's perspective and practice of global governance]. *Zhonghui shehui kexue [Social Sciences in China]*, (1), 94–106.

Cao, Y. B. (2015). 21 shiji yilai zhongguo canyu quanqiu zhili de lingyu fenxi' [Analysis of China's participation in global governance since the 21st century]. *Guoji guanxi yanjiu [Journal of International Relations]*, (3), 25–37.

Chen, F. Y. (2016). Yong "zhongguo fangan" tuidong quanqiu zhili tizhi gengjia gongzheng heli' [Using 'Chinese Solutions' to push forward a more just and reasonable global governance system]. *Ziguangge [Ziguangge]*, (8), 31–32.

Chen, F. Y. (2017). Shijiuda baogao quanshi quanqiu zhili zhi zhongguo fangan: zhongguo dui quanqiu zhili de gongxian yu zuoyong' [The 19th Party Congress Report interprets Chinese solutions for global governance: China's contribution to global governance]. *Dangdai shijie [Contemporary World]*, (12), 16–19.

Chen, J. Q., & Zhang, Y. (2017). Zhongguo tuidong quanqiu jingji zhili gaige de zhanlüe xuanze' [China's Strategic Choices to Promote Global Economic Governance Reform. *Tianjin shehui kexue [Tianjin Social Sciences]*, (3), 105–108.

Chen, W. G. (2017). Quanqiuhua nidong yu zhongguo de yingdui: jiyu quanqiuhua he quanqiu zhili guanxi de sikao' [Globalization reversal and China's response: Reflections on the relationship between globalization and global governance]. *Jiaoxue yu yanjiu [Teaching and Research]*, (4), 72–82.

Chen, Z. M. (2016). Guojia zhili, quanqiu zhili yu shijie zhixu jiangou' [National governance, global governance and the construction of the world order]. *Zhongguo shehui kexue [Social Sciences in China]*, (6), 14–21.

Chen, Z. M. (2014). Quanqiu zhili tixi de zhongguo shi zengliang gaijin zhanlüe' [China's incremental strategy for improving the global governance system]. *Dangdai shijie [Contemporary World]*, (8), 8–10.

Chen, D. X. (2009). Shilun quanqiu zhengzhi de xin fazhan he zhongguo duobian waijiao de zaisikao' [Comment on the new development of global politics and the rethinking on China's multilateral diplomacy]. *Guoji zhanwang [World Outlook]*, (2), 1–11.

Chen, H. X. (2008). Zhongguo ruhe zai guoji zhidu zhong mouqiu shengyu: yu Wang Xuedong shangque' [How China seeks reputation in the international institution: Discussing with Wang Xuedong]. *Dangdai yatai [Journal of Contemporary Asia-Pacific Studies]*, (4), 143–158.

Chu, L. S. (2001). Duobian waijiao: fanchou, beijing ji zhongguo de yingdui' [Multilateral diplomacy: Concept, background and China's response]. *Shijie jingji yu zhengzhi [World Economics and Politics]*, (10), 42–44.

Cong, R. Y. (2005). Quanqiu zhili, lianheguo gaige yu zhongguo zhengzhi fazhan' [Global governance, UN reform and China's political development]. *Zhejiang Xuekan [Zhejiang Academic Journal]*, (5), 108–115.

Du, Y. (2011). Quanqiu zhili zhong de zhongguo jincheng: yi zhongguo jianpin zhili wei li' [The Chinese process in global governance: Taking China's poverty reduction governance as an example]. *Guoji zhengzhi yanjiu [Studies of International Politics]*, (1), 90–99.

Fang, C. P. (2004). Duobian zhuyi yu zhongguo zhoubian anquan zhanlue' [Multilateralism and China's peripheral security strategy]. *Jiaoxue yu yanjiu [Teaching and Research]*, (5), 47–52.

Geng, B. J., & Shen, D. D. (2019). Lun quanqiu zhili de zhongguo fangan ji qi jiazhi jichu' [On Chinese solutions for global governance and their value basis]. *Jiangsu daxue xuebao (Shehui kexue ban) [Journal of Jiangsu University (Social Science Edition)]*, *21*(1), 13–18.

Guo, S. Y. (1999). 'Guoji zhidu de rongru yu guojia liyi: zhongguo waijiao de yizhong lishi fenxi' [The integration of international institutions and national interest: A historical analysis of Chinese diplomacy]. *Shijie jingji yu zhengzhi [World Economics and Politics]*, (4), 60–65.

Han, W. Q., & Jia, M. C. (2018). Taikong suipian zhili: quanqiu zhili jidai zhongshi de yiti ji zhongguo fangan' [Space debris governance: Issues for global governance and Chinese solutions]. *Guoji guanxi yanjiu [Journal of International Relations]*, (6), 108–125.

Hao, L. X., & Zhou, K. L. (2018). Goujian renlei mingyun gongtongti: quanqiu zhili de zhongguo fang'an' [Constructing community of shared future for mankind: Chinese solution to the global governance]. *Makesi zhuyi yu xianshi [Marxism & Reality]*, (6), 1–7.

He, F., Feng, W. J., & Xu, J. (2013). Quanqiu zhili jizhi mianlin de tiaozhan ji zhongguo de duice' [The challenges of global governance mechanisms and China's countermeasures]. *Shijie jingji yu zhengzhi [World Economics and Politics]*, (4), 19–39.

He, M. (2017). Guoji maoyi de quanqiu zhili yu zhongguo de gongxian' [Global governance in international trade and China's contributions]. *Shehui kexue [Social Sciences]*, (2), 45–55.

He, Z. P. (2016). Yidaiyilu' yu guoji zhidu de zhongguo gongxian' [The 'Belt and Road Initiative' and China's contribution to Internatioanl institutions]. *Xuexi yu tansuo [Study & Exploration]*, (9), 49–56.

He, Z. P. (2017). Guoji fazhi de zhongguo fangan: 'yidaiyilu'de quanqiu zhili shijiao' [Chinese solution to international rule of law: A global governance perspective of the "Belt and Road Initiative"]. *Taipingyang xuebao [Pacific Journal]*, *25*(5), 1–12.

Hu, J. (2015). Zhongguo canyu quanqiu zhili de zhiyue xing yinsu fenxi' [Analysis of the constraining factors of China's participation in global governance]. *Xueshuyuekan [Academic Monthly]*, (11), 63–73.

Hu, M. (2017). Yidaiyilu' changyi xia zhongguo canyu quanqiu zhili de lujing xuanze yu tidu buju' [Path selection and Gradient Layout of China's Participation in Global Governance under the 'Belt and Road Initiative']. *Beijing gongshang daxue xuebao (Shehui kexue ban) [Journal of Beijing Technology and Business University (Social Science Edition)]*, *31*(6), 8–13.

Huang, W. (2016). Quanqiu jingji zhili bianqian yu zhongguo yingdui zhanlüe' [Global economic governance changes and China's coping strategies]. *Dangdai shijie [Contemporary World]*, (2), 42–44.

Jiang, Y. (2003). Zhongguo de duobian waijiao yu shanghai hezuo zuzhi' [China's multilateral diplomacy and Shanghai Cooperation Organization]. *Eluosi dongou zhongya yanjiu [Russian, Central Asian & East European Studies]*, (5), 46–51.

Johnston, A. I. (1999). Zhongguo jiaru guoji tizhi de ruogan sikao' [Thoughts on China's entry into the international system]. *Shijie jingji yu zhengzhi [World Economics and Politics]*, (7), 4–10.

Li, D. (2018). Lun quanqiu zhili gaige de zhongguo fangan' [China's solutions for global governance reform]. *Makesi zhuyi yanjiu [Studies of Marxism]*, (4), 52–62.

Liu, F. M., & Liu, D. H. (2017). Guoji haidi quyu de quanqiu zhili he zhongguo canyu celüe' [Global Governance in the International Seabed Region and China's participation strategy. *Haiyang kaifa yu guanli [Ocean Development and management]*, (12), 56–60.

Liu, H. S. (2016). Zhengzhi jihui yu zhongguo zai ershiguo jituan jizhi zhong de zhengce changyi' [Political opportunities and China's policy initiatives in the G20 mechanism]. *Dangdai shijie yu shehui zhuyi [Contemporary World and Socialism]*, (4), 31–37.

Liu, S. Q. (2017). Shibada yilai zhongguo canyu quanqiu zhili de zhanlüe buju yu nengli jianshe tanxi' [Analysis of China's strategic layout and capacity building for participating in global governance since the Eighteenth Party Congress]. *Dangdai shijie yu shehui zhuyi [Contemporary World and Socialism]*, (2), 160–166.

Liu, X. L., & Yao, W. (2016). Guojia zhili de quanqiu zhili yiyi' [The significance of national governance for global governance]. *Zhongguo shehui kexue [Social Sciences in China]*, (6), 29–35.

Liu, Y., & Zhang, Y. W. (2018). Quanqiu jingji zhili huayuquan: shidai jingyu yu zhongguo c lüe' [Global economic governance discourse power: Current situations and China's strategy]. *Jinghai xuekan [Jiang Hai Academic Journal]*, (4), 232–237.

Liu, Z. Y., & Yang, T. Y. (2016). Zhongguo yu hulianwang quanqiu zhili tixi de biange' [China and the transformation of global governance system for internet]. *Xueshu qianyan [Academic Frontiers]*, (4), 6–13.

Liu, D. M. (2011). Lun guoji jizhi dui zhongguo shehui baozhang zhidu yu falü gaige de yingxiang: yi lianheguo, guoji laogong zuzhi he shijie yinhang de yingxiang weili' [Study on the impact of international regimes on China's Social Security System and Law Reform: Taking the impact of the UN, the International Labor Organization and the World Bank as Examples]. *Bijiaofa yanjiu [Journal of Comparative Law]*, (5), 22–36.

Liu, J. (2000). Lun jiaru WTO yu zhongguo canyu guoji jizhi zhanlue de chuangxin' [Analysis of joining WTO and the innovation of China's strategy of participating in international regimes]. *Shijie jingji yanjiu [Studies of World Economy]*, (10), 42–44.

Liu, Q. C., & Zhang, W. (2017). Zhongguo 'yidaiyilu' jianshe yu quanqiu zhili: quyu jingji hezuo de moshi chuangxin' [China's "Belt and Road" construction and global governance: Model Innovation of Regional Economic Cooperation]. *Tianjin shifan daxue xuebao (Shehui kexue ban) [Journal of Tianjin Normal University (Social Science Edition)]*, (2), 59–65.

Liu, X. L., & Sang, P. (2018). Yidaiyilu' jianshe yu zhongguo de quanqiu zhili linian: yi goujian zhuyi wei shijiao' [The 'Belt and Road Initiative' and China's Global Governance Concept: From the perspective of constructivism]. *Jilin daxue xuebao (Shehui kexue ban) [Journal of Jilin University (Social science Edition)]*, 59(6), 60–70.

Lu, J. (2015). Zhongguo canyu quanqiu zhili de juese zeren yu renwu' [The role, responsibilities and tasks of China's participation in global governance]. *Qianxian [Frontline]*, (9), 44–47.

Lu, J. (2019). Quanqiu jingji zhili tixi biange yu zhongguo de juese' [The transformation of the global economic governance system and China's Role]. *Dangdai shijie [Contemporary World]*, (4), 12–17.

Ma, J. Y. (2018). Cong minzu jingshen gongtoti dao renlei mingyun gongtongti: 'yidaiyilu' yu zhongguo tese de quanqiu zhili jiazhi' [From the National Spirit Community to the Community of Shared Future for Mankind: the 'Belt and Road Initiative' and the Value of Global Governance with Chinese Characteristics]. *Sixiang zhanxian [the Ideological Front]*, (5), 84–94.

Men, H. H. (2017). Yingdui quanqiu zhili weiji yu bainge de zhongguo fanglüe' [China's strategy for dealing with global governance crisis and changes]. *Zhongguo shehui kexue [Social Sciences in China]*, (10), 36–46.

Men, H. H. (2005). Yali, renzhi yu guoji xingxiang: guanyu zhongguo canyu guoji zhidu zhanlue de lishi jieshi' [Pressure, cognition and international image: A historical interpretation of China's strategy of participation in the international institution]. *Shijie jingji yu zhengzhi [World Economics and Politics]*, (4), 17–22.

Niu, J. S., & Liu   ,. (2019). Zhongguo canyu quanqiu zhili de "du" yu "lu"'['Depth' and 'way' of China's participation in global governance]. *Xueshujie, [Academia]*, (1), 161–169.

Niu, J. S., & Liu, M. (2019). Zhongguo yinling quanqiu zhili de wenti yu duice' [Problems of China's leading role in global governance problems and its countermeasures]. *Dongbeiya luntan [Northeast Asia Forum]*, (2), 33–46.

Pang, Z. Y. (2018). Quanqiu zhili zhongguo fangan" de leixing yu shishi fanglüe' [Types and implementation strategies of China's solutions for global governance]. *Xueshujie [Academia]*, (1), 5–12.

Pang, S. (2008). Gaige kaifang yu zhongguo de duobian waijiao zhengce' [Reform and opening up and China's multilateral foreign policy]. *Shijie jingji yu zhengzhi [World Economics and Politics]*, (11), 44–51.

Qiao, Y. Q. (2018). Renlei mingyun gongtongti: yingdui quanqiu zhili kunjing de zhongguo luoji' [Community of shared future for mankind: Chinese logic to deal with the dilemma of global governance]. *Makesi zhuyi yanjiu [Studies of Marxism]*, (4), 20–26.

Ren, H. P., & Xu, C. Y. (2017). Zhongguo ying zai quanqiu zhili zhong fahui gengjia zhongyao de jianshe xing zuoyong' [China should play a more important and constructive role in global governance]. *Quanqiuhua [Globalization]*, (3), 59–70.

Ren, J. (2018). Renlei mingyun gongtongti: quanqiu zhili de zhongguo fangan' [Community of shared future for mankind: The Chinese solution for global governance]. *Dongnan xueshu [Southeast Academic Research]*, (1)", 10–17.

Qiao, W. B. (2001). Lengzhan hou zhongguo yu guoji jizhi de hudong guanxi' [The interaction between China and international regimes after the Cold War]. *Taipingyang xuebao [Pacific Journal]*, 9(4), 13–19.

Ruggie, J. G. (1992). Multilateralsim: An anatomy of an institution. *International Organization*, 43(3), 561–598. doi:10.1017/S0020818300027831

Shen, Y. M. (2017). Tanxi quanqiu zhili zhuanxing zhong de "zhongguo fangan'"[Analysis of the "China's Program" in the transformation of global governance]. *Heping yu fazhan [Peace and Development]*, (6), 1–15.

Sheng, B., & Gao, J. (2018). Zhongguo canyu quanqiu jingji zhili: cong guize jieshou zhe dao guize canyu zhe' [China's participation in global economic governance: From Rule takers to rule shapers]. *Nankai xuebao (Zhexue shehui kexue ban) [Nankai Journal (Philosophy and Social Sciences Edition)]*, (5), 18–27.

Sheng, B., & Ma, B. (2018). Quanqiu jinrong zhili gaige yu zhongguo de juese' [Global financial governance reform and China's role]. *Shehui kexue [Social Sciences]*, (8), 13–26.

Song, G. Y. (2018). Zhongguo, meiguo yu quanqiu jingji zhili' [China, the United States and global economic governance]. *Shehui kexue [Social Sciences]*, (8), 27–34.

Song, J. X., & Ma, L. D. (2013). Goujian hexie guoji zhidu: yuanqi, gouxiang yu zhongguo zhanlue dingwei' [Building a harmonious international institution: Origin, conception and China's strategic positioning]. *Shehui zhuyi yanjiu [Socialism Studies]*, (2), 143–148.

Su, C. H. (2011). Zhongguo yu quanqiu zhili: jincheng, xingwei, jiegou yu zhishi' [China and global governance: Process, behavior, structure and knowledge]. *Guoji zhengzhi yanjiu [Studies of International Politics]*, (1), 35–45.

Su, C. H. (2016). Tansuo tigao woguo zhidu xing huayuquan de youxiao lujing' [Exploring the effective approach to improving China's institutional discourse power]. *Dangjian [Party Development]*, (4), 28–30.

Su, C. H. (2002). Zhongguo yu guoji zhidu: yixiang yanjiu yicheng' [China and international institutions: a research agenda]. *Shijie jingji yu zhengzhi [World Economics and Politics]*, (10), 5–10.

Su, C. H. (2005). Faxian zhongguo xin waijiao: duobian guoji zhidu yu zhongguo waijiao xin siwei' [Discovering China's New Diplomacy: Multilateral institutions and China's new thinking of diplomacy]. *Shijie jingji yu zhengzhi [World Economics and Politics]*, (4), 11–16.

Su, C. H. (2006). Zhoubian zhidu yu zhoubian zhuyi: dongya quyu zhili Zhong de zhongguo Tujin' [Peripheral institutions and peripheralism: The Chinese path in east asian regional governance]. *Shijie jingji yu zhengzhi [World Economics and Politics]*, (1), 7–14.

Su, C. H. (2007). Guoji-guonei xianghu zhuanxing de zhengzhi jingji xue: jianlun zhongguo guonei bianqian yu guoji tixi de guanxi (1978-2007)' [The political economy of domestic- international transformation: A discussion on the relationship between China's domestic changes and the international system (1978-2007)]. *Shijie jingji yu zhengzhi [World Economics and Politics]*, (11), 6–13.

Sun, J. S. (2019). Yidaiyilu' changyi shi canyu quanqiu zhili de zhongguo zhihui' [The 'Belt and Road Initiative' is a Chinese wisdom to participate in global governance]. *Guobie he quyu yanjiu [Journal of Area Studies]*, (1), 55–56.

Tan, Y. Z. (2013). Wangluo kongjian quanqiu zhili: guoji qingshi yu zhongguo lujing' [Global governance of cyberspace: The international situation and China's approach]. *Shijie jingji yu zhengzhi [World Economics and Politics]*, (12), 25–42.

Tang, W. (1998). 1949-1980 nian zhongguo duobian waijiao de shijian ji tedian' [The practice and characteristics of new China's Multilateral Diplomacy from 1949 to 1989]. *Guoji zhengzhi yanjiu [Studies of International Politics]*, (1), 15–22.

Tian, T., & Lin, J. (2009). Guoji laogong biaozhun yu zhongguo laodong zhili: yizhong zhengzhi jingjixue fenxi' [International Labor Standards and China's Labor Governance: An analysis of political economy]. *Shijie jingji yu zhengzhi [World Economics and Politics]*, (5), 6–16.

Tian, Y. (2011). Guoji zhidu, yusuan ruanyueshu yu chengnuo kexinxing: zhongguo jiaru WTO yu guoyou qiye gaige de zhengzhi luoji' [International institutions, soft budget constraint and credibilty of commitment: The Political Logic of China's Entry into WTO and Reform of State-owned Enterprises]. *Jiaoxue yu yanjiu [Teaching and Research]*, (11), 6–13.

Tian, Y. (2014). Guoji zhengce kuosai yu guonei zhidu zhuanhuan: Laozi jiti tanpan de zhongguo lujing' [International policy diffusion and domestic institutional transformation: China's path of collective bargaining]. *Shijie jingji yu zhengzhi [World Economics and Politics]*, (7), 118–138.

Wang, G. Y. (2018). Jiyu zhuquan de wangluo kongjian quanqiu zhili: "zhongguo fangan" ji qi shijian' [Global governance of cyberspace based on sovereignty: 'Chinese Solution' and its practice]. *Dangdai shijie yu shehui zhuyi [Contemporary World and Socialism]*, (5), 182–190.

Wang, H. X., & Liu, Y. (2019). Zhongguo canyu quanqiu zhili de dingwei yu kaoliang' [The positioning and consideration of China's participation in global governance]. *Guangxi shehui kexue [Guangxi Social Sciences]*, (1), 45–50.

Wang, M. G. (2017). Quanqiu zhili zhuanxing yu zhongguo de zhidu xing huayuquan tisheng' [Global governance transformation and the increase of China's institutional discourse power]. *Dangdai Shijie [Contemporary World]*, (2), 60–63.

Wang, Q. Y. (2018). Quanqiu zhili zhong de zhongguo fangan ji qi gongxian' [Chinese solutions and its contributions in global governance]. *Dangdai shijie [Contemporary World]*, (4), 54–57.

Wang, W., & Yao, L. (2018). Xinxing quanqiu zhili guan zhiyin xia de zhongguo fazhan yu nanji zhili: jiyu shidi diaoyan de sikao he jianyi' [China's development and Antarctic Governance under the guidance of the new global governance concept: Reflections and suggestions based on field research]. *Zhongguo renmin daxue xuebao [Journal of Renmin University of China]*, (3), 123–134.

Wang, X. Y. (2019). Zhongguo canyu quanqiu zhili de lishi jincheng ji qianjing zhanwang' [The historical process and prospects of China's participation in global governance]. *Makesi zhuyi yanjiu [Studies of Marxism]*, (1), 120–129.

Wang, J. M. (2004). Zhongguo dui duobian waijiao de renshi ji canyu' [China's understanding of multilateral diplomacy and its participation]. *Jiaoxue yu yanjiu [Teaching and Research]*, (5), 41–46.

Wang, R. H., & Chen, H. X. (2007). Guoji zhidu yu zhongguo hongshizihui lifa' [International institution and Chinese Red Cross Legislation]. *Guoji Zhengzhi Kexue [Science of International Politics]*, (1), 1–30.

Wang, X. D. (2007). *Waijiao zhanlue zhong de shengyu yinsu yanjiu: lengzhan hou zhongguo canyu guoji zhidu de jieshi [Research on reputation factors in diplomatic strategy: Interpretation of China's participation in international institution after the cold war]*. Tianjin: Tianjin renmin chuban she [Tianjin People's Publishing House].

Wang, X. D. (2009). Zhongguo canyu guoji zhidu de shengyu kaoliang: dui Chen Hanxi zhi xueshu piping de huiying' [The reputation of China's participation in the international institution: A response to Chen Hanxi's Academic criticism]. *Dangdai yatai [Journal of Contemporary Asia-Pacific Studies]*, (2), 147–160.

Wang, Y. (2018). Quanqiu zhili de zhongguo fangan: goujian renlei mingyun gong-tongti' [Chinese solution for global governance: Constructing community of shared future for mankind]. *Sixiang lilun jiaoyu [Ideological & Theoretical Education]*, (1), 25–29.

Wang, Y. Z. (1998). Zhongguo jueqi yu guoji guize' [The rise of China and inter-national rules]. *Guoji jingji pinglun [International Economic Review]*, (3-4), 32–34.

Wang, Y. Z. (2001). Zhongguo yu duobian waijiao' [China and multilateral diplo-macy]. *Shijie jingji yu zhengzhi [World Economics and Politics]*, (10), 4–8.

Wang, Y. Z. (2001). Xin shiji de zhongguo yu duobian waijiao' [China and multilateral diplomacy in the new century]. *Taipingyang xuebao [Pacific Journal]*, 9(4), 3–12.

Wang, Y. Z. (2002). Zhongguo yu guoji zuzhi guanxi yanjiu de ruogan wenti' [Some issues on the study of the relations between China and International Organizations]. *Shehui kexue luntan [Forum of Social Sciences]*, (8), 4–13.

Wang, Y. Z. (2003). *Mohe Zhong de Goujian: zhongguo yu guojizuzhi guanxi de duoshi-jiao toushi [Construction in run-in: A multi-perspective analysis on the relations between China and International Organizations]* Beijing: Zhongguo fazhan chu-banshe [China Development Press].

Wei, M. (2007). Buduan fazhan, riyi Shenhua de zhongguo duobian waijiao' [Constantly developing and deepening China's multilateral diplomacy]. *Dangdai shjie [Contemporary World]*, (5), 51–54.

Wu, X. M. (2017). Zhongguo fangan" kaiqi quanqiu zhili de xin wenming leixing' ['Chinese Solutions' open a new type of civilization for global governance]. *Zhonghui shehui kexue [Social Sciences in China]*, (10), 5–16.

Xie, L. Y. (2009). Zhongguo waijiao de duobian zhuyi zhuanxing jiqi jieshi' [The multi-lateralism transformation of China's diplomacy and its explanation]. *Hunan shehui kexue [Hunan Social Sciences]*, (5), 213–216.

Xu, Y. (2018). Zhongguo canyu zhishi chanquan quanqiu zhili de lichang yu duice' [China's position and countermeasures in participating in the global governance of intellectual property rights]. *Guoji jingjifa xuekan [Journal of International Economic Law]*, (4), 95–116.

Xu, D. Y. (2018). Yidaiyilu' jianshe yu quanqiu zhili zhong de zhongguo huayu' ["Belt and Road" construction and Chinese discourse in global governance]. *Shantou daxue Xuebao (Shehui kexue ban) [Journal of Shantou University (Social Sciences Edition)]*, 34(1), 5–9.

Yang, P., & Dong, J. G. (2018). Gaige kaifang yilai zhongguo canyu quanqiu jingji zhili de chengjiu, kunjing ji duice' [China's achievements, dilemmas and countermeas-ures for participating in global economic governance since reform and opening up]. *Guanli kexue [Management Science]*, (3), 131–136.

Yang, N. (2018). Gaige kaifang 40 nian: zhongguo canyu quanqiu zhili de tedian ji qishi' [40 years of reform and opening up: The characteristics and enlightenment of China's participation in global governance]. *Jiaoxue yu yanjiu [Teaching and Research]*, (8), 39–49.

Yu, J.P. (2018). Quanqiu jingji zhili tixi de biange yu zhongguo de zuoyong' [The transformation of the global economic governance system and China's role]. *Jianghai xuekan [Jiang Hai Academic Journal]*, (3), 80–86.

Yu, H. Y. (2008). Guoji zhidu he zhongguo qihou bianhua ruan nengli jianshe: jiyu liangci wenjuan diaocha de fenxi jieguo' [International Institutions and the Building of China's soft climate change capacity: Analysis based on the results of two questionnaires and surveys]. *Shijie jingji yu zhengzhi [World Economics and Politics]*, (8), 16–23.

Yu, J. J. (2009). Shenfen, guifan yu liyi: lijie zhongguo guoji zhidu xingwei zhuanbian de linian tujing' [Identity, norms and interests: An understanding of the idea and path of the change of China's international institutional behavior]. *Shijie jingji yu zhengzhi luntan [Forum of World Economics and Politics]*, (3), 9–15.

Zhang, H. B. (2017). Quanqiu zhili shijiao xia de zhongguo yu G20' [China and G20 from the perspective of global governance]. *Tongji daxue xuebao (shehui kexue ban) [Journal of Tongji University (Social Sciences Edition)]*, 28(2), 38–44.

Zhang, S. R. (2017). G20 hangzhou fenghui: quanqiu zhili yu zhongguo zeren' [G20 Hangzhou Summit: Global governance and China's responsibility]. *Guobie he quyu yanjiu [Journal of Area Studies]*, (1), 6–15.

Zhang, Y. (2017). Zhidu bianqian shiyu xia de quanqiu zhili xin quxiang yu zhongguo yingdui' [The new orientation of global governance from the perspective of institutional change and China's response]. *Lilun xuekan [Theory Monthly]*, (9), 96–102.

Zhang, J., & Wang, H. B. (2005). Lun heping jueqi de zhongguo dui goujian dangdai guoji zhidu de jianshexing yingxiang' [Comment on the constructive influence of China's peaceful rise on building contemporary international institutions]. *Dangdai shijie yu shehui zhuyi [Contemporary World and Socialism]*, (2), 82–87.

Zheng, Q. R., & Sun, J. W. (2001). Lun shiji zhijiao de zhongguo duobian waijiao' [Analysis on China's multilateral diplomacy at the turn of the century]. *Dangdai zhongguoshi yanjiu [Studies of Contemporary Chinese History]*, (6), 53–59.

Zhu, X. (2018). Quanqiu zhili biange yu zhongguo de juese' [The transformation of global governance and China's role]. *Dangdai shijie yu shehui zhuyi [Contemporary World and Socialism]*, (3), 158–165.

Zhu, X. F., & Wang, H. Y. (2012). Guoji zuzhi zai zhengce zhuanyi zhong de zuoyong yanjiu: yi UNDP canyu zhongguo xiaoe xindai zhengce weili' [The role of international organizations in policy diffusion: A case study of UNDP participation in China's Microcredit Policy]. *Zhongguo xingzheng guanli [Chinese Public Administration]*, (2), 45–49.

China debating the regional order

Dong Wang and Weizhan Meng

ABSTRACT

This article examines China's academic debates on the regional order in Asia since 2012, by surveying nine thematic issues. Those thematic issues are not exhaustive, yet they provide an overview of China's intellectual landscape on the key issue of the regional order in Asia. This study shows that the United States (US) might have exaggerated China's strategic intention. Rather than aiming to replace US hegemony with a Chinese-led *Tianxia*/tributary system in the region, Chinese scholars advocate mutual accommodation between China and the US.

The miraculous rise of China in the past few decades has greatly shaped the regional order in Asia. During this period, China's academia has advanced a variety of arguments regarding China's strategic thinking and objectives on the regional order. As the views of these intellectual elites will, to a varying degree, inform and influence China's policy choices in the future, it is therefore of importance to understand how Chinese scholars approach and debate the issue of the regional order, so as to help shed light on the future trajectory of the regional order in Asia. Since Xi Jinping became General Secretary of the Central Committee of the Communist Party of China (CC-CPC) in 2012, the new leadership has brought changes to China's foreign policies while keeping some policies consistent with those of previous leaders.

This article will survey China's academic debates from 2012 onward on the Asian regional order, made by mainstream Chinese scholars of international relations (IR). These debates consist of the following nine thematic issues: (1) whether or not China should build an alliance with Russia; (2) whether or not China should provide a security guarantee to neighboring countries; (3) the debate regarding how to 'break' or 'dismantle' the US alliance system in the region; (4) discussion centering on the New Asian Security Concept and its implications for the regional order; (5) debate over the 'Indo-Pacific' strategy and counter-measures against it; (6) debate over the expansion of the Shanghai Cooperation Organization (SCO) and the development of the BRICS countries; (7) debate regarding the role that the Association of Southeast Asian Nations (ASEAN) plays in shaping the regional order; (8) debate on the regional order of Northeast Asia; and (9) debate over the 'Tribute system' and the 'Tianxia order'. These thematic issues, reflecting the viewpoints of Chinese scholars on the regional order from varied perspectives, are not intended to be exhaustive. We believe, however, that by sampling these debates on some of the most important issues concerning the regional order, we should be able to gain an overview of China's intellectual landscape on the key issue of the regional order in Asia.

A China-Russia alliance?

Soon after the Obama administration came to power, Washington announced the 'pivot to Asia' strategy in 2009, which essentially led to the enhancement of the 'hub-and-spoke' system in Asia – wherein the US as a hub established bilateral security alliances with several Asian countries. Consequently, Chinese scholars' attention on the regional order shifted to focus on China's responses to the US-led alliance network. A heated exchange took place in Chinese scholarly and policy communities between 2012 and 2014. Some insisted on building a China-Russia alliance, whereas others were not strong advocates of such an alliance, but nevertheless supposed that the possibility of such an alliance should not be ruled out. Others suggested that China could maintain a 'quasi alliance' or 'weak alliance' with other countries in the region. Intriguingly, many Chinese scholars firmly opposed the idea of building a China-Russia alliance, although they provided markedly different rationales supporting their arguments.

Beijing has been continuously bolstering its bilateral ties with Moscow since the end of the Cold War. In 1996, Beijing and Moscow announced that the two countries shared a 'strategic partnership', while in 2011, China and Russia agreed to upgrade their relationship to a 'comprehensive strategic partnership'. Taking his first state visit to Russia after assuming the Chinese presidency in 2013, Xi Jinping remarked that China and Russia enjoyed one of the world's most important bilateral relationships and the best of major-country relationships (Xinhua, 2013). In 2014, the two countries issued a joint statement, declaring that their comprehensive strategic relationship had entered a 'new stage'. The upgrading of the China-Russia strategic partnership came at a time when conflict between China and Japan escalated due to territorial disputes over the Diaoyu Islands, and when Beijing was under increasing strategic pressure exerted by Washington's 'pivot to Asia' strategy. Clearly, China intended to send a message: Beijing had the option of strengthening relations with Russia to counter-balance the US strategic encirclement.

Yan Xuetong of Tsinghua University, one of China's most prominent IR scholars, is among the strongest advocates of a China-Russia alliance. Since 2011, Yan has published a series of writings expounding upon his arguments. He believes that Beijing and Moscow share the same strategic and security interests at present because the structural conflicts between China and the US are unlikely to be resolved anytime soon, while it is also hard to see an easing of tensions between Russia and the US. It is thus more beneficial for China to ally itself with Russia (Yan, 2012, pp. 21–25). Yan argues that an alliance with Russia could effectively alleviate security concerns faced on the northern and western borders of China and the strategic pressures placed on China by the US at the eastern and southern borders (Yan, 2013a, pp. 208–209).

Not every Chinese scholar endorses Yan's position. Indeed, there are scholars who have taken a more neutral stance on this issue. For instance, Feng Shaolei at East China Normal University, a leading Russia expert in China, has not endorsed an immediate China-Russia alliance but instead implies that there is 'no upper limit' for the China-Russia strategic partnership (Feng, 2016).

Besides, Sun Degang (Sun, 2011, pp. 70–79) from Shanghai International Studies University maintains that China could seek to develop a 'quasi alliance' with Russia. A strategy of establishing a 'quasi alliance' could bring more friends to China while at the same time avoiding the China-US relationship becoming more confrontational. Wang Dong of Peking University explains that China's strategic goal in Asia is not to 'push the US out of East Asia'. There is little chance for the emergence of a formal China-Russia alliance in the future unless the two countries are forced to pursue such a path due to increasing strategic and security pressures from the US. Before this happens, however, China and Russia may seek a hedging strategy instead of any rigid ones, so that they will encounter fewer strategic risks but enjoy more freedom of action (Wang, 2015, pp. 69–70).

Although a small number of Chinese scholars have argued that Beijing should ally with Moscow, the Chinese government nevertheless has not pursued such a policy option. Instead, Beijing has reiterated that in its nature, the China-Russia strategic partnership is 'non-aligned, non-confrontational, and not targeted at third parties' (People.com, 2014; Xinhua, 2014).

Moreover, even when the Crimean Crisis intensified in 2014, Russian President Vladimir Putin publicly brushed aside the possibility of a political and military alliance between China and Russia (Beijing News, 2014). In fact, as early as when this issue began to stir up controversy in 2011, many Chinese scholars strongly opposed the idea of pursuing an alliance with Moscow. Zhao Huasheng of Fudan University argues that China and Russia have formed an alliance three times in history, but that each time the alliance was short-lived and China's security ended up being seriously damaged. Today, the pubic on both sides harbor doubts on the issue. Long gone are the old days when China and Russia maintained a fraternal relationship in the 1950s. Moreover, the Russians are wary of becoming a 'junior partner' of China, and are keen to avoid being dragged into the confrontation between China and the US. Finally, the economic ties between the two countries are not as close as they were in the 1950s. Russia is worried that an excessive economic bond will make itself a 'vassal' of China (Zhao, 2013, pp. 66–71).

At present, the strategic pressure exerted by the US on China and Russia is still far from reaching the point where Beijing and Moscow believe that they must enter a formal alliance. 'Forging a partnership without forming an alliance' (*jieban bu jiemeng*) is considered by the two governments to be a strategic choice with lower costs but greater returns. Despite the fact that China-US relations have grown more tense amidst trade disputes in the past two years, Beijing and Moscow still appear to have no intention to forge a formal alliance. Nevertheless, there is still the possibility for China to form a tactical coalition with Russia over selective issues.

Should China provide security guarantee to neighboring countries?

Although only very few Chinese scholars advocate allying with Russia, a larger number consider that it is necessary for China to provide more security guarantees to neighboring countries, believing that it is not enough for China to just develop economic ties with its neighbors. Again, Yan Xuetong is among the strongest advocates for providing a security guarantee to China's neighbors. He argues that China has already become the second most powerful country in the world, and an increasing number of countries are asking China to assume greater international security responsibilities, or in other words, hope that China can provide them with a security guarantee. If China declines to do so, Yan warns that China might be considered by other countries to be an 'irresponsible' or even an 'immoral, unreliable' great power (Yan, 2013b, pp. 15–16; Yan, 2014, pp. 153–184).

Zhou Fangyin from Guangdong University of Foreign Studies makes the same argument using a slightly different rationale. Zhou contends (Zhou, 2013, pp. 20–24) that ensuring greater economic benefits for neighboring countries will hardly relieve their security concerns about China. Some US allies might mistakenly believe that China has given its neighbours economic benefits out of fear for their alliances with the US, so they will be more determined to 'fall to the US side' on security issues. Therefore, Zhou argues that pursuing economic policy alone cannot defuse the threat posed to China by the US-led alliances in the region.

However, except for the relatively close security cooperation with partners such as Pakistan, the Chinese government does not seem to have explicitly stated that it provides security protection for any other countries.

How to drive a wedge between the US and its allies?

Although most Chinese scholars agree that forming a military alliance with Russia is not in China's interests, how to deal with the US alliance system in Asia is an issue that Chinese scholars cannot ignore. After Washington announced the pivot to Asia strategy, many Chinese scholars explored counter-measures to break the US strategic encirclement of China, drive a wedge between the US and its allies, and alleviate the strategic pressure on China from the US.

Liu Feng of Nankai University contends that there are two ways for China to 'break' or 'dismantle' American allies. Calling the first a 'united front' approach, Liu argues that China should seek to form coalitions with different countries centered on different political, economic or military issues, and should unite as many friends as possible. The second is to use economic leverage to change the incentives of US allies and partners – in other words, by continuing to deliver economic benefits to countries that are friendly to China, while imposing economic punishment upon trouble makers (Liu, 2012, pp. 64–67).

In addition, Zhong Zhenming of the Shanghai-based Tongji University (Zhong, 2012, pp. 80–84) suggests that China can employ a 'wedge strategy' to split the opponents. For weaker members within the US alliance system, strategic measures such as engagement, reassurances, negotiation, and even 'moderate coercion' when necessary, can be employed. This will help wean them off their relationship with the US and create a more favorable external environment for China's rise. Gao Cheng at the National Institute of International Strategy (NISS) of the Chinese Academy of Social Sciences (CASS) argues that China should adopt varying policies toward different neighboring countries. The amount of benefits China offers to various countries should be consistent with the degree of friendship between these countries and China. The purpose of such an approach is to eliminate some neighboring countries' illusion of trying to pressure China for greater economic gains through strengthening security ties with the US. In particular, Gao argues that it is necessary to prevent some US allies or partners from attempting to take advantage of China's 'stability-first' (*weiwen*) mentality by creating troubles. China should continue to work hard to maintain the neutrality of those US allies without territorial disputes with China, and to avoid the formation of an offensive alliance surrounding China aimed at containing its long-term development (Gao, 2014, pp. 45–48).

Zhou Fangyin compared the effectiveness of 're-assurance' and 'pressuring'. In his view, even if China tries to re-assure an American ally, that state will likely not determine that US protection is no longer needed. This is because, facing a rising China, it is beneficial for them to obtain more security protection from the US. On the contrary, if China exerts security pressure on the US allies, they will soon realize that maintaining alliances with the US is not cost-free; rather, it may bring risks in the security sphere. Zhou adds a caveat that China should not impose excessive pressure; otherwise it will lead to unpredictable consequences and even strategic isolation (Zhou, 2013, pp. 20–22). By contrast, Qi Huaigao of Fudan University holds that, given the fairly large power gap between China and the US at present, China should not adopt a 'hard balancing' strategy toward the US, arguing that 'soft balancing' or 'institutional balancing' is the preferred strategy. Interestingly, Qi suggests that the multilateral cooperation advocated by China is compatible and should coexist with the US-led alliance system in the region (Qi, 2011, pp. 70–74).

Believing that the two determinant factors of the configuration of the future East Asian order are the continuation of the US alliance system in East Asia and the rise of China, Sun Xuefeng and Huang Yuxing of Tsinghua University argue that the key to determining the future of the regional order is how the existing US alliance system responds to a rising China. To consolidate and deepen what the two authors call 'the regional coordination and co-governance order', they believe it is also necessary for the US and its regional allies to make a 'good-will strategic response' to China's 'self-restraint policy' (Sun & Huang, 2011, pp. 30–34).

A number of scholars have taken note of the declining US capability in dominating the regional order. Wu Xinbo, a prominent US expert at Fudan University, holds that the US ability to shape the regional order has fallen dramatically. One case in point: the US has failed to dominate the East Asia Summit. Clearly, the US is no longer the preeminent hegemonic power that it was during the 1990s (Wu, 2013, pp. 66–67). However, another prominent IR scholar, Zhu Feng of Nanjing University, offers a different view. Predicting that in the foreseeable future, the US will remain in a 'proactive and advantageous' position in the unfolding strategic competition between China and the US in the Asia-Pacific, Zhu advises against 'strategic adventurism' on the part of China, cautioning that any assertive actions by China may invite strong counter-measures from the US (Zhu, 2013, pp. 23–26).

There are also scholars who provide an analysis from the geopolitical perspective. Seeing the East Asian security order as based on a 'separated continental-maritime structure', Wei Zongyou of Fudan University argues that China and the US should, like what Beijing and Washington did in 1972, make concessions and reach a second 'strategic compromise'. China should recognize the legitimate interests and military presence of the US in the Western Pacific, while the US should acknowledge China's legitimate maritime interests in the coastal areas of East Asia and accept the peaceful transition of China from a 'land power' to a 'land-sea composite power'. China should pledge not to resolve territorial disputes by force and, in reciprocity, the US should commit itself to restraining unilateral provocations by some of its East Asian allies (Wei, 2014, pp. 54–56). Wei's logic is echoed by the influential view of 'co-evolution of two orders', put forward by Wang Jisi, one of China's most renowned US experts. The idea is that the US should respect and not actively challenge China's basic political system and domestic order. Only then can China be convinced that it should respect and not challenge the preeminent leading position enjoyed by the US and the existing international order advocated by Washington (Wang, 2014).

Both Zhou Fangyin (Zhou, 2013, p. 23) and Ling Shengli of Foreign Affairs University, a leading university affiliated with China's Ministry of Foreign Affairs, (Ling, 2015, pp. 46–50) suggest that China, facing the US-led regional security alliance system in East Asia, should actively develop 'minilateral' cooperation in the region. Such an approach may provide greater security reassurance and help establish a more open and inclusive regional security mechanism. For example, promoting minilateral cooperation between China, the US and Japan; or China, the US and the Republic of Korea (ROK); or China, the US and Australia, may help alleviate the security concerns of these US allies toward China.

Interestingly, some Chinese scholars regard the ROK as a possible 'breakthrough' or 'breach' for China to dismantle the US alliance system. Huang Fengzhi and his co-author from Jilin University argue that China should strengthen military and economic cooperation with the ROK in order to reduce the latter's dependence upon the US. They contend that China could, when necessary, impose moderate economic sanctions and strategic punishment against the ROK to prevent it from continuing to bolster its ties with the US (Huang & Liu, 2013, pp. 33–34). Yan Xuetong took a step further by advocating an alliance between China and the ROK. If China succeeds in aligning itself with the ROK, Seoul, despite being an ally of the

US, will likely take a neutral standing on China-US competition rather than take the sides of the US or turn against China. Yan nevertheless concedes that an immediate military alliance between China and the ROK is unlikely (Yan, 2015, pp. 25–27). Cao Wei, Yang Yuan and Zhou Fangyin (Cao & Yang, 2015, pp. 85–87; Zhou & Wang, 2016, pp. 41–43) attempt to seek strategic implications for contemporary China by looking into international relations in ancient East Asia. Their studies show that there were times in ancient Asian history where a small power formed alliance relations with two competing great powers simultaneously; a particular strategic pattern they define as 'two-sided alliancing' (liangmian jiemeng). Specifically, they investigate the cases of two successive ancient kingdoms on the Korean peninsula, Goryeo (918–1392 AD) and Chosŏn (1392–1910 AD), with the former having had simultaneously formed alliances with both Liao and North Song – two competing continental great powers – and the latter with the two contending powers, the Ming Dynasty and the Manchurian Hou Jin. They conclude that the spheres of influence of two competing great powers are not necessarily clear-cut or zero-sum and there are possibilities that a small power can swear allegiance to two competing big powers at the same time; an interesting finding clearly at odds with conventional alliance theory. Their research seems to imply that despite the alliance between the ROK and the US, there still exists the possibility in which China can strengthen its relationship, if not forming an alliance with the ROK.

Discussion on the new Asian security concept

At the 4th Conference on Interaction and Confidence Building Measures in Asia (CICA) Summit held in May 2014, Chinese President Xi Jinping proposed a New Security Concept for Asia, calling for a common, comprehensive, cooperative and sustainable security strategy in Asia. President Xi stated that 'we need to innovate in our security concept, establish a new regional security cooperation architecture, and jointly build a shared, win-win road for Asian security'. Opposing the Cold War and zero-sum mentality, Xi argued that 'no country should attempt to dominate' the region, advocating a 'multi-pronged and holistic approach and enhance regional security governance in a coordinated way'. In particular, Xi stated that 'in the final analysis, it is for the people of Asia to run the affairs of Asia, solve the problems of Asia and uphold the security of Asia' (Xi, 2014).

Jiang Zhida of the China Institute of International Studies, a leading think tank affiliated with China's Ministry of Foreign Affairs, argues that the core values of the New Asian Security Concept are openness, inclusiveness and win-win cooperation; implying that all countries have an equal right to engage in regional security affairs and no country should seek to monopolize regional security affairs (Jiang, 2014, pp. 1–11). Han Aiyong of the Institute for International Strategic Studies at the Central Party School, a prominent think tank affiliated with the CC-CPC, concurs that the new order advocated by China is characterized by openness, elasticity and flexibility rather than closedness and exclusiveness. Han acknowledges that the US has long had a strong presence in East Asia and that cooperation with the US and the US-led alliance system should be an important feature of any future security order in Asia (Han, 2015, pp. 63–64).

Xi's 'Asia for Asians' remarks have been criticized by some Western observers as proof that China is pursuing its own version of the 'Monroe Doctrine' (Navarro, 2014; Pei, 2014). Chinese scholars, however, do not share this view. Shen Dingli of Fudan University argues that the New Asian Security Concept advocates multilateral security and collective security in Asia, which provides a strong impetus for shaping an Asian cooperative security system. Shen believes that CICA should continue to draw lessons from the Organization for Security and Co-operation in Europe (OSCE) to evolve into a more substantive region-wide security architecture (Shen, 2014, pp. 1).

In an interview published by *South Reviews* (*Nan feng chuang*) – a leading Chinese news magazine that enjoys a large elite readership among the government, academia and business – Zhou Fangyin notes that there is a fundamental difference between China's proposal and the Monroe Doctrine, as President Xi never made the argument that Asian affairs should be run by China or any other big powers of Asia. The statement of President Xi is bold yet prudent, in fact bolder than that of the academia. The upgrading of the CICA mechanism would, to some extent, have a psychological impact on regional countries and weaken the expectation of a US strategy of encircling China (Lei, 2014, pp. 26–28). In the same interview, Jin Canrong of Renmin University, a leading US specialist, argued that although the New Asian Security Concept is categorically different from the Monroe Doctrine, the possibility cannot be ruled out that China might intend to leverage it to 'hedge' against the US 'pivot to Asia' strategy (Lei, 2014, pp. 26–28).

Indo-Pacific strategy and countermeasures

After Donald Trump took office in January 2017, the new US administration quickly unveiled the 'Indo-Pacific' Strategy, posing new challenges to the changing regional order. What are the implications of the Trump administration's Indo-Pacific strategy? How should China respond to such a strategy? Chinese scholars have been engaged in a heated debate on these issues.

Wei Zongyou (Wei, 2018, pp. 18–22) notes that the Indo-Pacific strategy is premised on the explicit recognition that China is a major strategic competitor of the US, therefore foreseeing a head-to-head contest between the

Indo-Pacific strategy and China's Belt and Road Initiative (BRI), a large-scale connectivity project perceived by Washington as aimed at expanding China's sphere of influence. Sun Ru of the China Institute of Contemporary International Relations (CICIR), a leading government-affiliated think tank in China, argues that China should adopt a 'greater neighborhood' (*da zhou-bian*) strategy to counter America's Indo-Pacific strategy. Beefing up diplomatic investments in neighboring countries, China should make more efforts to not only consult and coordinate with regional great powers such as Russia but also try to 'win over' small and middle powers in the region (Sun, 2017, pp. 27–29).

There are a small number of Chinese scholars who believe that India is where breakthroughs can be made in response to the US Indo-Pacific strategy. For instance, Lin Minwang, an India specialist at Fudan University highlights India's lack of strategic trust in the US (Lin, 2018a). Trump's trade protectionism has impacted the Indian economy negatively, which indirectly provides an incentive for New Delhi to improve Sino-Indian relations. Since Beijing and New Delhi share strong opposition to protectionism, Lin argues that as long as China maintains a good diplomatic relationship with neighboring countries including India, there is not too much to worry about regarding the Indo-Pacific strategy (Lin, 2018b, pp. 32–35). Ye Hailin, another India expert at the Institute for South Asia Studies, the CASS, however, holds a different view. Ye worries that there is a risk in pursuing an overly-accommodating policy toward India: that if China goes too far in an attempt to 'win over' India, it may be 'blackmailed' by New Delhi (Ye, 2018, pp. 1–14).

Quite a few Chinese scholars predict that the US Indo-Pacific strategy may not be implemented smoothly. For instance, Ling Shengli (Ling, 2019, pp. 14–16) notes that as President Trump's 'America First' policy and his hostility toward multilateralism estrange many Asian countries, China should seize the opportunity to improve ties with other major powers in the region. China's improvement in relationships with India and Japan since 2018 has increased Beijing's influence in the 'concert of great powers', which Ling believes will play a pivotal role in the development of a future regional order in Asia. Zhao Minghao, a researcher affiliated with the International Department of the CC-CPC argues that some ASEAN countries, such as Indonesia and Thailand, fear that the Indo-Pacific strategy will challenge ASEAN centrality in the regional architecture, adding that the ROK is also prudent enough to choose to 'sit on the sidelines' (Zhao M., 2019, pp. 55–57). Zhao's view is shared by Wang Peng of Renmin University who notes that ASEAN is a 'weak link or loophole' in the US Indo-Pacific strategy that China can exploit (Wang, 2018, pp. 47–52). Zhang Jie, a Southeast Asia specialist at the CASS, holds that ASEAN's vision of the Indo-Pacific is aimed at striking a balance between China and the US. With an emphasis on maintaining the inclusiveness of the

Indo-Pacific region, it is different from the US Indo-Pacific strategy character-ized by strong geopolitical flavor and China focus. Therefore, Zhang argues that China should uphold ASEAN's Indo-Pacific vision so as to counter the US Indo-Pacific strategy (Zhang, 2019, pp. 1–13).

Unlike the above-mentioned scholars, Song Wei of Renmin University (Song, 2018, pp. 30–34) holds a more pessimistic view, believing that the Indo-Pacific strategy may put China at a disadvantage. He notes that the roll-out of the Indo-Pacific strategy may have paved the way for the Quadrilateral Security Dialogue (also known as QUAD), an informal security mechanism composed of four powers – the US, Japan, Australia, and India – to evolve into a more formal alliance targeting China. It is no longer easy for China to prevent the emergence of such an alliance, Song warns.

Intriguingly, unlike in the official Indo-Pacific Strategy document unveiled by the Trump administration, Chinese scholars do not see a zero-sum relationship between the BRI and the Indo-Pacific strategy. For example, Pang Zhongying at the Qingdao-based Ocean University of China argues that China should take the 'if you cannot beat them, join them' approach toward the US Indo-Pacific strategy. As a 'peaceful and artful' way to deal with the Indo-Pacific strategy, China should actively consider joining the Indo-Pacific alignment, Pang contends; although without specifying how China could succeed in doing it (Pang, 2019, p. 7). Similarly, Zhao Huasheng of Fudan University argues that the linkage between the Asia-Pacific and the Indian Ocean indeed serves the interests of China. Therefore, China should consider the Indo-Pacific agenda as a way to 'penetrate into' the Indian Ocean region. Moreover, the Indo-Pacific agenda will not stand in the way of the BRI undertakings and is economically bene-ficial to China. Therefore, China should partake in the kind of economic cooperation prescribed by the Indo-Pacific strategy (Zhao H., 2019, pp. 43–46). Zhang Jiadong, Director of the Center for Indian Studies at Fudan University, concurs that there is no need for China to completely reject the Indo-Pacific strategy. The BRI and the Indo-Pacific strategy are compatible with each other and China can choose to selectively cooperate with 'reasonable content' of the Indo-Pacific strategy (Zhang, 2018, pp. 1–26).

Debate over the SCO and the BRICS

Debate over the SCO expansion

The establishment of the Shanghai Co-operation Organization (SCO) in 2001 was an important hallmark for China and like-minded regional coun-tries to pursue a more balanced regional order. Six members joined the SCO upon its founding: China, Russia, Kazakhstan, Kyrgyzstan, Tajikistan and Uzbekistan. Since 2012, membership expansion has become an important issue on the SCO agenda. Some Chinese scholars believe that an enlargement would give China an edge on shaping the future regional order, while others adopt a much more prudent attitude towards the SCO expansion.

The discussion over membership expansion of the SCO has heated up since 2012. Chen Xiaoding, a Central Asia specialist from Lanzhou University, in a co-authored article, argues that despite the inevitable tendency of the SCO enlargement, cons of the rush to expand outweigh the pros. While an enthusiastic Russia hopes to compete with the US by promoting the SCO enlargement, China should be concerned that an expansion may lower the organizational efficiency of the SCO, destabilize China's northwest border, and even turn the organization into an anti-US bloc (Chen & Wang, 2013, pp. 100–101). Zeng Xianghong, another Central Asia specialist from Lanzhou University, worried that China's political influence might be undermined if India and Iran joined the SCO. Zeng and his co-author caution that in the worst case scenario, Russia and India might join hands in 'squeezing' China's influence in the SCO (Zeng & Li, 2014, pp. 152–155).

There are, however, also scholars in favor of the SCO expansion. Wang Xiaoquan, a Russia and Central Asia specialist at the CASS, argues that on balance, an expansion of the SCO would be positive for China. Although the US intends to sow internal divisions and ruin the political cooperation of the SCO on the occasion of Indian accession, the joining of India and Pakistan would facilitate the 'trilogy of China, Russia and India' in promoting the development of the SCO, greatly improve its overall strength and international influence, and spread the New Asian Security Concept (Wang, 2015, pp. 94–100). Li Jinfeng, another specialist on Russia and Central Asia at the CASS, holds that the membership expansion of the SCO presents valuable opportunities but poses severe challenges, too. On the whole, there are more opportunities than challenges. The prospects of the post-expansion development of the SCO will primarily depend on whether China and Russia can establish an effective interactive mechanism (Li, 2015, pp. 42–44).

So far, with India and Pakistan having joined the SCO in 2017, the views of pro-expansion scholars seem to have been favored by the Chinese government. The SCO is likely to continue to grow as Beijing sees it as an important institution in helping to produce a multipolar and more balanced regional order.

BRICS

Jim O'Neill, the chief analyst of Goldman Sachs, coined the term BRIC in 2001, referring to an association of four major emerging economies: Brazil, Russia, India, and China. The acronym was expanded to become BRICS when South Africa was included in the grouping in 2010. After the 2008 Global Financial Crisis, emerging economies such as BRICS were regarded as an important force reshaping the regional and international orders. Particularly since June 2009 when BRIC leaders established a mechanism to meet on a regular basis, at their first formal summit in Yekaterinburg, Russia, BRIC(S) has become a hot topic within both the Chinese scholarly and policy communities.

Some Chinese scholars are optimistic about the prospects of BRICS. Zhu Jiejin of Fudan University notes that the establishment of the BRICS Development Bank in 2012 marked a step from 'concept' to 'reality' in BRICS cooperation, which will help promote the reform of traditional international financial institutions such as the International Monetary Fund (IMF) and the World Bank, and thus help shape a new international economic order (Zhu, 2014, p. 6; Zhu, 2015, pp. 24–25). Pu Ping of Renmin University (Pu, 2014, pp. 56–59) notes that all BRICS countries agree to build a fair and equal world order and uphold the UN-based multilateral mechanism. Therefore, the BRICS mechanism is of strategic value to China's multilateral diplomacy.

However, other scholars take a more cautious attitude on the prospect of the BRICS. Guo Shuyong from Shanghai International Studies University holds that even though the US dominance of the regional order would be further weakened by the continued growth of the BRICS countries, the BRICS will not be able to challenge the hegemony of the US (Guo & Shi, 2015, pp. 28–29). Similarly, Pang Zhongying argues that since the BRICS cooperation is still at an initial stage, with many uncertainties and fragilities, it is ill-advised to overestimate the influence of BRICS cooperation on the existing global and regional governance structures. The BRICS Bank or the New Development Bank and the Emergency Reserve Fund are far from being 'challenges' to or 'substitutes' for the World Bank and the IMF (Pang, 2014, pp. 33–35; Pang, 2017, pp. 40–41).

ASEAN and the regional order

Chinese scholars' discussions about ASEAN integration started from around 2000. Since 2012, most Chinese scholars have supported ASEAN integration, although a minority remain skeptical.

Men Honghua of Tongji University makes it clear that China should support ASEAN taking the driver's seat in regional integration. The reason being that neither China, nor Japan, or ROK is able to assume the leading role, and that the US' attempt to dominate the East Asian order has roused widespread vigilance among East Asian countries. On this basis, it is in the strategic interests of most East Asian countries, including China, to continue supporting ASEAN centrality in the shaping of the future regional order (Men, 2015, pp. 59–62).

Zhai Kun, a Southeast Asia expert at Peking University, holds that ASEAN, in an attempt to strike a balance among great powers, advocates the East Asia Summit (EAS)'s central position in the development of the regional order. The development of the EAS will help promote a more balanced regional order, and therefore China should seize the momentum to redesign a proactive strategy for participating in the EAS, thus harvesting 'positive interactions' and 'adaptable win-win outcomes' for all parties concerned (Zhai & Wang, 2016, pp. 43–46). Wu Xinbo notes that both China and ASEAN share similar outlooks on the regional order, advocate inclusiveness and openness, and stress the principles of equality and consensus-building. Such similarities, Wu argues, are the embodiment of the 'Asian way' or 'Asian experiences'. China, the US and ASEAN are three key players whose preferences and policy behaviors will greatly shape the future Asian regional order. Interestingly, Wu contends that the combined power of China and ASEAN will be greater than that of the US alone; therefore any future regional order will likely bear a more 'Asian imprint' (Wu, 2017, pp. 32–36). Ren Yuanzhe of Foreign Affairs University sees the emergence of a 'tripod' in Southeast Asia – with China providing economic public goods, the US strengthening military alliances, and ASEAN playing a leading role in regional integration. In a nutshell, China, due to its geographic advantages, still has the initiative in cooperating with ASEAN, and it is an irresistible trend for China to expand its influence in Southeast Asia (Ren, 2017, pp. 27–28).

However, a minority of scholars maintain a cautious attitude toward ASEAN integration. Specifically, Cao Yunhua, a leading Southeast Asia specialist at the Guangzhou-based Ji'nan University, notes that ASEAN has always regarded itself as the 'host', and other great powers the 'guests', when it comes to regional integration. While benefiting from China's robust economic growth, ASEAN still remains wary of China's growing military power and hopes to woo the US to counter-balance China (Cao, 2011, pp. 12–13). No great power would be able to dominate the future regional order without support from ASEAN. Thus, ASEAN plays an indispensable role in building a new regional order (Cao, 2018, pp. 13–17). Ge Hongliang, a Southeast Asia expert from Guangxi University for Nationalities, holds that ASEAN always prefers to be 'in the driver's seat' in regional affairs and to maintain regional peace through balance of power. In recent years, ASEAN, reflecting its rising suspicion of China, has adopted a soft balancing strategy against China through regional multilateral mechanisms (Ge, 2015, pp. 60–65).

The regional order of Northeast Asia

The regional order of Northeast Asia is another important topic that Chinese scholars have debated over the years. After 2012, a minority of

Chinese scholars proposed to eliminate or dilute US influence in Northeast Asia. Most Chinese scholars, however, do not advocate the exclusion of the US from Northeast Asia; rather, they believe that China should pursue 'co-leadership' with the US on the Northeast Asia regional order or otherwise establish a new regional security architecture in a gradual way.

Zhou Yongsheng of Foreign Affairs University contends that given that China, the ROK, and Japan retain profound Confucian traditions, Confucianism should be promoted as the dominant ideology for the regional order in Northeast Asia (Zhou, 2012, pp. 124–126). Similarly, Xue Li of the Institute of World Economics and Politics, the CASS, also proposes to rebuild a Chinese *li* (ritual)-based order. But instead of replacing the existing international order, Xue believes that such a Chinese *li*-based order should be compatible and coexist with it (Xue, 2018, pp. 135–138).

Believing that the Northeast Asian region needs to build a new security architecture, Shen Dingli nevertheless holds that such a goal does not require the immediate removal of the bilateral military alliance system built by the US. In fact, Shen acknowledges that the US-led bilateral military alliances are likely to co-exist with a Northeast Asia security architecture for a long time to come (Shen, 2011, pp. 26–27). Wang Junsheng, a Korea expert at the NIIS of the CASS, advises that China-US 'dual leadership' could be an ideal solution to Northeast Asian security problems; and that China and the US should develop mutual trust instead of staying suspicious of or trying to undermine each other (Wang, 2013, pp. 108–113). Likewise, Shi Yuanhua, a Korea expert at Fudan University contends that now and for a long time to come, the so-called 'compatible co-existence' of two security cooperation systems led by China and the US, respectively, will be a major characteristic of regional security dynamics, as well as an important precondition of regional cooperation in Asia. To fundamentally change the status quo and ask the US to withdraw from Northeast Asia is unrealistic if not impossible, and such a move will undermine not only China's economic development but also Asia's political stability (Shi, 2016, pp. 25–28). Such a view is echoed by Dong Xiangrong, another Korea specialist from the NIIS, CASS. Dong uses a vivid metaphor – 'renovating the temple rather than demolishing it' – to illustrate China's approach; China has been advocating gradual reform of the US-dominated regional order of Northeast Asia instead of seeking to overthrow the existing system (Dong, 2016, pp. 20–22).

There are still other scholars advocating the importance of the 'concert of great powers' in building the regional order in Northeast Asia. Believing that the concert of powers should be the main approach to solve the issue of order in Northeast Asia, Ren Jingjing from the CASS contends that China should not advocate completely eliminating US military presence in Northeast Asia (Ren, 2018, pp. 16–18; Ren, 2019, pp. 24–25). Gao Cheng also notes that in the domain of regional security, China's strategic purpose is to form a mechanism of concert of great powers led by China and the US, allowing them to jointly exert influence upon regional countries (Gao, 2014, pp. 42–48).

The approach of gradually facilitating the transformation of the regional order has been endorsed by most Chinese scholars. Moreover, many further conclude that it is an effective approach for China to promote the transformation of the international order. For instance, Tang Shiping, a preeminent IR theorist at Fudan University, argues that China should work with other countries including the hegemon – the US – as much as possible to jointly facilitate the steady improvement and transformation of the international order, thus bringing benefits to the world. Tang holds that China has never attempted to challenge the fundamental 'bedrock institutions' of the existing international order, but rather seeks their gradual transformation through cooperation, in order to bring benefits to both developing and developed countries. Tang cautions that China should conduct careful assessments on the costs and risks associated with its policies to avoid falling into 'strategic over-extension' or 'strategic overdraft' (Tang, 2019, pp. 201–203).

Debate over the "Tributary system"/"*Tianxia* order"

As China rises rapidly, some Western analysts and politicians have come to believe that China is trying to restore the 'Tributary system' or the '*Tianxia* order' from ancient China. A typical example is former US Secretary of Defence James Mattis. Speaking at the Naval War College's graduation ceremony in June 2018, Mattis said China 'harbored long-term designs to rewrite the existing global order', adding that 'the Ming Dynasty appears to be their model, albeit in a more muscular manner, demanding that other nations become tribute states kowtowing to Beijing' (Taylor, 2018).

In 2005 and 2009, Chinese political philosopher Zhao Tingyang published two books in which he tries to develop a *Tianxia* theory. In an attempt to renew the old Confucian concept, Zhao defines '*Tianxia*' as a world consisting of three levels: the physical world (all lands under the sky); the psychological world (the general sentiments of peoples); and the institutional world (Zhang, 2010, p. 109). Claiming 'the world' is the highest level of political unit, Zhao argues that '*Tianxia*' (all under heaven) is a better system than the Western-led international order (Zhao, 2005). Zhao's works, along with the idea of a tributary system, have generated heated debate within the IR community in China.

Seeing fundamental conflicts and contradictions between the Confucian *Tianxia*/Tributary system and the existing international order, Wang Qingxin of Tsinghua University argues that Confucian ethics or the *Wangdao* (humane authority) does not have to be reflected by establishing the 'Tianxia system'; nor is the 'Tianxia system' necessarily better than the modern international order. Wang contends that it is impossible to restore the Confucian 'Tianxia system', though acknowledges that there are many similarities between Confucian ethics and Christian cultural values, both of which are universal and therefore are able be adopted as the guidance for contemporary international relations (Wang, 2016, p. 73).

Another criticism of Zhao is offered by Hu Jian of Shanghai Academy of Social Sciences, who argues that Tianxia was actually a tool for the rulers of ancient China to construct legitimacy and promote nationalism. Disputing Zhao's claim that Tianxia is a political unit that is beyond the state, Hu contends that Tianxia is indeed a political unit within the Chinese empire, and an ideological instrument for the rulers to maintain the 'grand unification' (dayitong) of the Chinese empire. Therefore, Hu insists that the term Tianxia should not be used in the vocabulary of contemporary Chinese foreign policy (Hu, 2017, pp. 195–203) (Wang 2015).

There are also many critics of the tributary system. For instance, Yang Shu of Gansu University argues that the maintenance of the tributary system relied upon China's authority and cultural influence rather than its power. In fact, however, most of the surrounding countries did not culturally or politically identify with the Middle Kingdom as much as the Middle Kingdom expected. The tributary system therefore was a loose system which did not have the same binding power of the multilateral institutions in modern international relations (Yang & Li, 2017, pp. 72–75). Yang Baoyun of Peking University contends that the BRI is not an attempt to restore the 'Chinese-barbarian order' based on the China-led tributary system in history; rather, it is indeed an inclusive cooperation process (Yang, 2014, p. 3).

In conclusion, the 'Tianxia system' proposed by Zhao Tingyang has not been widely accepted by Chinese IR scholars, who – although believing that some of the political philosophies from ancient China could benefit today's international system – oppose the restoration of the hierarchical Tianxia/tributary system.

Conclusion

The rise of China will not only pose a challenge to US hegemony in East Asia, but also reshape the regional order in East Asia. Our survey on the Chinese scholarly debate on the regional order suggests that Washington might have exaggerated China's strategic intention. In the National Security Strategy Report released in December 2017, the Trump administration officially identified China as a major strategic competitor, claiming that China's strategic goal was to challenge the US-led 'Liberal International Order' and to establish a 'parallel order' dominated by China. In fact, our examination of the scholarly debate in China shows that the majority of Chinese scholars do not advocate building a competing alliance to counter the US-led alliance system in East Asia. Indeed, China has always responded to the US alliance system in the region with defensive policies. Since 2009, there have been discussions among Chinese academia about how to deal with or even dismantle the US-led military alliance networks in the region, but these discussions were mostly 'reactive' responses as China's threat perception of the US increased with the unfolding of the US' pivot to Asia strategy. China has no strategic intention of pushing the US out of East Asia, and few, if any, Chinese scholars advocate a Chinese version of the Monroe Doctrine. Interestingly, Chinese scholars generally take a non-zero sum perspective on the relationship between the BRI and the Indo-Pacific strategy, and maintain that the two are not mutually exclusive. In fact, most Chinese scholars explicitly recognize the leading role of the US in the regional order. Meanwhile, most Chinese scholars also believe that China should actively participate in the process of reforming the existing regional and international orders.

Since the new leadership took office in 2012, there has been both continuity and change in China's foreign policy. China's diplomacy is still fundamentally guided by the principles of peace and development. With the increase of China's national strength in recent years, China does believe that the US-led East Asian order needs to become more balanced, which has been prominently reflected in the discussions among Chinese academia and policymakers on issues such as the expansion of the SCO membership, China-ASEAN relations and the New Asian Security Concept. Nevertheless, it should be noted that these discussions are not aimed at displacing American primacy or promoting an alternative order, but rather at easing the strategic pressure from the US and achieving a more balanced distribution of power in Asia. This can also be observed in Chinese scholars' predilection for the concept of 'concert of great powers' in discussion on the regional order. Essentially, Chinese scholars advocate mutual accommodation between China and the US, rather than replacing US hegemony with a Chinese-led *Tianxia*/tributary system in the region.

Disclosure statement

No potential conflict of interest was reported by the authors.

Funding

The article was funded by Beijing Outstanding Young Scientists Program (BJJWZYJH01201910001007).

References

Beijing News. (2014). *Zhong E jian junshi zhengzhi tongmeng?* Pujing: Yi guoshi [Putin suggested that the idea of a military and political alliance between China and Russia is outdated]. April 18. Retrieved from http://www.bjnews.com.cn/world/2014/04/18/313523.html.

Cao, W., & Yang, Y. (2015). Mengguo de diren haishi mengguo? [Is the enemy my ally also an ally?]. *Dangdai Yatai [Journal of Contemporary Asia-Pacific Studies], 5*, 49–87.

Cao, Y. (2011). Lun Dongnanya diqu zhixu [On the regional order of Southeast Asia]. *Dongnanya Yanjiu [Southeast Asian Studies], 5*, 4–13.

Cao, Y. (2018). Zhongguo-Dongmeng hezuo yu yatai quyu zhixu de goujian [China-ASEAN cooperation and the construction of the Asia-Pacific Regional Order]. *Dangdai Shijie [Contemporary World], 12*, 13–17.

Chen, X., & Wang, Y. (2013). Dongmeng kuoyuan dui Shanghai hezuo zuzhi de qishi yu jiejian [The lessons of the ASEAN expansion for the SCO]. *Dangdai Yatai [Journal of Contemporary Asia-Pacific Studies], 2*, 100–127.

Dong, X. (2016). Guize, zhixu yu Dongbeiya guoji tixi de yanbian [Rules, order and the evolution of Northeast Asian International System]. *Huanghai Xueshu Luntan [Yellow Sea Academic Forum], 2*, 8–22.

Feng, S. (2016). Zhong E lianhe shengming biaoming huoban guanxi bu fengding [The "China-Russian Joint Statement" shows that there is no limit to the partnership between the two countries], Guancha.cn, June 27. Retrieved from https://www.guancha.cn/FengShaoLei/2016_06_27_365523.shtml.

Gao, C. (2014). Zhongguo jueqi beijing xiade zhoubian geju bianhua yu zhanlue tiaozheng [The pattern evolution and strategic adjustments of neighboring countries against the backdrop of China's rise]. *Guoji Jingji Pinglun [International Economic Review], 2*, 32–48.

Ge, H. (2015). Zhongguo "xin anquan guan" jiqi mianxiang Dongnanya de waijiao shijian [China's new security concept and its practices toward Southeast Asia]. *Gonggong Waijiao Jikan [Public Diplomacy Quarterly], 3*, 60–65.

Guo, S., & Shi, M. (2015). Jianshe xinxing guoji guanxi tixi de keneng [The possibility to build a new IR system]. *Guoji Guancha [International Review], 2*, 15–29.

Han, A. (2015). Dongya anquan kunjing yu Yazhou xin anquan guan de qidi [East Asia's security dilemma and the inspiration of the New Asian Security Concept]. *Guoji Wenti Yanjiu [International Studies], 5*, 51–64.

Hu, J. (2017). Tianxia zhixu: yizhong wenhua yixiang [The Tianxia Order: A Cultural Image]. *Xue Hai [Academia Bimestrie], 4*, 195–203.

Huang, F., & Liu, B. (2013). Meihan tongmeng qianghua yu Zhongguo de zhanlue yingdui [The strengthening of the U.S.-ROK alliance and China's strategic response]. *Guoji Luntan [International Forum], 15*(2), 28–34.

Jiang, Z. (2014). Yazhou xin anquan guan jiqi zhixu yihan [The new Asian Security concept and its implications for order]. *Heping yu Fazhan [Peace and Development], 5*, 1–11.

Lei, M. (2014). Cong yaxin fenghui kan Zhongguo waijiao xin dongxiang [Looking at the new trends of China's diplomacy from the CICA Summit]. *Nan Feng Chuang [South Review], 12*, 26–28.

Li, J. (2015). Shanghai hezuo zuzhi kuoyuan: Tiaozhan yu jiyu [Expansion of the SCO: Challenges and opportunities]. *Eluosi Dong'ou Zhongya Yanjiu [Russian, East European & Central Asian Studies], 6*, 36–44.

Lin, M. (2018a). Lishun Zhong Yin guanxi, Yintai zhanlue bugong zipo [Streamlining relationship between China and India will make the "Indo-Pacific strategy" difficult to sustain]. *Shijie Zhishi [World Affairs]*, 10, 74.

Lin, M. (2018b). Yintai de jiangou yu Yazhou diyuan zhengzhi de zhangli [The construction of "Indo-Pacific" and the tension of Asian geopolitics]. *Waijiao Pinglun [Foreign Affairs Review]*, 35(1), 16–35.

Ling, S. (2015). Xiezi zhanlue yanjiu [A study of the wedge strategy]. *Guoji Guanxi Yanjiu [Journal of International Relations]*, 5, 39–50.

Ling, S. (2019). Telangpu chongji yu Yatai diqu zhixu tiaozheng [The Trump shock and the adjustment of the Asia-Pacific order]. *Heping yu Fazhan [Peace and Development]*, 4, 1–16.

Liu, F. (2012). Guoji zhengzhi zhongde lianhe zhenxian [The United Front in the International Politics]. *Waijiao Pinglun [Foreign Affairs Review]*, 29(5), 56–67.

Men, H. (2015). Dongya zhixu jiangou de qianjing [Prospects for the construction of the East Asian order]. *Jiaoxue yu Yanjiu [Teaching and Research]*, 2, 56–62.

Navarro, P. (2014). China's real goal: A 'Monroe Doctrine' in Asia. *The National Interest*, September 2. Retrieved from http://nationalinterest.org/blog/the-buzz/ chinas-real-goal-monroe-doctrine-asia-11179.

Pang, Z. (2014). Yaoyou butongyu xifang de quanqiu zhili fang'an [To raise a global governance program that is different from the West]. *Renmin Luntan: Xueshu Qianyan [People's Tribune: Frontiers]*, 18, 26–35.

Pang, Z. (2017). Jinzhuan hezuo miandui de shijie zhixu he quanqiuhua tiaozhan [BRICS Cooperation facing challenges from the international order and globalization]. *Guoji Guancha [International Review]*, 4, 32–41.

Pang, Z. (2019). Zhongguo huo keyi jiaru "Yintai" lai yingjie he yingdui "Yintai" de tiaozhan [Join the "Indo-Pacific" strategy is a way to deal with it]. *Huaxia shibao [China Times]*, June 10, 7.

Pei, M. (2014). China's Asia? *Project Syndicate*, December 3. Retrieved from http:// www.project-syndicate.org/commentary/asia-for-asians-political-rhetoric-by-min-xin-pei-2014-12.

People.com. (2014). Waijiaobu: Zhong E anquan hezuo bujiemeng, buchongtu, buzhendui disanfang [Foreign Ministry: Security Cooperation between China and Russia is not Aimed at Forming an Alliance, or Confrontation, or against Third Parties]. November 27. Retrieved from http://world.people.com.cn/n/2014/1127/ c1002-26107741.html.

Pu, P. (2014). Jinzhuan guojia jizhi zai Zhongguo duobian waijiao zhongde dingwei [The status of BRICS mechanism in China's multilateral diplomacy]. *Jiaoxue yu Yanjiu [Teaching and Research]*, 10, 52–59.

Qi, H. (2011). Zhongmei zhidu junshi yu Dongya liangzhong tixi de jianrong gongcun [The institutional balance between the U.S. and China and the coexistence of two different East Asian Systems]. *Dangdai Yatai [Journal of Contemporary Asia-Pacific Studies]*, 6, 55–74.

Ren, J. (2018). Guoji anquan zhili yu Dongbeiya diqu anquan zhixu goujian [International security governance and the construction of Northeast Asia Security Order]. *Dongbeiya Xuekan [Journal of Northeast Asia Studies]*, 2, 16–18.

Ren, J. (2019). Tuidong Dongbeiya zhixu chonggou zhengdang qishi [Now is the time to promote the reconstruction of Northeast Asia Order]. *Shijie Zhishi [World Affairs]*, 1, 24–25.

Ren, Y. (2017). Meiguo Dongmeng guanxi de "sanjitiao" yu Dongnanya diqu zhixu [The "Triple Jump" of American-ASEAN relations and the regional order of Southeast Asia]. *Nanyang Wenti Yanjiu [Southeast Asian Affairs]*, 1, 17–28.

Shen, D. (2011). Dongbeiya anquan tizhi [Security institution of Northeast Asia]. *Fudan Journal (Social Sciences Edition)*, 6, 19–27.

Shen, D. (2014). Suzao Yazhou gongtong yishi yu Yazhou jiti anquan [Shaping Asia's common consciousness and Asia's collective security]. *Zaobao*, May 23, 1.

Shi, Y. (2016). Zhonggong shibada yilai Zhongguo zhoubian waijiao de lishixing xin jinzhan [New historical developments of China's neighboring diplomacy since CCP's 18th National Congress]. *Zhongguo Zhoubian Waijiao Xuekan [Journal of China's Neighboring Diplomacy]*, 1, 25–59.

Song, W. (2018). Cong Yintai diqu dao Yintai tixi [From the indo-pacific region to the indo-pacific system]. *Taipingyang Xuebao [Pacific Journal]*, 26(11), 24–34.

Sun, D. (2011). Lun "zhun lianmeng" zhanlue [On "Quasi-alliance" strategy]. *Shijie Jingji yu Zhengzhi [World Economics and Politics]*, 2, 55–79.

Sun, R. (2017). Xinshidai Zhongguo yinling Yatai heping fazhan mianlin de tiaozhan [The challenges facing China in leading peaceful development in the Asia-Pacific]. *Xiandai Guoji Guanxi [Contemporary International Relations]*, 12, 27–29.

Sun, X., & Huang, Y. (2011). Zhongguo jueqi yu Dongya diqu zhixu yanbian [China's rise and the evolution of the East Asia Regional Order]. *Dangdai Yatai [Journal of Contemporary Asia-Pacific Studies]*, 1, 6–34.

Tang, S. (2019). Guoji zhixu bianqian yu Zhongguo de xuanxiang [The transformation of the international order and China's choices]. *Zhongguo shehui kexue. Social Sciences in China*, 3, 187–203.

Taylor, A. (2018). Mattis compared Xi's China to the Ming Dynasty. *The Washington Post*, June 20. Retrieved from https://www.washingtonpost.com/news/worldviews/wp/2018/06/20/mattis-compared-xis-china-to-the-ming-dynasty-xi-might-be-happy-to-hear-it/?noredirect=on&utm_term=.7c979d333934.

Wang, D. (2015). Zhong Mei guanxi yu Dongya zhixu [China-US relations and the East Asian order]. *Zhongguo Guoji Zhanlue Pinglun [China International Strategy Review]*, 14, 69–70.

Wang, J. (2014). Zhong Mei ying gongtong jinhua [China and the United States should Pursue "Coevolution"]. Caijing.com.cn, June, 16. Retrieved from http://misc.caijing.com.cn/chargeFullNews.jsp?id=114266114&time=2014-06-16&cl=106.

Wang, P. (2018). Duichong yu xiezi: Meiguo Yintai zhanlue de neisheng luoji [Hedging and wedging strategies: The internal logic of America's Indo-Pacific strategy]. *Dangdai Yatai [Journal of Contemporary Asia-Pacific Studies]*, 3, 4–52.

Wang, Q. (2016). Rujia wangdao lixiang, Tianxia zhuyi yu xiandai guoji zhixu de weilai [Confucian "Kingly War", Tianxiaism and the future of the modern international order]. *Waijiao Pinglun [Foreign Affairs Review]*, 33(3), 73–99.

Wang, X. (2015). Daguo boyi xia, Shanghai hezuo zuzhi zouxiang hefang [Against the backdrop of great power game, where will the SCO be heading?]. *Jingji Daokan [Economic Herald]*, 3, 94–100.

Wei, Z. (2014). Zhong Mei zhanlue tuoxie yu Dongya anquan zhixu goujian [Strategic compromises between China and the United States and the construction of the East Asian Security Order]. *Guoji Guancha [International Review]*, 4, 43–56.

Wei, Z. (2018). Telangpu zhengfu de Yintai zhanlue gouxiang jiqi dui diqu zhixu de yingxiang [The Trump Administration's Indo-Pacific strategic concept and its impact on the regional order]. *Dangdai Shijie [Contemporary World]*, 12, 18–22.

Wu, X. (2013). Aobama zhengfu yu Yatai diqu zhixu [The Obama Administration and the order in the Asia-Pacific Region]. *Shijie Jingji yu Zhengzhi [World Economics and Politics]*, 8, 54–67.

Wu, X. (2017). Lun Yatai da bianju [On the great changes in the Asia-Pacific]. *Shijie Jingji yu Zhengzhi [World Economics and Politics]*, 6, 32–59.

Xi, J. (2014). Jiji shuli Yazhou anquan guan [We should actively promote the Asian Security Concept]. Xinhuanet.com, May 21. Retrieved from http://www.xinhuanet.com/world/2014-05/21/c_126528981.htm.

Xinhua. (2013). Xi Jinping zai mosike guoji guanxi xueyuan de yanjiang [Xi Jinping's speech at MGIMO University, March 24. Retrieved from http://www.xinhuanet.com/politics/2013-03/24/c_124495576.htm.

Xinhua. (2014). Waijiaobu fayanren jiu jianli Zhong E junshi tongmeng zuochu huiying [The Foreign Ministry Spokesman Answered Whether a Military Alliance with Russia should be Established], September 17. Retrieved from http://politics.people.com.cn/n/2014/0918/c70731-25684725.html.

Xue, L. (2018). Zhongguo de xin shijie zhixu yu jiu shijie de guanxi [The relationship between China's new world order and the old world]. *Zhongyang Shehui Zhuyi Xueyuan Xuebao [Journal of the Central Institute of Socialism]*, 1, 135–138.

Yan, X. (2012). *Eluosi kekao ma? [Is Russia reliable?]. Guoji Jingji Pinglun [International Economic Review]*, 3, 21–25.

Yan, X. (2013a). *Lishi de guanxing [Inertia of history]*. Beijing: CITIC Press Group.

Yan, X. (2013b). Zhongguo waijiao quanmian gaige de kaishi [The beginning of China's comprehensive reform of foreign affairs]. *Shijie Zhishi [World Affairs]*, 24, 15–16.

Yan, X. (2014). From keeping a low profile to striving for achievement. *The Chinese Journal of International Politics*, 7(2), 153–184. doi:10.1093/cjip/pou027

Yan, X. (2015). Zhonghan jiemeng shi "shidai qushi" [China-ROK alliance is the trend of the times]. *Lingdao Wencui [Leaders' Digest]*, 2, 25–27.

Yang, B. (2014). Xin haishang silu bingfei yao huifu "huayi zhixu" [The New Maritime Silk Road is not to restore the "Chinese-Barbarian Order"]. *Zhongguo Haiyang bao [China Ocean Newspaper]*, May 19, 3.

Yang, S., & Li, L. (2017). Fansi chaogong tixi de anquan gongneng [Reflections on the security function of the tributary system]. *Nanjing Daxue Xuebao (Zhexue Shehui Kexue) [Journal of Nanjing University (Philosophy & Social Sciences)]*, 54(2), 61–75.

Ye, H. (2018). Yintai" gainian de qianjing yu Zhongguo de yingdui celue [The prospects of the "India-Pacific" concept and China's coping strategies]. *Yinduyang Jingjiti Yanjiu [Indian Ocean Economic and Political Review]*, 2, 1–14.

Zeng, X., & Li, T. (2014). Shanghai hezuo zuzhi kuoyuan de xueli yu zhengzhi fenxi [Membership expansion of the SCO: Theoretical and political analysis]. *Dangdai Yatai [Journal of Contemporary Asia-Pacific Studies]*, 3, 120–155.

Zhai, K., & Wang, L. (2016). Zhongguo ying chongxin sheji Dongya fenghui canyu celue [China should redesign its strategy for participating in the East Asia Summit]. *Guoji Guanxi Yanjiu [Journal of International Relations]*, 1, 43–46.

Zhang, F. (2010). The Tianxia system: World order in a Chinese Utopia. *Global Asia*, 4(4), 108–112.

Zhang, J. (2018). Meiguo "Yintai" changyi jiqi dui Zhongguo de yingxiang [US "Indo-Pacific" initiative and its impact on China]. *Yinduyang Jingjiti Yanjiu [Indian Ocean Economic and Political Review]*, 3, 1–26.

Zhang, J. (2019). Dongmeng ban "Yintai" yuanjing [ASEAN's vision of the "Indo-Pacific"]. *Taipingyang Xuebao [Pacific Journal]*, *27*(6), 1–13.

Zhao, H. (2013). Zhong E jiemeng weihe quefa xianshi kexingxing [Why "China-Russia Alliance" lacks feasibility]. *Renmin Luntan: Xueshu Qianyan [People's Tribune: Frontiers]*, *10*, 62–71.

Zhao, H. (2019). Yintai zhanlue yu da ouya ["Indo-Pacific" strategy and great Eurasia]. *Eluosi Dong'ou Zhongya Yanjiu [Russian, East European & Central Asian Studies]*, *2*, 27–46.

Zhao, M. (2019). Meiguo zheng fuyu "Yintai zhanlue" shizhi neirong [The United States is injecting substantive content into the "indo-pacific strategy"]. *Shijie Zhishi [World Affairs]*, *5*, 55–57.

Zhao, T. (2005). *Tianxia tixi: Shijie zhidu zhexue daolun [The Tianxia System: An introduction to the philosophy of world institution]*. Nanjing: Jiangsu jiaoyu chubanshe.

Zhong, Z. (2012). Xiezi zhanlue lilun ji guoji zhengzhi zhongde zhiheng xiaoneng [The theory of wedge strategy and the effectiveness of balancing in international politics]. *Guowai Shehui Kexue [Social Sciences Abroad]*, *6*, 76–84.

Zhou, F. (2013). Meiguo de Yatai tongmeng tixi yu Zhongguo de yingdui [The US Asia-Pacific alliance system and China's coping strategy]. *Shijie Jingji yu Zhengzhi [World Economics and Politics]*, *11*, 4–24.

Zhou, Y. (2012). Dongbeiya de lishi jiegou, waijiao linian yu weilai qiantu [Historical structure, diplomatic ideas and the future of Northeast Asia]. *Waijiao Pinglun [Foreign Affairs Review]*, *29*(1), 114–126.

Zhu, F. (2013). Zhongmei zhanlue jingzheng yu Dongya anquan zhixu de weilai [China-U.S. strategic competition and the future of East Asian Security order]. *Shijie Jingji yu Zhengzhi [World Economics and Politics]*, *3*, 4–26.

Zhu, J. (2014). Jinzhuan yinhang lishixing tuijin guoji jingji xin zhixu [The BRICS Bank is promoting a new international economic order]. *Wen Wei Po*, July 15, 6.

Zhu, J. (2015). Jinzhuan yinhang de zhanlue dingwei yu jizhi sheji [The strategic and mechanism design of the BRICS Bank]. *Shehui Kexue [Journal of Social Sciences]*, *6*, 24–34.

Foreign aid study: Chinese schools and Chinese points

Meibo Huang and Jianmei Hu

ABSTRACT

China is playing an increasingly important role in the international aid system, attracting widespread attention both at home and abroad. Chinese scholars, based in China, have a deeper understanding of China's political and economic system and China's foreign aid policies and practices. This article analyzes China's academic schools and points in foreign aid. National leaders' Philosophy of foreign aid is the core of Chinese aid policy. But Chinese scholars have different views on whether China has formed a systematic foreign aid theory. They also have conflicts in the scale of China's foreign aid and its status in the international aid system. Some Chinese scholars put forward 'new modes' for its aid. Through a review of the literature, this article explores China's four core motivations: political, diplomatic and strategic motivation, economic motivation, development motivation, and humanitarian motivation.

Since the 21st Century, patterns of international aid have been gradually diversified by the world economy's rapid growth and transformation. China and other emerging donors are playing an increasingly important role in the international aid system, attracting widespread attention both at home and abroad. On one hand, Western researchers use existing Western foreign aid theories, principles, and standards to analyze China's foreign aid policies and practices, which has led to many questions and criticisms. On the other hand, Western studies are mostly based on secondary sources or even media reports, such as the AidData database, widely used in the current empirical research. This database is extracted from multi-channel news reports. It lacks a fundamental understanding of the concept, sources of funds and modes of Chinese foreign aid. Therefore, although this database appears to be rich in form, it can often lead to incorrect judgments and confused conclusions. Chinese scholars, based in China, have a deeper understanding of China's political and economic system and China's foreign aid policies and practices. Through the understanding of leaders' speeches, government policies and aid projects, they have established a deep understanding of the nature and characteristics of China's foreign aid, and raised this perceptual knowledge to the theoretical level through deep research.

In order to better present the views of Chinese scholars on China's foreign aid, we searched Chinese academic articles from China's largest journal database, China National Knowledge Infrastructure (CNKI), with the time span 1984–2019 (up to 8 July, 2019). We comprehensively retrieved journal articles from CNKI's Chinese Social Sciences Citation Index (CSSCI) source journals and Chinese core journals, but excluded masters and doctoral degree dissertations, conference papers and newspaper articles. The Chinese government and scholars use different terms when they discuss 'foreign aid' (duiwai yuanzhu). Searching papers by their 'theme', we employed terms such as 'China + aid' (zhongguo + yuanwai), 'China + foreign aid' (zhongguo + duiwai yuanzhu), 'China + economic and technical assistance' (zhongguo + jingji jishu yuanzhu), and 'China + aid to Africa' (zhongguo + yuanfei).

In order to avoid omitting important sources not retrieved using these keywords, we also conducted literature retrieval on the authors of the above-mentioned and previously accumulated documents. After reading these papers one-by-one, removing unrelated papers, we added new documents cited by existing articles and created a database with 498 valid results. It can be seen from Figure 1 that prior to 1990, Chinese research on

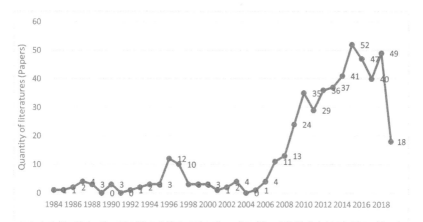

Figure 1. Quantity of papers published by Chinese scholars on "Foreign Aid": 1984–2019.
Source: China National Knowledge Infrastructure (CNKI).

foreign aid was very rare. After 1995, Chinese scholars gradually began to study the theoretical and policy issues of foreign aid. Since 2005, Chinese scholars have gradually increased their research on foreign aid, especially after 2010.

There are two theoretical and policy systems in the field of foreign aid. The mainstream is Organization for Economic Co-operation and Development–Development Assistance Committee's (OECD-DAC's) relatively mature and complete system. Chinese scholars have come into contact with these theories and policies at international conferences and by reading academic scholarship, and have learned a lot of useful knowledge, particularly regarding the content and framework of international development, the specific methodologies of international development research, and the concrete operations of international development assistance management. However, China's foreign aid is fundamentally different from that of DAC. China cannot use Western theories and principles to transform China's foreign aid, but can only borrow some elements from Western aid practices to reform and upgrade China's foreign aid management. China has its own foreign aid philosophy, motives, principles and practices. As a developing country, China has established unique practices of economic and social development in its own development process, and also explored a set of experiences and practices in its foreign aid. The expansion of the scale of China's foreign aid and influence and China's rising status in the international development assistance system will certainly drive the theoretical research of China's domestic scholars. Has the Chinese academic community formed 'China's foreign aid theory'? From what perspective do current Chinese scholars research on China's foreign aid? And, what is the Chinese academic community's view on China's foreign aid? The discussion of the above issues is the focus of this paper.

1. The concept of Chinese foreign aid and its academic schools

Searching CNKI with 'foreign aid theory' (duiwai yuanzhu lilun) reveals limited literature.[1] In fact, Chinese scholars use 'foreign aid theory' less and use 'foreign aid concept' (duiwai yuanzhu linian) more to summarize the nature of China's foreign aid, its goals, interests, functions, methods, and strengths. Qu (2019, p.95) believes that Chinese scholars mainly study China's foreign aid concept from three aspects: the first one is based on the perspective of character research, mainly national leaders' ideas and strategies for foreign aid; the second one is based on the perspective of time research, paying attention to different policies and concepts of China's foreign aid at different stages; the third one is based on the perspective of regional research, mainly focusing on aid to Africa. Some scholars have explored cultural factors in the formation of the above-mentioned foreign aid ideology from Chinese ethical thoughts and traditional culture. This research perspective can better reflect the fertile ground of China's foreign aid thinking, at a deeper level.

1.1. National leaders' philosophy of foreign aid

Due to the collective governance system in China, the Party and national leaders' concept of foreign aid reflects that of the top leadership of the Communist Party at any given time, and the whole country. We can also say that the foreign aid concept of the Party and the state is known to the public through the public statements of the Party and state leaders.

In the study of the foreign aid concept of the Party and state leaders, the words 'thoughts' (sixiang), 'ideas'(linian), and 'points' (guandian) (such as world view, international cooperation outlook) are commonly used, mainly for Mao Zedong (Qin, 2016), Zhou Enlai (Xue, 2013), Deng Xiaoping (Wu & Zhang, 2005; Cai, 2018) and Xi Jinping (Liu, 2018; Su & Li, 2019). These studies are usually based on the leaders' anthologies, chronologies, biographies, summary of speeches and other historical materials that are related to China's foreign aid, and combined with the situation at home and abroad. Through these analyses, we can understand the motives and principles of China's foreign aid in different time periods.

Mao Zedong saw providing foreign aid as an inescapable internationalist obligation. On June 27, 1950, when Mao met with the Vietnam Military Advisory Group, he pointed out that 'to help the oppressed nations and their liberation struggle is an issue of internationalism and a duty of the Communists. There are still many nations being oppressed and invaded by the aggressor countries and under the iron hoof of imperialism, we are not only sympathizing with them, but also reaching out to help them' (Zhongguo junshi guwentuan yuanyue kangfa shilu, 2012, pp.38–39). During that period, China's foreign aid not only helped the national independence and economic development of the third world countries, but also reduced the pressure placed on the new socialist China. Such help was seen as mutual, not unilateral. On February 21, 1959, Mao said in a conversation with the youth representatives of Africa: 'You need support, we also need support, and all socialist countries need support ... so we are mutual support. Your anti-imperialist movement is support for us ... we can contain imperialism and disperse its power, making them unable to concentrate on oppressing Africa' (Ministry of Foreign Affairs of the People's Republic of China & Literature Research Office of the CPC Central Committee, 1994, p.370). Mao followed the peaceful diplomatic thought of not interfering in other nations' internal affairs and opposing great powers. This idea is still the cornerstone of China's foreign aid policy up to today.

Zhou Enlai's foreign aid thinking was mainly reflected in his 'Eight Principles of Foreign Economic and Technical Assistance' proposed during his visit to Asia and Africa in 1963-1964. On one hand, China 'provides assistance on the basis of the principle of equality and mutual benefit. It does not regard aid as a unilateral gift, but believes that aid is mutual.' China's foreign aid 'strictly respects the recipient countries' sovereignty, does not attach any conditions, and never asks for any privileges' (Xue, 2013; Zhouenlai zongli fangwen feizhou, 8–9). On the other hand, Zhou made it clear that 'the purpose of providing assistance to foreign countries is not to cause the recipients to rely on China, but to assist the recipients to gradually embark on the road of self-reliance and economic independence.'

Deng Xiaoping's foreign aid ideology reflected his diplomatic thought of actively avoiding confrontation, and the unity of national interests and morality (Wu & Zhang, 2005). He believed that foreign aid was an objective need to promote international morality and safeguard national interests; the formulation of foreign aid policy should be based on the international situation and national conditions and strength; foreign aid should adhere to the principle of treating each other equally, respecting the sovereignty of recipient countries, and not interfering in the internal affairs of other countries; and that foreign aid management should expand functions, optimize structure, enrich forms, and enhance efficiency (Cai, 2018).

Xi Jinping's theory of foreign aid can be characterized as practical and realistic, and is based on China's national conditions, relying on the overall pattern of international relations and the 'Belt and Road' initiative, advancing with the times and constantly reforming and innovating. Su and Li (2019) believe that Xi's theory is 'rational thinking and practical summary of China's foreign aid, basing on New China's foreign aid concept and practice, combining with changes in the international situation and changes within China's national strength and international status.' Xi's approach to foreign aid mainly reflects that major countries need to pursue common development, while maintaining China's primary principle not to interfere in other countries' internal affairs; 'teaching one to fish is better than giving him fish' (shouren yiyu buru shouren yiyu). Mentioning the international aid system, Xi mainly advocates the role of the United Nations and conducts bilateral and multilateral assistance cooperation in an open and transparent manner. Liu (2018, p. 38) believes that Xi's foreign aid thinking is pragmatic, strategic, scientific and responsible.

1.2. The theory of foreign aid in Chinese academic circles

China's foreign aid theory is the key concept and theoretical core of 'China's foreign aid', and a set of coherent theoretical statements have developed around the core concept (Ren, 2016, p. 56). Chinese scholars have different views on whether China has formed a systematic foreign aid theory. Pan (2013, p92) believes that China has formed the 'the theory of foreign aid with Chinese characteristics' (zhongguo tese duiwai yuanzhu lilun), that is, the ontology with altruism and win-win spirit as the core, the development purpose-oriented epistemology, the equal and open method-ology, and the emphasis on comprehensive means and gradual practice. But some scholars hold the opposite view. Hu (2011) points out that China's foreign aid is misunderstood by Western society because China lacks a systematic theoretical system to explain the aid relationship between China and recipient countries, especially in Africa. This aid relation-ship is different from the West in two aspects. Firstly, the Western realist view of aid theory emphasizes aid conditions, whereas China does not attach conditions to foreign aid. Secondly, Western humanitarian aid theory dictates that international morality is the basis for providing aid, whereas China's foreign aid takes into consideration national interests. 'The foreign aid theory with Chinese characteristics' should be built in the traditional culture of China, such as its core worldview of 'harmony and difference', its communication criteria of 'self-denial and ritual', its traditional methodology 'teaching people to fish' and its spirituality in 'feeling for others' and 'emphasis on affection and righteousness'.

From the perspective of discipline foundation, research perspective and research methodologies, China's research teams focusing on foreign aid mainly include: the research team of Li Xiaoyun in the College of Humanities and Development, China Agricultural University, from the per-spective of international development public policy; the research team of Huang Meibo in the International Development Cooperation Academy, Shanghai University of International Business and Economics (formerly School of Economics, Xiamen University before February 2018), from the perspective of economics and management; scholars in the Institute of International Development Cooperation of the Chinese Academy of International Trade and Economic Cooperation, from the perspective of international political economy and international relations. Figures 2 and 3 illustrate China's research institutions and major scholars on foreign aid:

Note on acronyms in Figure 2: CAITEC: Chinese Academy of International Trade and Economic Cooperation; XMUdieb: Department of International Economics and Business, Xiamen University; XMUse: School of Economics, Xiamen University; XMUcidrc: China International Development Research Center, Xiamen University; HEBUTsem: School of Economics and Management, Hebei University of Technology; UCASS: University of Chinese Academy of Social Sciences; CASSiwaas: Institute of West-Asian and African Studies, Chinese Academy of Social Sciences; CAUcohd: College of Humanities and Development Studies, China Agricultural University;

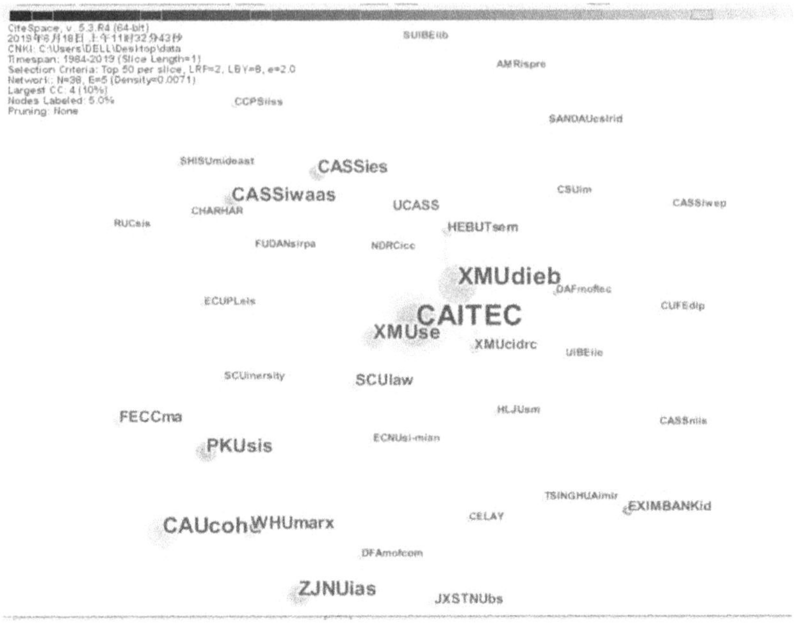

Figure 2. Display Degree of China's Research Institutions on 'Chinese Foreign Aid', 1984–2019.
Source: China National Knowledge Infrastructure （CNKI） .

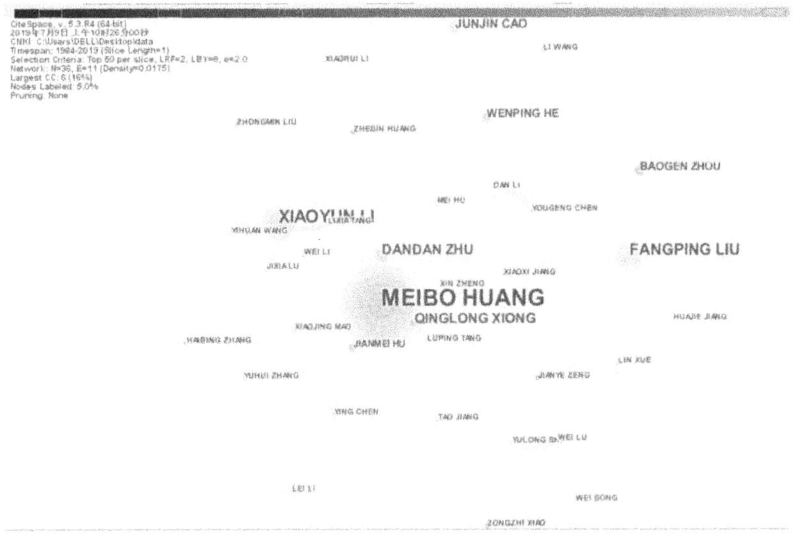

Figure 3. Display Degree of Chinese Scholars on 'Foreign Aid', 1984–2019.
Source: China National Knowledge Infrastructure （CNKI） .

CASSies: Institute of European Studies of Chinese Academy of Social Sciences; ZJNUias: Institute of African Studies Zhejiang Normal University; PKUsis: School of International Studies, Peking University; SCUlaw Sichuan University law School; FECCma: Foreign Economic Cooperation Center, Ministry of Agriculture; EXIMBANKid: International Department of the Export- Import Bank of China.

The team led by Li mainly studies China's foreign aid from the perspective of international development public policy. It focuses on micro-level research, using the ethnographic field survey methodology, using agricultural technology demonstration centers and Chinese aid personnel in Africa as its main research objects. Li's team believes that China's foreign aid is an extension of its domestic development approach overseas (Li, 2017). There are many differences in value and form between China's foreign aid practice and existing Western-based international development practice. China has provided an alternative development model with solutions to global development issues. China's development knowledge construction path is an empirical construction, which is different from Western theoretical construction (Li, Zhang, & Liu, 2017). China should provide a scheme to reinvent the global development program under the main path of 'new South-South Cooperation' informed by its experience of development, new development resources and new development system (Li & Xiao, 2017, p. 1).

Huang and her research team mainly study China's foreign aid from the perspective of economics and management. The team was based at Xiamen University and transferred to Shanghai University of International Trade and Economics in early-2018. On the one hand, the team conducted a systematic study of China's foreign aid management system (Huang, 2007), and studied the foreign aid management mechanisms of major traditional donors and emerging donors, and found lessons for China to learn from. On the other hand, they studied the effects of China's foreign aid and development financing from an economic perspective, including the impact of aid and development financing on trade, investment, economic growth and poverty alleviation. The team believes that on the basic principles of South-South Cooperation, China's foreign aid policy can learn from the aid management experience of DAC countries and advocate for a combination of 'aid effectiveness' and 'development effectiveness', to strengthen the management of China's foreign aid and attach importance to the actual economic, social and environmental effects of China's aid on recipient countries.

The team of the Institute for International Development Cooperation of China Academy of International Trade and Economic Cooperation conducts empirical and applied research on China's foreign aid policy from the perspective of international political economy and international relations, and has provided relevant policy advisory services to China's foreign aid management and implementing departments for a long time. It has accumulated a rich portfolio of research in China's foreign aid policy planning, data, statistics, country analysis, domain topics, and foreign aid evaluation.

There are many Chinese scholars in political science who have studied Chinese foreign aid. Zhou Hong from the Institute of European Studies of Chinese Academy of Social Sciences is a scholar who has conducted foreign aid research for a long time. She originally focused primarily on China's recipient status. As China's foreign aid advanced, she shifted her research perspective to China's foreign aid and she has comprehensively studied China's aid's concept, structure, quality and management (Zhou, 2010, 2013). Drawing upon the theory of the interaction between foreign relations and domestic politics in international politics, Ren and Guo (2016) constructed a preliminary theoretical framework for China's foreign aid, namely the 'motivation-relationship' interpretation mechanism.

2. The China foreign aid mode

Chinese scholars put forward new concepts to define China's development cooperation mode basing on summarizing the principles and practice of China's foreign aid. They also have conflicts in the scale of China's foreign aid and its status in the international aid system.

2.1. China's foreign aid under the principle of South-South cooperation

China's foreign aid follows the main principles of South-South Cooperation (SSC). Huang and Tang (2013a, p.66) believe that China's foreign aid is carried out within the SSC framework, and its aid principles, policies and concepts are consistent with SSC's core essence. Ren and Guo (2016) hold that China's foreign aid and SSC are closely linked, stating 'the unequal international economic order makes China consciously strengthen SSC through foreign aid'. Zhou (2010) pointed out that China's foreign aid 'puts forward a series of concepts and policies with Chinese characteristics, such as people-oriented, paying attention to the livelihood of the recipients, and sets an example of SSC' in the new century.

The most important principle of China's foreign aid is political equality without political conditions attached. Non-conditionality is the greatest feature of China's foreign aid policy. Premier Zhou unveiled three cornerstones of foreign aid in 1956, with the second being 'mutual assistance without any economic or political conditions attached' (CPC Central Research Office, 1998, p. 576).[2] The principle of non-conditionality is theoretically consistent with the basic norms of international law and international codes of conduct, and it has also been universally recognized by developing recipients in practice (Ding, 2016, p. 46). In the new era, 'China should continue to adhere to the principle of without attaching (any) political conditions and carry out foreign aid under the SSC framework' (Bai, 2015, p. 61). Han (2018, p. 112) believes that in the new era China's foreign aid policy should continue the principle of no additional political conditions, but it should be narrowly defined. 'No additional political conditions' does not mean that the recipient countries do not commit to any obligations – the recipients should be required to undertake corresponding obligations based on the contract and international law (such as providing legal facilities) in order to ensure aid effectiveness. Based on a series of facts about aid to Africa, by Chinese and Western donors, He (2007) pointed out that the development of China and Africa should not be directed by any third country, and that China and Africa were equal and had established a mutually beneficial SSC partnership.

2.2. "New mode" of China's foreign aid

The ultimate objective of China's foreign aid is to promote Southern countries' common development, and to contribute to SSC among China and other developing economies, 'using "package" approaches combining trade, investment, preferential loans and commercial loans to boost growth of developing countries' (Huang, 2018, p.39). In this process, China's foreign aid has reflected many new modes.

Li and Xiao (2017, p.10) put forward the concept of 'New South-South Cooperation', which 'inherits the political legacy of non-interference in domestic affairs in SSC and emphasizes respect for national demand orientation and the principle of reciprocity and mutual benefit in the new era of global development'. It is a global development mode under the new development experience, new resources and new system and emphasizes the integration of aid, trade and investment.

Zhang (2012b, p. 78) defined the model of China's aid to Africa as 'development-oriented aid', which helps and guides recipient countries to achieve self-development through equal 'aid + cooperation' and ultimately realizes mutual development between recipient and donor states. The theoretical pillars of this model include peaceful development, equal treatment of state relations, mutually beneficial and win-win cooperation and common development goals. Huang and Tang (2013b) further defined China's foreign aid as 'growth-driven aid' which is without any political conditions, advocating mutual benefits, and promoting economic growth and poverty alleviation in recipient countries. This new aid mode advocates 'development effectiveness' and emphasizes direct economic promotion to recipients.

Cheng (2016) generalized Sino-Africa development cooperation as 'official development finance with Chinese characteristics' (ODF-CC) which simultaneously meets three requirements of officially, development-oriented and concessionality. He advocates that ODF-CC is a 'South-South' development cooperation mode, which is provided by the Chinese Government and is geared to developing countries with high preferential components and highly dependent on various financial credit instruments.

Xu, Li, and Ma (2015) used the concept of "parallel experience transfer" and regarded China as the representative of providing development-oriented public goods which include mutually beneficial infrastructures, technology transfer and parallel experience sharing. Liu (2014, p. 91) regards China's aid to Africa as "relation aid", which is different from the "dominant aid" of traditional donors. China's aid to Africa aims at relations building and attaches importance to the emotional significance and relationship building in exchange process. Such assistance is a process of two-way interaction, and a natural extension of friendly relations between the two sides, emphasizing mutual benefit and assistance, in order to achieve sustainable relationship progress in the form of aid and cooperation.

2.3. The scale of China's foreign aid: too much or too little?

In the 1970s, China's foreign aid accounted for 7.5% of the national fiscal expenditure (Shi, 1994, p. 298). Beginning with its reform and opening-up policy in 1978, Chinese foreign aid has been adjusted to coordinate with domestic fiscal revenue. According to the White Paper (2011) on China's Foreign Aid, China had provided a total of 256.3 billion yuan in aid by the end of 2009. From 2010 to 2012, China's foreign aid amounted to 89.3 billion yuan (White Paper, 2014).

In recent years, the increasing scale of China's foreign aid has attracted widespread attention in the international community, and whether China should expand its foreign aid at this stage has also become a focus of domestic public opinion (Luo & Li, 2019, p. 62). The appropriate scale of aid is an important basis for giving full consideration to the role of aid and achieving the objective of aid (Luo & Liu, 2007, p.29). There are three views on the scale of China's foreign aid at this stage: too much, too little, or just enough.

One view is that the current scale of China's foreign aid is in line with China's development level. Ding (2016, p. 47) argued that China's aid scale has eliminated the previous excessive expenditure which was incompatible with China's level of economic and social development, and the scale of

China's current foreign aid (total amount and its proportion in government fiscal expenditure) currently matches its socio-economic development level and policy objectives.

Some scholars believe that the scale of China's foreign aid is still far behind that of Western countries (Xie, Tian, & Haung, 2012, p. 155) and that China's current foreign aid is too little. Luo and Liu (2007, p.30) pointed out that 'African countries generally welcome all kinds of aid from China and hope that such aid will continue to increase with the strengthening of China's economy and the continuous development of Sino-Africa relations', which was an implicit expression of China's relatively small scale of aid to Africa at the time. Ye (2013) argued that although China's contribution to the global multilateral development had increased rapidly, its scale was still relatively small. Hu, Zhang, and Gao (2017, p. 5) pointed out that 'although China's foreign aid has grown rapidly and ranks fourth in the world, it still has a large asymmetry with the proportion of China's total economic output, foreign trade and foreign investment in the world, which is also inconsistent with China's international status and has become a shortboard of China's "going out" strategy'. Therefore, China should learn from the Marshall Plan of the United States (Hu et al., 2017, p. 10) and expand the relative scale of its foreign aid.

But most Chinese scholars think that China's foreign aid policy is totally different from the Marshall Plan (such as Jin, 2015). They think that China's foreign aid policy embodies many 'self-interest motivations' such as China's economy, politics, diplomacy and strategy, and other 'altruistic motivations' such as development, livelihood and humanitarianism. It is not scientific to simply require the scale of China's foreign aid in terms of the proportion of total economic output, foreign trade and foreign investment in the world. Moreover, the international measurement of a country's aid obligations is generally based on the percentage of foreign aid in GNI, rather than on indicators of opening-up such as exports. Huang and Xiong (2014, p. 60) even argued that it is not feasible to measure a country's responsibility or obligations related to foreign aid based on its total economic output. China is currently exceeding its international aid obligations if the level of its per capita income and the problem of its poverty reduction are considered. Dong (2018, p. 101) believes that China's aid to Africa should not blindly be expanded in scale, but should pay more attention to optimizing its impact, through adjusting aid structure and focusing more on improving livelihoods.

He and Tang (2007, p. 84) held that the scale of China's foreign aid will increase with the further improvement of its economic strength, arguing that with the rise of China's national power, 'the Government can gradually increase the proportion of ODA to GNI in a planned and systematic way'. In

2016, foreign aid was incorporated into the National Five-year Development Plan for the first time. The 13th Five-Year Plan stated that China would 'expand the scale of foreign aid'. The report of the 19th National Congress of the CPC in 2017 pointed out that China will increase its aid to developing countries, especially the least developed countries. China should recognize its own current status as 'a responsible great developing country' and provide foreign aid based on its own strength (Luo, 2014, p. 42).

2.4. The status of China's Foreign Aid in the international aid system: challenge or complement?

Chinese academia generally agrees with China's status as an emerging donor and believes that China belongs to the Southern donor countries. China has become the most concerned emerging donor because it provides the most aid and its recipient countries have the widest scope (Mao, 2010, p. 59). The international community regards China as an 'emerging donor', reflecting the view that China's foreign aid activities began in recent years (Xie et al., 2012, p. 148). In fact, China's foreign aid has a long history, beginning in the 1950s. Like Brazil, India and other emerging donors, China invests most of its grants and concessional loans in infrastructure construction, mainly through project assistance and technical cooperation. With the fundamental difference of concepts and principles with DAC countries, is China's foreign aid a challenge or a complement to the traditional aid system?

2.4.1. China's foreign aid is a challenge to the traditional international development assistance system

Some Chinese scholars believe that due to differences in aid principles and practices, the rise of emerging donors, including China, is a challenge to the traditional development assistance system. Southern donors have emphasized independence and the uniqueness of their own forms of development cooperation. Yao argues that China's foreign aid scale ranked at the forefront of the world, and that China has the strength to compete with traditional donors. The collective rise of emerging donors, including China, poses a structural challenge to the Western-led international development assistance order (Yao, 2019, p. 31). The establishment of development *financing* institutions such as the Asian Infrastructure Investment Bank (AIIB), the BRICS New Development Bank (NDB) and the Silk Road Fund (SRF), constitutes a challenge to the traditional system dominated by *financial* development institutions such as the World Bank and the Asian Development Bank (ADB). Li and Xiao (2017, p. 7) point out that China has become the main supplier of new global development resources. The G20 Hangzhou Summit in 2016 marked that the development proposition of the Southern countries represented by the 'China Program' was gradually becoming an important substitute for global development (Li & Xiao, 2017, p. 9).

2.4.2. China's foreign aid complements the existing international development assistance system

Other Chinese scholars have argued that China's foreign aid is not a challenge to the existing development assistance system. Firstly, China has not attempted to challenge the mainstream economic development theory (Ye, 2013, p. 54). Secondly, China's foreign aid belongs to SSC among developing countries, which is essentially different from DAC development assistance. Chinese scholars mainly put forward corresponding policy recommendations under the SSC framework. As an emerging donor, China is a leader in SSC (Yao, 2019, p. 37) and should strengthen communication and coordination with emerging aid powers, maintain its foothold and develop SSC assistance (Mao, 2010, p. 58). In terms of the multilateral global aid system, China also has no intention to challenge the historical norms and policies advocated and implemented by multilateral development agencies (Ye, 2013, p. 54). Thirdly, in terms of aid scale, DAC donors are still the main force of development assistance, and the scale of aid from developing countries, including China, remains limited (Huang & Tang, 2013b, p. 23) and is not enough to challenge the dominant position of the largest traditional donors (Pang, 2013, p. 34). Although China's aid to sub-Saharan Africa is of considerable scale, these areas were originally neglected by traditional donors (Pang, 2013, p. 36). Therefore, China's foreign aid is a complement to the existing international development assistance system.

3. The purpose and motivation of China's foreign aid

Academia usually divides foreign aid motivation into self-interest motivation and altruism motivation, in which self-interest includes political motivation and economic motivation, while altruism includes development motivation and humanitarian motivation (Huang & Tang, 2013b, pp. 10–13). Through a review of the literature, we will explore these four core motivations. The first category, political motivation, is also taken to encompass diplomatic and strategic motivations.

3.1. Political, diplomatic and strategic motivation

Political and diplomatic motivations are important for China's foreign aid strategy, which is fundamentally an integral part of its overall national strategy. Zhou and Liu (2009, p. 46) pointed out that China's foreign aid is aimed at serving national strategic interests, which is similar to that of Western countries. Chinese scholars also regard foreign aid as an important component of China's peaceful diplomacy strategy (Zhang, 2008, p. 38) and a strategic decision of several generations of Chinese leaders (Xue, 2011).

Foreign aid has been provided since the founding of the New China in 1949. The main motivation of China's foreign aid in 1950-1970s was political (diplomatic) motivation. Seeking the widest possible international support from developing countries was the primary purpose of China's foreign aid during that time period, when Chinese foreign aid won favors from recipient countries and the 'Albania-Algeria proposals' made it possible for China to resume its legitimate seat in the United Nations.

Deng had always stressed that foreign aid was an indispensable strategic expenditure for China, with foreign aid strategy related closely to national interests (Chen, 2009, p. 78). With the constant adjustment and change of national strategic needs, China's foreign aid strategy has generally undergone a transformation from focusing on internationalism to paying attention to both internal and external situations and coping with both internal and external challenges. The year of 2013 can be regarded as the beginning of a new era in China's foreign aid policy, in which Chairman Xi put forward the 'Belt and Road' initiative. Over the past seven years, China has consistently abided by the principles of non-conditionality, equality and mutual benefit in foreign aid, and foreign aid work has been guided by the concepts of inclusive growth, consultation, contribution, shared benefits and strengthened communication and connection between China and other countries and international organizations participating in the 'Belt and Road' initiative. China's foreign aid has gone from the stage of scale expansion to intensive development. In 2017, the 32nd Session of the CPC Central Committee's Deep Restructuring Group deliberated and adopted 'Opinions on the Implementation of Foreign Aid Reform', emphasizing the need to optimize the strategic layout of foreign aid. This is the first time in recent years that the Chinese Government has emphasized the strategic role of foreign aid. The goal of China's foreign aid at present should be to fully cooperate with the implementation of its overall national strategy (Liu, 2015, p. 88, p. 91). China's foreign aid will help to usher in a new period of growth, while there is an objective need for China to change from being a passive responder to global challenges to actively participating in global governance after 40 years of reform and opening-up (Liu, 2018, p. 38).

However, while facets of Chinese diplomacy seek to serve its national economy, China has not yet formulated a foreign aid strategy to serve its overall economic development (Liu, 2015, p. 89). Wang (2019, p. 78) points out that China's foreign aid lacks strategic planning. Zhang (2012a) believed that China's aid to Africa was facing five strategic balance issues against the background of major adjustments in the current international pattern and international development assistance trends. China 'should adjust its foreign aid system in time to meet the strategic requirements of participating in global governance, satisfy the strategic needs of aid to Africa, and focus on promoting China's development concept and experience.' Bai (2013, p. 70; 2015, p. 53) studied the strategic choice of China's foreign aid and suggested China's foreign aid strategy be reformed in line with the Belt and Road Initiative. He considered that 'in the new era of the Belt and Road Initiative, China's foreign aid has undergone significant changes and is in an important transition period' (Bai, 2015, p. 53), while 'foreign aid has increasingly become a policy tool and governing strategy for the transformation of China's economic resources and power into influence and soft power' (Bai, 2013, p. 70). After Xi put forward the 'Overall National Security Concept' in April 2014, China's foreign aid strategy going forward should pay full consideration to security pressures and moral needs, while at the same time serving national economic development. As an international public good, foreign aid is also an important means for China to fulfil its responsibilities and build its image as a strong and capable country (Wang, 2015, pp. 55, 57–58, 59).

3.2. Economic motivation

The focus of Chinese foreign policy shifted from opposing imperialism to enabling domestic economic growth after 1978. And the form of foreign aid has also changed from one-way aid to mutually beneficial cooperation (White Paper, 2011). Economic motivation has gradually replaced political (diplomatic) motivation as the primary motive, while mutual benefits and the notion of win-win co-operation have become the most important principles of China's foreign aid. Chinese scholars often use such terms as 'foreign economic and technological cooperation' (duiwai jingji jishu hezuo) and 'foreign economic cooperation' (duiwai jingji hezuo) while studying foreign aid. Most scholars believe that foreign aid is the main form of China's participation in international economic cooperation. Zhang (2009, p. 4) regarded the provision of economic and technical assistance to foreign countries as the beginning of China's foreign economic cooperation. The Academic Committee on Development Assistance, which was set up under the Chinese Society for International Economic Cooperation in 1987, also included development assistance in the scope of foreign economic cooperation. In reform of foreign aid policy since the mid-1990s, China has further emphasized economic motivation, while a major purpose of foreign aid has been to ensure the supply of energy and resources, and to seek international markets for domestic products. Huang and Tang (2013a, p. 66) clearly pointed out that 'in the view of "aid + cooperation", China does not shy away from economic interests in foreign aid. Mutual benefit and assistance are the basic purposes of China's foreign aid'.

When studying the role of China's foreign aid, Chinese scholars often associate foreign aid with foreign trade and foreign investment. The results of empirical analysis show that China's foreign aid has a significant role in promoting trade with and investment in recipient countries. Zhang, Yuan, and Kong (2010, p. 73) argued that China's aid to Africa has greatly promoted China's exports to Africa. Meanwhile, China's foreign aid and FDI to Africa are complementary in scale, and China's long-term assistance to Africa has promoted Chinese enterprises investment in Africa. Peng and Lin (2019, p. 2) argued that China's foreign aid could promote China's exports to 'Belt and Road' countries through the infrastructure effect, the systems friction easing effect, the political relations improvement effect and cultural integration effect. Hu, Ding, and Deng (2015) found that 'China's aid to Africa is conducive to promoting China's FDI. In particular, the promotion effect of aid on FDI is more obvious when China's investment enters a smaller host country'. Chen and Wu (2019, p. 45) also found, via an analysis of 39 African states, that China's infrastructure aid to Africa has significantly boosted China's FDI in Africa. Zhou, Hong, and Wang (2018) found that China's aid to Africa can regulate the political risk of FDI in diversified African economies. From the perspective of public goods, Huang (2015, p. 97, 103) believes that goods or services provided by aid projects have obvious positive externalities, which can reduce external costs of donors' FDI enterprises in recipient countries, thereby promoting donors' investment in recipients. Case studies also show that China's foreign aid has become an important channel for Chinese enterprises to 'go out' and realize industrial transfer (Luo, 2019, p. 74; Zhang, 2007a, p. 30). However, some scholars have argued that China's foreign aid is not conducive to China's own economic growth (Yu & Kan, 2017), while some Chinese scholars have put forward suggestions and other perspectives on how to use foreign aid to promote China's economic development, such as using foreign aid to promote the internationalization of the Renminbi (Yang, 2012; Yang, 2015).

3.3. Development motivation

The ultimate goal of China's foreign aid is to promote recipients' development and focus on improving their independent development capacities. With the introduction of the Belt and Road Initiative in 2013 and the establishment of the United Nations' Sustainable Development Goals in 2015, China's foreign aid attaches greater importance to SSC, and development and humanitarian motivations have been further enhanced in China's foreign aid policy. Huang and Liu (2013, p. 62) believe that the ultimate goal of China's foreign aid is to reduce poverty, which should be the single goal. Zhang (2007b, p. 79) argues that China's aid to Africa is 'centered on promoting African economic development', and that aid projects 'were determined through consultation between the two sides and played a positive role in promoting African development'. Zhang further argued that China's aid to Africa has achieved the goal of promoting development through assistance, and promoting cooperation through development, and ultimately realizing common development between China and Africa. Luo (2013, p. 22) said that China's foreign aid and economic cooperation with Africa 'should not only alleviate poverty and provide humanitarian relief, but also focus on promoting African industrialization and modernization and enhance their capacity to develop independently'. Wang and Zhao (2014) showed that China's aid to Africa has significantly promoted Africa's economic growth.

In recent years, China has further strengthened its aid in the livelihood field and provided livelihood aid projects to Southern countries. Zhu and Huang (2017, p. 88) demonstrate that China's livelihood aid covers eight areas: living material assistance, education, medical treatment, water supply, environmental sanitation, employment, housing, and urban and rural public facilities – which are mainly used to meet basic survival needs and boost the basic development opportunities and capabilities of recipients. Hu and Liu (2009) regarded China's policy of providing 'livelihood aid to Africa' as being aligned with the goals of economic growth, improving livelihoods and pursuing mutual benefits. Some scholars argue that China's aid policy, prioritizing development aid and putting livelihoods first, has brought real and tangible benefits to both sides. However, some scholars hold a different view regarding the development motivation of China's foreign aid. For example, Liu (2015, p. 89) believes to the contrary that China's foreign aid attaches too much importance to economic interests and neglects livelihood projects, having a negative impact on social development and environmental protections in recipient countries.

3.4. Humanitarian motivation

Foreign aid concerned with humanitarian motivation is predominantly used to help recipient countries 'cope with international unexpected events and emergencies, alleviate the unfortunate situation of backward countries and save lives' (Huang & Tang, 2013b, p. 11). Li (2012, pp. 48–50) argues that China's foreign humanitarian assistance has progressed through three distinct stages: revolutionary humanitarian assistance (1950–1978), pragmatic humanitarian assistance (1979–2003) and non-discriminatory humanitarian assistance (2004–present). China provides emergency humanitarian assistance on its own initiative or at the request of recipient countries, including materials, cash and rescue workers. In September 2004, the Chinese Government established a formal emergency mechanism for humanitarian emergency relief assistance. Almost 200 emergency aid operations have been carried out by the end of 2009 (White Paper, 2011), while from 2010 to 2012, China provided emergency humanitarian assistance to the value of 1.5 billion renminbi, to more than 30 countries (White Paper, 2014). Li (2012, pp. 50–52) argues that China's foreign humanitarian assistance has gradually been in line with international practices.

The 2030 Agenda for Sustainable Development adopted by the United Nations in September 2015 provided a 'truly transformative international development framework' (Huang, 2016, p. 78). China's emergency humanitarian assistance abroad has helped the recipient countries and regions maintain social order and maintain stability in spite of testing circumstances (Liu, 2015, p. 89). Such assistance 'reflects a humanitarian spirit of poverty alleviation and relief, and a harmonious world concept of "some people and some regions getting rich first, then the rich help the poor, in pursuit of common development".' (Luo, 2014, p. 39).

Huang and Liu (2013, p. 62) proposed that with the growing strength of China's economy and the rise of its international political and economic profile, China should shift its main objective of foreign aid and gradually strengthen foreign aid as a component of diplomatic relations, within a broader international perspective. While realizing its own interests, China should help the world's less-developed countries reach the UN Millennium Development Goals (and then Sustainable Development Goals) and ultimately achieve the coordinated development of the world economy as a whole. In April 2018, the China International Development and Cooperation Agency (CIDCA) was established to oversee China's foreign aid affairs as a sub-ministerial organ, directly under the State Council. On the one hand, the establishment of CIDCA reflects the transformation of China's foreign aid role from promoting global economic cooperation to serving great power diplomacy. China's foreign aid will play a greater role in serving its foreign strategy and promoting the construction of the Belt and Road in the future (Yao, 2019, p. 35), and it is an important manifestation of China's image as a large, responsible developing country. On the other hand, China's foreign aid in the new era will pay greater attention toward enhancing the independent development capacity of recipient countries, promoting the establishment of series a new win-win bilateral relationships and propelling the creation of a *Community of Shared Future for Mankind* at the global level, through the Belt and Road Initiative.

4. The evaluation of Chinese foreign aid impact and effectiveness: aid effectiveness and development effectiveness

4.1. Aid effectiveness: standards and norms of aid

The existing international aid system is complex. There are many differences in procedures for assessment, approval, reporting, and valuation between donor and recipient countries, making transaction costs very high. To make aid more effective, efficiency, governance and transparency must all be improved. DAC members have made a clear commitment to their 'aid effectiveness' agenda by signing the *Paris Declaration (2005)* and the *Accra Agenda for Action (2008)*. Most DAC members have formulated clear, actionable, and time-bound aid effectiveness action plans. Improving 'aid effectiveness' depends upon the strict evaluation of the entire foreign aid process.

The developed countries have put huge resources into foreign aid, but outcomes are not always satisfactory. This makes the international community rethink whether 'aid effectiveness' is a reality and whether it should consider changing the concepts and methods of international development assistance. Wang& Liu (2012) argues that aid effectiveness is a process-driven development approach which is more focused on the Western-style democratic political process of good governance, accountability, transparency, and participation in recipient countries. But this kind of development assistance has not succeeded in poverty reduction in recipient countries. Sun (2008) pointed out that international development assistance has gone through seven decades, but most of the recipients – especially recipients in SSA – have not achieved the level of development they hope for. On the contrary, their economies have stagnated or regressed, their poverty-stricken populations have increased not decreased, and they still rely on assistance in varying degrees.

4.2. Development effectiveness: the actual effect of China's foreign aid

Different from the 'aid effectiveness' standard emphasized by developed countries and the evaluation index system of the Global Partnership for Effective Development Co-operation (GPEDC), Chinese scholars advocate 'development effectiveness' focused on the 'results' of foreign aid. 'Development effectiveness' focuses more on whether aid can bring faster economic growth, higher employment and reduce poverty rates in recipient countries within a relatively short period of time. However, China has not established a specific evaluation index system for 'development effectiveness'. The lack of data makes it difficult to conduct an in-depth evaluation of the effectiveness of China's foreign aid. Judging from the current domestic evaluation of Chinese aid, case studies are used to evaluate the concrete impact of an aid program on recipient countries.

Chinese scholars have analyzed the economic and social impacts of China's foreign aid on recipient countries. Huang, Xu, and Mao (2018) edited a case set on China's aid projects, including a case series on Madagascar General Hospital Project, China's Agricultural Technical Cooperation on *juncao* aid projects to Papua New Guinea and Fiji, Sino-Tanzania Village-based Poverty Reduction Learning Center and Joint Learning Center. These projects were found to have generated favorable economic and social impacts in recipient countries.

Chinese scholars have established econometric models to evaluate the specific effectiveness of China's foreign aid. Therefore, many Chinese scholars have studied the economic and poverty reduction effects, and most of the existing literature links foreign aid with trade and investment. Some scholars have found that China's foreign aid has increased recipient countries' economic growth, promoted their exports and enlarged FDI inflows. Zhu and her collaborator are the first Chinese scholars to study the effects of China's foreign aid from a combination perspective of trade and aid. Their relevant conclusions show that China's aid to Africa can significantly reduce recipient countries' export and import costs (Zhu & Huang, 2015), increase the total exports of recipient countries to China, significantly promote the economic growth of African recipient countries (Zhu & Huang, 2018). Liu and Tang (2018) found that China's aid to Africa has significantly increased bilateral trade scale between China and Africa. Sun, Xu, and Liang (2019) found that China's foreign aid has enabled African recipient countries to increase the proportion of exports that are appropriate to their level of development, and to reduce the proportion of exports that are not suitable for their level of development, and that China's foreign aid will help recipient countries' export structure adjust to a direction more suitable for the recipients' development level, which is conducive to promoting the healthy development of the recipients' economies. Wu and Dai (2019, pp. 32–35) found that China's aid to Africa has promoted Africa's export process upgrades in the global value chains, and the marginal effects on export upgrades of China's aid and FDI to Africa are complementary.

Some scholars have argued that China's foreign aid has a limited effect on recipients' trade development. Based on existing data, Xiong and Huang (2014) found that there does not exist a co-integration relationship between China's foreign aid and foreign trade. In other words, China's foreign aid does not promote recipients' foreign trade, and has little effect on recipients' growth. Dong and Fan (2016, p. 60) believe that China's combination of aid, trade and investment has promoted African local economies.

Their research found that overall, China's aid to Africa has significantly improved the level of social and economic development of host countries in the early stage, and created certain favorable conditions for foreign capital inflow; however, the effect of aid on investment is not sustainable, and the marginal efficiency declined over time. From the perspectives of Sino-Africa trade, investment, technology and experience transmission, tourism and other aspects, Zhang (2006, p. 66) affirmed the role of China's aid to Africa in promoting African economic development.

An important goal of foreign aid is poverty reduction. Zhang (2018) argues that China's poverty reduction cooperation model – combining aid and investment – helps poverty alleviation in Latin America, but that the poverty reduction effects of different types of aid are different. Other official funds, economic aid, infrastructure aid, science and education humanity assistance have significant poverty reduction effects. Xiong and Wu (2016) used dynamic stochastic general equilibrium (DSGE) to construct a three-sector international poverty reduction model including family, firm and government, and found that in the absence of technology shocks, positive aid volatility can reduce poverty, while negative aid volatility is not conducive to poverty reduction.

In addition, Chinese scholars have analyzed the role of China's foreign aid in promoting recipients' economic and social development from a theoretical perspective. For example, Huang and Zhu (2013, pp. 25–26) proposed the concept of 'knowledge cooperation' and argued that China can provide its rich and accumulated development knowledge and experience to countries which receive its aid, and other developing states, through South-South forms of knowledge cooperation and tripartite knowledge cooperation, thus promoting their economic and social development.

5. Conclusions

The global financial crisis that erupted in 2008 further increased the contradiction between international aid supply and demand. In the post-crisis era, global issues such as climate change, food security, energy and resource security, environmental pollution, major natural disasters and pandemics have become more prominent. At the same time, development and economic imbalances between developed and developing states have become increasingly serious. The gap between rich and poor is widening. China has provided a large scale of aid, and has the largest number of recipients among emerging donors. Emerging donors such as China should actively shoulder the necessary international responsibilities and help underdeveloped countries to eradicate poverty, improve their development capabilities, and promote the achievement of the UN SDGs. In recent years,

Chinese scholars have gradually increased their research on foreign aid, and universities and research institutions have gradually established specialized research institutions for international development, forming a Chinese school and a Chinese perspective of foreign aid.

First of all, regarding the model and motivations of China's foreign aid, Chinese scholars believe that China's foreign aid is very different from that of DAC countries. China's foreign aid is under the SSC framework, and has the nature and characteristics of SSC. It emphasizes equality, mutual benefits and non-interference in other countries' internal affairs. In China's foreign aid, development finance such as preferential loans account for a considerable proportion of aid funds, including project aid and technical cooperation. The strong participation of emerging donors and their strength embodied in this process has challenged the existing international development assistance system dominated by developed countries, which no longer fully reflects the current status of diversified international aid entities and providers. Therefore, the reform of the international development cooperation management system is imminent.

Secondly, regarding the evaluation of the effectiveness of foreign aid, the Western 'aid effectiveness' standard is not comprehensive enough. Foreign aid evaluation must also emphasize the 'development effectiveness' perspective, which pays greater attention to the role of foreign aid in promoting recipients' economic development and poverty reduction. China's foreign aid model is 'growth-driven', focusing on whether it can bring about 'development effectiveness' via direct economic growth, technological progress and poverty reduction in partner countries. An important part of international aid system reform is to re-constitute the aid effectiveness evaluation system, and to examine the effectiveness of foreign aid from both the perspective of aid effectiveness and development effectiveness, and from the perspective of aid process and aid impact.

Finally, in the future, the development of China's foreign aid system should, on the one hand, adhere to its own principles, focus on the role of aid in economic growth and poverty alleviation, and promote the transformation of the evaluation of international aid from 'aid effectiveness' to 'development effectiveness'. On the other hand, in terms of specific aid management and practices, Chinese foreign aid can learn from Western foreign aid management and promote the reform of China's foreign aid management system.

Notes

1. Pan (2013, pp.95-97) analyzed theoretical research on China's foreign aid by searching CNKI (up to May, 2013). We disagree with her in the following two aspects: first, she regarded the articles on the reform and adjustment stage of China's foreign aid (e.g.,

Liu, 1998) as theoretical research; second, she thought that the theoretical research on China's foreign aid accounts for 20–40% of the total research. We believe that Pan (2013) confused the relationship between "China's foreign aid theory" (zhongguo duiwai yuanzhu lilun) and "theoretical discussion on China's foreign aid" (guanyu zhongguo duiwai yuanzhu de lilun tantao), so she analyzed a high proportion of theoretical research on China's foreign aid. We believe that Chinese scholars do not have much research on the theory of China's foreign aid.

2. The other two are "helping recipient countries build independent industries" and "teaching technology to other countries to achieve independence, not replace it".

Acknowledgments

The authors would like to thank Xiaoshuang Lang, Jie Hao and Lei Shan for their helpful assistance in data processing. They are master degree candidates in School of Economics and Management, Hebei University of Technology, Tianjin, China.

Disclosure statement

No potential conflict of interest was reported by the authors.

Funding

This work is supported by the Major Project of the National Social Science Foundation of China (No. 16ZDA037) and the Youth Project of the National Social Science Foundation of China (No. 17CGJ013).

References

Bai, Y. Z. (2013). zhongguo duiwai yuanzhu de zhanlue fenxi [Strategic analysis of China's foreign aid]. *shijie jingji yu zhengzhi [World Economics and Politics]*, (5), 70–87.

Bai, Y. Z. (2015). yidai yilu" changyi yu zhongguo duiwai yuanzhu zhuanxing [The "Belt and Road Initiative" and China's foreign aid transformation]. shijie jingji yu zhengzhi]. *World Economics and Politics*, (11), 53–71.

Cai, Y. (2018). dengxiaoping duiwai yuanzhu sixiang tanxi [An analysis of Deng Xiaoping's thoughts on foreign aid]. *dengxiaoping yanjiu [Deng Xiaoping Research]*, (4), 88–89.

Chen, J. M. (2009). zhongguo waiyuan zhanlue xin geju de jiagou [The structure of the new pattern of China's foreign aid strategy]. *changjiang luntan [Yangtze Tribune]*, (5), 78–82.

Chen, W. B., & Wu, J. (2019). dui fei jichu sheshi yuanzhu yu zhijie touzi de chuandao jizhi yanjiu - jiyu feizhou 39 guo mianban shuju [A study on the impact of China's infrastructure assistance on direct investment in Africa: Based on panel data from 39 countries in Africa]. *Shanghai duiwai jingmao daxue xuebao [Journal of Shanghai University of International Business and Economics*, 26(4), 38–46.

Cheng, C. (2016). zhongguo tese de guanfang kaifa jinrong: zhongfei fazhan hezuo de xinmoshi [Official Development Finance with Chinese Characteristics: A new model of China-Africa development cooperation]. *fudan guoji guanxi pinglun [Fudan International Studies Review]*, 19(2), 1–34.

CPC Central Research Office. (1998). *zhouenlai nianpu (1949-1976) [Zhou Enlai's Chronicle (1949-1976)]*. Beijing: zhongyang wenxian chubanshe [Central Party Literature Press].

Ding, S. B. (2016). oumei dui zhongguo duiwai yuanzhu de renzhi jiqi qishi [European and American recognition on China's Foreign aid and its revelation]. *dongbeiya luntan [Northeast Asia Forum, 25*(3), 40–48.

Dong, T. M. (2018). zhongguo dui feizhou yuanzhu de zhengce zhuanxiang yu xiaoying pingjia [Policy shift and effect evaluation of China's aid to Africa]. *Beijing keji daxue xuebao (shehui kexue ban) [Journal of University of Science and Technology Beijing (Social Sciences Edition, 34*(1), 101–111.

Dong, Y., & Fan, C. J. (2016). yuanzhu hui cujin touzi ma - jiyu zhongguo dui feizhou yuanzhu ji zhijie touzi de shizheng yanjiu [Can aid promote investment - An empirical study based on China's aid and direct investment in Africa]. *guoji maoyi wenti [Journal of International Trade]*, (3), 59–69.

Han, Y. H. (2018). lun woguo duiwai yuanzhu jibenfa de goujian—jiyu guoneifa he guojifa tongchou sikao de shijiao [The construction of China's basic law of foreign aid: From the perspectives of national law and international law]. *wuda guojifa pinglun [Wuhan University International Law Review], 2*(4), 99–115.

He, F., & Tang, Y.H. (2007). lengzhan hou guanfang fazhan yuanzhu de jueding yinsu [Determinants of official development assistance after the cold war]. *guoji zhengzhi kexue [Quarterly Journal of International Politics], 12*(4), 61–84.

He, W. P. (2007). xin zhimin zhuyi lun" shi dui zhongfei guanxi de dihui ["New Colonialism" is a smashing of China-Africa relations]. *xuexi yuekan [Study Monthly]*, (3), 46–47.

Hu, A. G., Zhang, J. Y., & Gao, Y. N. (2017). duiwai yuanzhu yu guojia ruanshili: zhongguo de xianzhuang yu duice [Foreign assistance and national soft power: China's status quo and countermeasures]. *Wuhan daxue xuebao (renwen kexue ban) [Wuhan University Journal (Arts & Humanity)], 70*(3), 5–13.

Hu, B., Ding, X. P., & Deng, F. H. (2015). zhongguo duifei yuanzhu nengfou tuidong duifei touzi [Can China's aid to Africa promote investment in Africa?]. *dangdai jingji yanjiu [Contemporary Economic Research]*, (1), 67–73.

Hu, M. (2011). zhongguo yuanfei wushinian yu guoji yuanzhu lilun chuangxin [China's aid to Africa for 50 years and international aid theory innovation]. *shehui zhuyi yanjiu [Socialism Studies]*, (1), 141–146.

Hu, M., & Liu, H. W. (2009). yishi xingtai xianxing haishi minsheng gaishan youxian?-lengzhan hou xifang "minzhu yuanfei" yu zhongguo "minsheng yuanfei" zhengce zhi bijiao [Ideology first or livelihood improvement first? A comparison between the "democracy aid to Africa" of the west and "Livelihood Aid to Africa" of China]. *shijie jingji yu zhengzhi [World Economics and Politics]*, (10), 17–24.

Huang, C. (2016). 2030 nian kechixu fazhan yicheng kuangjia xia guanfang fazhan yuanzhu de biange [The reform of ODA under the Framework of the 2030 Agenda for Sustainable Development]. *guoji zhanwang [Global Review], 8*(2), 78–93.

Huang, C. (2018). quanqiu fazhan zhili zhuanxing yu zhongguo de zhanlue xuanze [Transformation of global development governance and Chinese strategic choices]. *Guoji zhanwang [Global Review, 10*(3), 153–154.

Huang, M. B. (2007). zhongguo duiwai yuanzhu jizhi: xianzhuang he qushi [China's foreign aid mechanism: Status quo and trends]. *guoji jingji hezuo [Journal of International Economic Cooperation]*, (6), 4–11.

Huang, M. B., & Liu, A. L. (2013). zhongguo duiwai yuanzhu zhong de jingji dongji he jingji liyi [Economic motivation and economic benefits in China's foreign aid]. *guoji jingji hezuo [International Economic Cooperation]*, (4), 62–67.

Huang, M. B., & Tang, L. P. (2013a). nannan hezuo yu zhongguo duiwai yuanzhu [South-south cooperation and China's foreign aid]. *guoji jingji hezuo [Journal of International Economic Cooperation*, (5), 66–71.

Huang, M. B., & Tang, L. P. (2013b). nannan hezuo yu nanbei hezuo - dongji, moshi yu xiaoguo bijiao [On South-South Cooperation and North-South Cooperation in international aid architecture]. *guoji zhanwang [Global Review]*, (3), 8–26.

Huang, M. B., & Xiong, Q. L. (2014). cong renjun shouru shijiao kan zhongguo duiwai yuanzhu yiwu de lvxing [Viewing the implementation of China's Foreign Aid obligation from the perspective of per capita income]. *guoji jingji hezuo [Journal of International Economic Cooperation]*, (6), 55–61.

Huang, M. B., Xu, X. L., & Mao, X. J. (2018). *South-South Corporation and Chinese foreign aid*. Singapore: Palgrave Macmillan.

Huang, M. B., & Zhu, D. D. (2013). zhishi hezuo zai guoji fazhan yuanzhu zhong de zuoyong [The role of knowledge cooperation in international development assistance]. *guoji luntan [International Forum*, 15(2), 21–27.

Huang, N. (2015). lun duiwai zhijie touzi yu fazhan yuanzhu de hudong fazhan [The interactive development of foreign direct investment and development aid]. *yinduyang jingjiti yanjiu [Indian Ocean Economic and Political Review]*, (1), 96–108.

Jin, L. (2015). "yidai yilu": zhongguo de maxieer jihua? [The "One Belt and One Road" Initiative: China's Marshall plan?]. *guoji wenti yanjiu [International Studies]*, (1), 88–99.

Li, X. R. (2012). zhongguo duiwai rendao zhuyi yuanzhu de tedian he wenti [Characteristics and problems of China's foreign humanitarian aid]. *xiandai guoji guanxi [Contemporary International Relations]*, (2), 48–54.

Li, X. Y. (2017). zhongguo yuanfei de lishi jingyan yu weiguan shijian [Historical experience and micro practice of China's aid to Africa. *wenhua zongheng [Beijing Cultural Review]*, (2), 88–96.

Li, X. Y., & Xiao, J. (2017). xin nannan hezuo de xingqi: zhongguo zuowei lujing [Emergence of new South-South Cooperation: The path of China]. *huazhong nongye daxue xuebao (shehui kexue ban) [Journal of Huazhong Agricultural University (Social Sciences Edition)]*, (5), 1–11.

Li, X. Y., Zhang, Y., & Liu, W. Y. (2017). zhishi he jishu de qianru yu zaoyu: zhongguo yuanzhu shijian xushi [The embedding and encounter of knowledge and technology: The narrative of Chinese aid practice]. *xinan minzu daxue xuebao (renwen sheke ban) [Journal of Southwest Minzu University(Humanities and Social Science)]*, 38(11), 1–8.

Liu, A. L., & Tang, B. (2018). US and China aid to Africa: Impact on the donor-recipient trade relations. *China Economic Review, 48*, 46–65. doi:10.1016/j.chieco.2017.10.008

Liu, F. P. (2015). yidai yilu" shijiao xia de zhongguo yuanwai zhanlue tiaozheng [China's foreign aid strategy adjustment from the perspective of "Belt and Road"]. *guoji jingji hezuo [Journal of International Economic Cooperation]*, (9), 87–92.

Liu, F. P. (2018). xijinping duiwai yuanzhu zhongyao lunshu de yanjiu [A study of Xi Jinping's important discussion on foreign aid]. *makesi zhuyi yanjiu [Studies on Marxism]*, (9), 38–45.

Liu, X. Y. (1998). Zhongguo duiwai yuanzhu gaige yu tiaozheng ershinian [Twenty years of reform and adjustment of China's foreign aid]. *guoji jingji hezuo [Journal of International Economic Cooperation]*, (10), 87–92.

Liu, Y. (2014). guanxi quxiang, liwu jiaohuan yu duiwai yuanzhu de leixingxue [Relationship orientation, gift exchange and typology of foreign aid]. *shijie jingji yu zhengzhi [World Economics and Politics]*, (12), 71–94.

Luo, C. G. (2019). anhuisheng shouge yuanwai gongye chengtao xiangmu lishi huigu. [Historical review of the first foreign aid industrial project in Anhui Province]. *chizhou xueyuan xuebao [Journal of Chizhou University]*, 33(2), 73–76.

Luo, J. B. (2013). xifang duifei yuanzhu xiaoguo ji zhongfei jingji hezuo [Western aid to Africa and China-Africa economic cooperation]. *guoji zhengzhi kexue [Quarterly Journal of International Politics]*, (1), 1–32.

Luo, J. B. (2014). fuzeren de fazhanzhong daguo: zhongguo de shenfen dingwei yu daguo zeren [Responsible big developing country: China's identity and big country responsibility]. *xiya feizhou [West Asia and Africa]*, (5), 28–45.

Luo, J. B., & Liu, H. W. (2007). lun zhongguo dui feizhou yuanzhu de jieduanxing yanbian ji yiyi [On the phased evolution of China's aid to Africa and its significance]. *xiya feizhou [West Asia and Africa]*, (11), 25–30.

Luo, Y. F., & Li, W. (2019). guoheshu chengli yizhounian: zhongguo yuanzhu waijiao "zhuanxing shengji" [The first anniversary of the establishment of China International Development and Cooperation Agency: China's Aid Diplomacy "Transformation and Upgrading"]. *shijie zhishi [World Affairs]*, (8), 60–62.

Mao, X. J. (2010). guoji yuanzhu geju yanbian qushi yu zhongguo duiwai yuanzhu de dingwei [The evolution trend of international aid pattern and the position of China's Foreign Aid]. *guoji jingji hezuo [Journal of International Economic Cooperation]*, (9), 58–60.

Ministry of Foreign Affairs of the People's Republic of China, Literature Research Office of the CPC Central Committee. (1994). Maozedong waijiao wenxuan [Mao Zedong's Diplomatic Selection]. Beijing: Zhongyang wenxian chubanshe [Central Literature Publishing House].

Pan, Y. L. (2013). zhongguo tese duiwai yuanzhu lilun jiangou chutan [On the construction of foreign aid theory with Chinese characteristics]. *dangdai yatai [Journal of Contemporary Asia-Pacific Studies]*, (5), 92–110.

Pang, X. (2013). xinxing yuanzhuguo de "xing" yu "xin" –chuizhi fanshi yu shuiping fanshi de shizheng bijiao yanjiu [An empirical study of the "rising" and "new" of emerging donor countries: Vertical paradigm and horizontal paradigm]. *shijie jingji yu zhengzhi [World Economics and Politics]*, (5), 31–54.

Peng, D. D., & Lin, Y. (2019). yidai yilu" changyi xia zhongguo duiwai yuanzhu de maoyi cujin xiaoying [The trade promotion effect of China's foreign aid under "the Belt and Road" Initiative]. *Suzhoushi zhiye daxue xuebao [Journal of Suzhou Vocational University]*, 30(2), 2–13.

Qin, C. J. (2016). maozedong de duiwai yuanzhu sixiang yu shijian [Mao Zedong's thought of foreign aid and its practice]. *dang de wenxian [Literature of Chinese Communist Party]*, (6), 50–58.

Qu, C. Y. (2019). xin zhongguo 70 nian duiwai yuanzhu linian de fazhan, jicheng yu chuangxin [Development, inheritance and innovation of the concept of foreign aid in the past 70 years of new China]. *tongyi zhanxian xue yanjiu [Journal of United Front Science]*, 3(1), 95–105.

Ren, X. (2016). xueke, lilun yu zhongguo xuepai jianshe [Discipline, theory and con-struction of Chinese school]. *guoji guanxi yanjiu [Journal of International Relations]*, (2), 55–59.

Ren, X., & Guo, X. Q. (2016). jiexi zhongguo duiwai yuanzhu: yige chubu de lilun fenxi [Interpreting China's foreign aid: A preliminary theoretical analysis]. *fudan xuebao (shehui kexue ban). Fudan Journal (Social Sciences Edition)*, 58(4), 155–165.

Shi, Z. F. (1994). *Zhonghua renmin gongheguo duiwai guanxi shi yijiu sijiu—yijiu bajiu [History of the People's Republic of China on Foreign Relations 1949 - 1989]*. Beijing: Beijing daxue chubanshe [Peking University Press].

Su, R. X., & Li, Y. (2019). xijinping duiwai yuanzhu lilun yu zhongguo duiwai yuanzhu shijian [Xi Jinping's theories on foreign aid and Chinese practices of foreign aid. *wenhua ruanshili [Cultural Soft Power]*, 4(2), 5–12.

Sun, C. R., Xu, J. Q., & Liang, J. (2019). zhongguo duifei yuanzhu yu shouyuanguo chukou jiegou zhuanhuan [China's aid to Africa and the transformation of export structure of recipient countries]. *caimao jingji [Finance & Trade Economics]*, 40(7), 82–94.

Sun, T. Q. (2008). guoji fazhan yuanzhu zhong "yuanzhu yilai" de chengyin [The causes of "aid dependence" in international development assistance]. *guoji jingji hezuo. [Journal of International Economic Cooperation]*, (6), 55–58.

The State Council Information Office of the People's Republic of China. (2011). zhongguo duiwai yuanzhu baipishu [China's Foreign Aid White Paper]. Retrieved from http://www.scio.gov.cn/zfbps/ndhf/2011/Document/896983/896983.htm.

The State Council Information Office of the People's Republic of China. (2014). zhongguo duiwai yuanzhu baipishu [China's Foreign Aid White Paper]. Retrieved from http://www.scio.gov.cn/zfbps/ndhf/2014/Document/1375013/1375013.htm.

Wang, W. Q., & Zhao, Z. X. (2014). zhongfei hezuo dui sahala yinan feizhou guojia jingji zengzhang de yingxiang - maoyi, zhijie touzi yu yuanzhu zuoyong de shiz-heng fenxi [Impact of China-Africa cooperation on economic growth of Sub-Saharan African Countries: An empirical analysis on roles of Trade, FDI and Aid]. *guoji maoyi wenti [Journal of International Trade]*, (12), 68–79.

Wang, X. K. (2015). zongti anquanguan shijiao xia de zhongguo yuanwai zhanlue fenixi [An analysis of China's foreign aid strategy from the perspective of the over-all national security concept]. *taipingyang xuebao [Pacific Journal]*, 23(2), 55–62.

Wang, X. L., & Liu, Q. Q. (2012). zhongfei hezuo: tigao fazhan youxiaoxing de xinfang-shi [China-Africa Cooperation: A new way to improve the effectiveness of devel-opment]. *guoji wenti yanjiu [International Studies]*, (5), 69–81.

Wang, Z. F. (2019). guoji geju zhuanhuan xia zhongguo jingwai hezuoqu yu duiwai yuanzhu de zhanlue xietong [The strategic synergy between foreign economic zones and foreign aid of China]. *taipingyang xuebao [Pacific Journal]*, 27(3), 75–85.

Wu, L. F., & Dai, J. P. (2019). zhongguo duifei yuanzhu, zhijie touzi yu feizhou zai quanqiu jiazhilian de diwei tisheng [China's aid and outward direct investment in Africa and African global value chain upgrading]. *Shanghai duiwai jingmao daxue xuebao [Journal of Shanghai University of International Business and Economics]*, 26(7), 27–37.

Wu, S. Y., & Zhang, X. X. (2005). lun zhongguo xina waiyuan, duiwai yuanzhu de wai-jiao guanxi—yi dengxiaoping de yuanzhu linian jiqi yuanzhu shixiao wei shijiao [Study on China's diplomatic relations concerning receiving and providing foreign aid: Take Deng Xiaoping's aid idea and aid effectiveness as the visual angle]. *Dongbei shida xuebao [Journal of Northeast Normal University]*, (4), 27–34.

Xi, J. P. (2019). jianchi zongti guojia anquanguan, zou zhongguo tese guojia anquan daolu" [Adhere to the Overall National Security Concept and Take the National Security Road with Chinese Characteristics]. Renmin ribao [People's Daily].

Xie, Q., Tian, F., & Haung, M. B. (2012). chengqing dui zhongguo duiwai yuanzhu de jizhong wujie [Clarifying misunderstandings about China's foreign aid]. *guoji jingji pinglun. [International Economic Review]*, (4), 147–157.

Xiong, Q. L., & Huang, M. B. (2014). duiwai yuanzhu neng cujin guoji maoyi ma [Can foreign aid promote international trade?]. *guoji jingmao tansuo [International Economics and Trade Research*, *30*(10), 4–12.

Xiong, Q. L., & Wu, G. H. (2016). guoji yuanzhu bodong dui jianpin yingxiang de jizhi fenxi-jiyu DSGE de moni yanjiu [Mechanism Analysis of international aid fluctuations impact on poverty reduction: A simulation study based on DSGE]. *Jiangxi keji shifan daxue xuebao [Journal of Jiangxi Science & Technology Normal University]*, (3), 68–76.

Xu, X. L., Li, X. Y., & Ma, J. L. (2015). zhongguo shifou chongsu guoji fazhan jiagou [Does China reshape the international development architecture?]. *guoji yuanzhu [International Development Cooperation]*, (5), 52–59.

Xue, H. (2011). duiwai yuanzhu: jidai lingdaoren de zhanlue juece [Foreign aid: Strategic decisions of several generations of leaders]. *shijie zhishi [World Affairs]*, (13), 14–16.

Xue, L. (2013). zhouenlai duiwai yuanzhu sixiang yanjiu [Zhou Enlai's research on foreign aid]. *dangshi yanjiu yu jiaoxue [CPC History Research and Teaching]*, (3), 68–77.

Yang, S. J. (2015). zhongguo duiwai yuanzhu yu renminbi guojihua - jiyu riben de jingyan fenxi [China's foreign aid and RMB internationalization: An empirical analysis based on Japan. *Fujian jinrong [Fujian Finance]*, (8), 54–59.

Yang, Z. H. (2012). waibu chongji xia zhongguo yuanwai gongzuo de jinronghua zhanlue tuijin [The promotion of financialization of China's foreign aid with external shocks]. *kexue fazhan [Scientific Development]*, (9), 13–20.

Yao, S. (2019). biange yu fazhan: 2018 nian guoji fazhan hezuo huigu yu zhanwang [Review of the current trend of international development cooperation and performance of China's economic assistance to other developing countries]. *guoji jingji hezuo [Journal of International Economic Cooperation]*, (1), 29–37.

Ye, Y. (2013). zhongguo yu duobian fazhan tixi——cong shouyuanzhe dao gongxianzhe [China and the multilateral development system: From a taker to a contributor]. *guoji zhanwang [Global Review]*, (3), 45–62.

Yu, B. W., & Kan, D. X. (2017). zhongguo duiwai yuanzhu dui jingji zengzhang yingxiang de shizheng yanjiu [An empirical study of the impact of China's foreign aid on economic growth]. *Jiangxi shehui kexue [Jiangxi Social Sciences]*, *37*(10), 97–103.

Zhang, C. Y. (2009). duiwai jingji hezuo liushinian: huigu yu qianzhan [Sixty years of foreign economic cooperation: Retrospect and prospect]. *guoji jingji hezuo [Journal of International Economic Cooperation]*, (2), 4–8.

Zhang, H. B. (2006). zhongfei hezuo yu nannan hezuo [China-Africa Cooperation and South-South Cooperation]. *maozedong dengxiaoping lilun yanjiu [Studies on Mao Zedong and Deng Xiaoping Theories]*, (12), 65–68.

Zhang, H. B. (2007). guanyu zhongguo dui feizhou yuanzhu nengyuan daoxiang de guandian fenxi [An analysis of the energy orientation of China's aid to Africa]. *shijie jingji yanjiu [World Economy Study]*, (10), 76–80.

Zhang, H. B. (2012a). zhongguo dui feizhou yuanzhu de "zhanlue pingheng" wenti ["The strategic balance" problems of China's aid to Africa]. *xiya feizhou [West Asia and Africa]*, (2), 39–52.

Zhang, H. B. (2012b). fazhan yindaoxing yuanzhu: zhongguo dui feizhou yuanzhu moshi tantao [Development-oriented Assistance: China's Assistance Model for Africa]. *shijie jingji yanjiu [World Economy Study]*, (12), 78–83.

Zhang, H. L., Yuan, J., & Kong, Y. (2010). zhongguo dui feizhou ODA yu FDI guanliandu yanjiu [A Study on the Linkage between China's ODA and FDI to Africa]. *shijie jingji yanjiu [World Economy Study*, (11), 69–74.

Zhang, X. M. (2008). zhongguo heping waijiao zhanlue shiye zhong de duiwai yuanzhu [China's Foreign Aid in the Perspective of Its Foreign Policy for Peace]. *guoji luntan [International Forum]*, 10(3), 38–43.

Zhang, Y. (2007). dui zhongguo yuanzhu tanzan tielu de lishi kaocha [A Historical Investigation of China's Assistance to the Tazara Railway]. *Liaocheng daxue xuebao (shehui kexue ban) [Journal of Liaocheng University (Social Sciences Edition]*, (1), 28–31.

Zhang, Y. (2018). xinshiji yilai zhongguo dui lamei yuanzhu he touzi jianpin xiaoying yanjiu [Poverty reduction effect of China's foreign aid and investment in Latin America and the Caribbean since the new century]. taipingyang xuebao. *[Pacific Journal]*, 26(12), 61–73.

Zhongguo junshi guwentuan yuanyue kangfa shilu [Record of the Chinese Military Advisory Corps's Assistance to Vietnam in Resistance to France]. (2012). *Dangshiren de huiyi [Memories of the Parties]. beijing: zhonggong dangshi chubanshe* [Beijing: Communist Party History Press].

Zhou, B. G., & Liu, Q. (2009). jiaoxun yi manzu shouyuanguo xueqiu wei xian: maxieer jihua de jingyan yu [Meeting the Needs of Recipient Countries: The Experience and Lessons of the Marshall Plan]. *guoji jingji hezuo [Journal of International Economic Cooperation]*, (11), 44–47.

"Zhouenlai zongli fangwen feizhou: yu baguo youguan jingji yuanzhu he maoyi fangmian de huitan zhaiyao" [Premier Zhou Enlai's visit to Africa: Summary of talks on economic assistance and trade with eight countries"]. waijiaobu danganguan [Ministry of Foreign Affairs Archives], "203-00494-01," 8–9.

Zhou, H. (2010). zhongguo yuanwai liushinian de huigu yu zhanwang [Retrospect and prospect of China's foreign aid for 60 years]. *waojiao pinglun (waijiao xueyuan xuebao) [Foreign Affairs Review, 27*(5), 3–11.

Zhou, H. (2013). *zhongguo yuanwai liushinian [60 years for China's foreign aid].* Beijing: Shehui kexue wenxian chubanshe [Beijing: Social Science Academic Press (China)].

Zhou, J., Hong, J., & Wang, K. (2018). Zhengzhi fengxian, jingji yuanzhu yu zhongguo dui feizhou zhijie touzi - jiyu kuaguo mianban shuju de shizheng yanjiu [Political risk, economic aid and China's OFDI to Africa——An empirical analysis based on cross-country panel data]. *xiandai jingji tantao [Modern Economic Research]*, (6), 51–59.

Zhu, D. D., & Huang, M. B. (2015). zhongguo duiwai yuanzhu de maoyi chengben xuejian xiaoying yanjiu [Impacts of Chinese foreign aid on recipients' trade costs]. *shijie jingji yanjiu [World Economy Studies]*, (7), 100–107.

Zhu, D. D., & Huang, M. B. (2017). zhongguo de minsheng yuanzhu: jingyan, pingjia he gaijin jianyi [China's livelihood assistance: Experience, evaluation and improvement suggestions]. *guoji jingji hezuo. [Journal of International Economic Cooperation]*, (3), 88–95.

Zhu, D. D., & Huang, M. B. (2018). zhongguo duiwai yuanzhu nenggou cujin shouyuanguo de jingji zengzhang ma?-jianlun "cumao yuanzhu" fangshi de youxiaoxing [Does China's foreign aid enhance recipients' economic growth: Effectiveness of "aid for trade"]. *zhongguo jingji wenti [China Economic Studies]*, (2), 24–33.

International law debates in China: traditional issues and emerging fields

He Zhipeng

ABSTRACT

There have been many academic debates in the Chinese academic circle of international law during the past few decades. Both positive and negative attitudes were presented on the functioning of international law within the world order, while different understandings were provided on China's dealings with international law and various views were expressed on frontier issues of international law. The debates were also reflected in and through China's diplomatic position and discourse, and have influenced China's stance and concepts in relation to international affairs.

Many studies by Chinese international law researchers are closely related to China's national interests and national policies.[1] Although the process of China coming into contact with modern international law started only in the 1840s, and there have been many twists and turns in this process, spurring many Chinese researchers to think broadly on the interactions between China and international law. This academic atmosphere has led to a very interesting phenomenon: in Chinese universities, many doctoral and master's theses on international law have naturally paid attention to China's position, or China's counter-measures, in relation to international law. This phenomenon reflects that Chinese scholars generally combine the study of international law and its application to – or in – China. This paper will elaborate on several areas of international law that Chinese scholars are concerned about: the status of international law and its influence on China, China's attitude toward international law, current frontier topics of international law within global society, and China's proposals in international law and international relations. This paper strives to allow its readers to ascertain a general understanding of the main concerns and viewpoints within the Chinese international law academia.

1. Debates on the status and role of international law

Scholars from various states have long discussed the role of international law (Lauterpacht, 1933); even in China, this discussion has continued for at least 100 years.[2] However, in recent years, the function of international law in general – and for some specific states – is still of concern to Chinese scholars. Traditional studies in China paid attention to the importance of international law to China based on the political and positive law approach, while newer studies have discussed more the involvement of China in the systems and processes of international law, in an interdisciplinary perspective between international law and international relations (Liu, 2003). In general, Chinese scholars believe that international law is very important for the international order and for China's development (Che, 2009), and that from historical experience, international law is especially important for great powers (Cai, 2009). Scholars have pointed out that there is a close benign interaction between the international rule of law and the rule of law in China, and that China should seek to coordinate these two sets of rules. In the international society, China should become accustomed to expressing the language of law, in order to enhance China's ability to safeguard its interests via international law and improve China's image in international society. The discussion of these issues can be understood from the following three aspects:

First, what is the significance of international law for states and the international society? In other words, how should the function of international law be determined? Based on the previous general understanding of the operational conditions of international law (Vos, 2013), Chinese international law scholars have recognized that international law has a function at the discourse level (Che, 2016). This view, recognizing the function of international law as 'soft restraint on hard power' and 'hard support for soft power' for states (He, 2018a), became popular among Chinese international lawyers. Meanwhile, it is widely accepted that under certain time and space conditions, international law could be unfair and unreasonable, and bring losses to the state(s) concerned. On this issue, very influential researchers reviewed the history of international law, and found that sometimes international law expressed the will and interest of great powers and sacrificed the interest of small states. When the United States (US) launched the Afghanistan war in 2003, Professor Liang (2004) believed that international law was at risk and was likely to become a tool for power politics. Qin Yaqing (1998) believes that the international system should reflect more international cooperation, as the existing international system is insufficient in this regard (Qin, 2010). From the perspective of future development, international relations should move from 'power politics' to 'rights politics' (Qin, 2014), meaning that fairer treatment of the more vulnerable states and the rules of law should be given greater importance. There is an opportunity for international rules to shift focus in the new era (Che, 2019). He (2014b) believes that since the mid-20th century, international law has brought about progress with the values of 'peace and development', but that there have also been one-sided considerations which have facilitated passive coexistence among states, and hinder the possibilities of cooperation and pursuing joint interests. A one-sided emphasis on peace and development may also have led to a neglect of the diversity between civilizations, a neglect of the differences in social environments, and intolerance and even conflict between civilizations.

Second, how should the history of China's access to and understanding of international law be evaluated? The vast majority of Chinese scholars believe that although there were some traces of international law in China's pre-Qin era, China did not create international law in the modern sense due to its unique international relations pattern (Cheng, 1989). China has long adopted the tributary system to interact with neighboring countries, and there was a marked difference with the international law system that stemmed from the Western political and cultural environment (Yang, 1999). The first formal and systematic contact between China and modern international law can be traced mainly to the late Qing Dynasty, after 1842 (Liu, 2001). Western powers have arguably used international law to crush China, deprive China of its interests, and bring a lot of suffering to China. At the same time, such contacts have brought great excitement to Chinese society, spurred the spread of international law in China (Tian, 2000), and also stimulated China's overall reflection on diplomacy and domestic governance (Tian, 2006). Exposure to international law has gradually brought China into modernization.

At the macroscopic level, assessing the relationship between international law and China, the two major factors determining the importance that Chinese scholars attach to international law are the government's demand for international law, and the government's attitude toward international law. This recognition of its importance can be roughly divided into three stages: the first stage was in 1978, when Deng Xiaoping proposed to vigorously strengthen the study of international law. The second stage was at the end of the 20th Century, when China was actively preparing to join the World Trade Organization (WTO). Supported by the central leadership, this development triggered a new wave of research on international law. The third stage began from the second decade of the 21st Century, when the government and international lawyers in China begun to pay greater attention to China's position within international society, and gave a higher evaluation of the status of international law within China's great power diplomatic strategy.

In 1997, Professor Lu Song, an expert on international law, gave a lecture on the knowledge of international law to the central leadership (Lu, 1997; Lu et al. 1997). On 29 April 2000, Chinese leader Li Peng presided over the 'Lecture on Law' of the Standing Committee of the National People's Congress and invited Dr. Jiang Guoqing, Deputy Director of the Institute of International Law of the Foreign Affairs College, to give a speech on international law and international treaties. The lecture comprised four parts: (1) The concept of international law and contemporary development; (2) International Treaty is the most important source of contemporary international law; (3) Constitutional Procedures for the Treaty; and (4) Compliance and Application of the Treaty (Jiang, 2000). After the lectures, the national leaders highly elevated the status and role of international law. During the event, Chinese President Jiang Zemin said that 'in recent years, the Chinese government had repeatedly stressed that leading cadres at all levels must work hard to learn legal knowledge, which of course includes knowledge of international law.' He acknowledged the importance of international law to China and added, 'We must pay attention to learning the knowledge of international law and strive to improve the ability to use international law. In dealing with inter-state relations and international affairs, in the exchanges and cooperation in the political, economic, scientific, and cultural fields, in the struggle against hegemonism and power politics, we must be good at using international law as a weapon to safeguard our national interests and national dignity, to promote international justice, and firmly grasp the initiative of international cooperation and struggle.' The current system of international law is conducive to maintaining world peace and promoting economic development. However, it should also be noted that due to the conditions of the formation of the international society, and certain political factors, that the international legal system also contains unacceptable elements that need to be further improved and perfected. New and reasonable rules need to be established for new situations and problems that have arisen in the development process of the international society. We must abide by and uphold the norms of international law, and work with representatives of other states to continue to work for the improvement and development of international law, and to advance international law in a direction that is conducive to the establishment of a new international political and economic order that is peaceful, stable, just and reasonable (Lu, Liu, & Qin, 1997).

Third, has China (mainly since 1949) effectively participated in the operation and development of international law, and made important contributions to international law? From the perspective of future development, should China further actively participate in the formulation and operation of international law? On this issue, most scholars positively evaluate China's role and contribution to international law and tend to give a positive answer to this question. For example, Dr. Xu Hong, former director of the Department of Treaty and Law of the Ministry of Foreign Affairs, believes that 'after long-term efforts, as China's international status has improved, China's influence in the field of global governance has also increased, from the participants of international rules', adding that China has experienced a gradual shift toward becoming a contributor and leader in international law. 'China's participation and contribution in the field of international law is not only a process of integration into the international system, but also a process of continuous innovation and development, leaving more and more Chinese imprints. In this process, we use international law weapons to maintain and expand national interests while contributing to all mankind' (Xu, 2019).

Most international lawyers in China believe that despite difficulties and obstacles, China has made positive and beneficial contributions to international law. Concerning whether there are negative attitudes and perceptions regarding China's engagement with international law, or in the process of participating in the operation of international law, many scholars have proposed that due to China's great power mentality (Jiang, 2009), or the state of mind outside the international system (Xu, 2006), that it is likely China holds a degree of distrust or feeling of alienation toward international law (He, 2014a). At present, in the field of practice, as the problems and challenges encountered by the international society become more prominent (Huangying, 2011; Shao & Huangying, 2011), it is necessary for China to pay greater attention to international law, respect international law (Wang, 2015) and contribute to the further civilization and progress of the world (Yu & Heng, 2010). From a theoretical point of view, it is necessary to further expand the research horizon of international law (Zhou, 2004), deepen the degree of theoretical exploration of international law (Liu, 2011), enhance the theoretical research level of international law (Xiao, 2015), and reflect the research style of international law with (Yu and Heng 2010) Chinese characteristics (He, 2010). From the perspective of future development, it is necessary for China to participate more actively in agenda setting and process setting in relation to international law, and make efforts for the rationalization and fairness of international law.

2. The interpretation of the international law advocated by China's world order

As a major power in East Asia, China has been proposing its own series of ideas in international relations since 1949. These ideas mainly originate from the perspective of Chinese diplomacy and the international order that China expects. These ideas initially belong to the field of international relations, but all of them have connotations relative to international law and embody requirements and directions in international law. Therefore, Chinese scholars have also understood and analyzed these aspects from the perspective of international law.

2.1. The five principles of peaceful coexistence

The Five Principles of Peaceful Coexistence (hereinafter referred to as 'the Five Principles') were proposed by Chinese leaders at the end of 1953 (Qiu, 1984), and were made public in 1954 through the bilateral agreements between China and India, and China and Myanmar. The Five Principles became of great significance after their emergence (He & Sun, 2014). It was not only incorporated into Chinese Constitutional law, reflected in many bilateral agreements, but also formed an important legal basis for Chinese diplomacy (Cheng, 1984). These five principles are regarded as important propositions in the field of Chinese international law and one of the outstanding contributions of New China's first-generation leaders in the field of diplomacy and international law. On 27 October 1989, Deng Xiaoping remarked in a conversation with the Thai Prime Minister, 'For a long time to come, the Five Principles should serve as an international political norm guiding the relationship between countries'. China's Government Work Report in 1988 stated, 'the Five Principles of Peaceful Coexistence have stood the test of time and have shown that it has a strong vitality'. 'If all countries in the world follow the Five Principles of Peaceful Coexistence in their mutual relations, the international situation can be stabilized, the purposes of the UN Charter can be realized, and world peace can be safeguarded' (Zhao, 1990). In a speech celebrating the 40th anniversary of the founding of the People's Republic of China, Jiang Zemin pointed out that 'we advocate the establishment of a new international political and economic order based on the Five Principles of Peaceful Coexistence' (Zhu, 1995).

After the Five Principles of Peaceful Coexistence were initiated in mid-1950s, scholars conducted extensive research (Zhou, 1955),and a considerable number of research achievements appeared after the 1980s. A series of papers in this field highly appraised the Five Principles of Peaceful Coexistence (Wang and Wang 2000). Views are varied in their theoretical levels. Some pay greater attention to the interpretation of the contents of the Five Principles, while some focus on historical analysis; mainly concerning why this set of principles was put forward in the historical context of the 1950s (Liu 1984). Liu (1994) believed that the Five Principles were born while the national liberation movement flourished after the Second World War and many colonial countries successively became independent. In the 1990s and in the 21st Century, Chinese scholars made greater effort to link the Five Principles and the fundamental norms of international law based on the UN Charter (Zhao 2014).

Both approaches attracted attention, while more studies dwelt on what the significance of the Five Principles should be in the context of the new era (Liu, 1990). According to these studies, the Five Principles are an innovation of traditional international law, and generalization and development of the principles of the UN Charter. To deal with contemporary international relations, states must strictly abide by the Five Principles (Xi, 2014). Authors have carried out in-depth and thorough research on the historical significance of the Five Principles since they endeavored to establish and maintain the basic operation system for international society (Pan, 1984). Scholars also discussed how to adhere to these principles in the late 20th Century and the beginning of the 21st Century – to avoid hegemony, disprove intervention based on excuses tied to human rights, and promote international cooperation – reflecting China's understandings and advocated positions with respect to international rule of law. Analysis has also been conducted on the status and function of the Five Principles in the evolving global order as the cornerstone of international relations, in the perspective that it tries to maintain peace and security (Su, 2014). The Five Principles demonstrate the possibility of peaceful coexistence within the international system, and have played a key role in driving the development of China's international law theory (Liu 1984). It seems that there is widespread consensus on adhering to the Five Principles, with very few exceptions advocating replacing or revising the principles during academic conferences.

2.2. Harmonious world and China's peaceful development

At the beginning of the 21st Century, from the perspective of its own development, China has proposed the concepts of 'peaceful rise', 'peaceful development',[3] the 'Chinese dream' and 'national rejuvenation'. Many books and articles were published as analysis and explanation from international law perspectives. According to the literature, on the one hand, in the 'global village' where states are interdependent and economic globalization reigns, international law provides the external environment for China's peace and security. It also aims to construct a fair and equitable international competition order, and provide legal guarantees for international cooperation. On the other hand, China's internal and external development strategies for peaceful development will inevitably make an important contribution to the key themes and pace of changes within international law.

In relation to the future of international relations, the Chinese government has put forward the idea of building 'a harmonious world'. Many writing shave discussed the manifestation of a harmonious world in the field of international law (Zeng, 2006). Other writing shave analyzed the ways in which international law should help to realize a harmonious world, and studied China's international law position. It is proposed that the harmonious world that China wants to build is actually a state of harmonious coexistence between states based on the UN Charter, which also adheres to the basic principles and rules of existing international law (Gong, 2006).

In the context of the difficulties of traditional international law, the concept of harmony with the characteristics of Oriental culture may be integrated into the values of international law, and drive the transcendence of current norms and functions of international law. 'Harmonious development', emphasizing the pursuit of common prosperity and development in the context of respect for diversity and coexistence of civilization, is a sublimation of Western mainstream values. In order to achieve harmonious development, the international society needs to carry out gradual improvement in concepts and systems. China also needs to establish a harmonious view which respects diversity, helps to resolve conflicts, advocates humanism and supports the rule of law. The world in harmony should be a stage after the rule of law. A harmonious world is an important external social foundation for China's peaceful development, and international law is an indispensable legal foundation and guarantee for building a harmonious world (He, 2011).

2.3. Human community with a shared future

In the second decade of the 21st Century, China put forward the concept of a 'human community with a shared future'. It belongs to the concepts and approaches of diplomacy and international relations that President Xi Jinping has sought to advance. These ideas succeeded the thoughts and terms of previous leaders and expressed more clearly the role of China within the international order. Xi has not only inspired a lively discussion among Chinese scholars on issues related to international law, but has also provided many materials in the dimension of general practice as the basis of customary international law. It is still relatively early to judge whether Xi has altered the ideas of domestic and international governance in China, since the Xi era is still underway, and his ideas are still being developed and discussed. However, his notions on world order, and China's role within it, are no doubt of great significance for international law scholars in China.

With traditional Chinese cultural characteristics and close to Western philosophy, Xi's proposals intend to reflect China's role in the international society in the 21st Century. At the 19th National Congress of the Chinese Communist Party, an in-depth analysis of the content of the human destiny community was provided. These analyses guided people to understand the term and actively construct such a community. Many scholars have explored this term in the dimension of international law, considering what international law can contribute in building a human community with a shared future.

Che (2018)argues that the 'human community with a shared future' ideasummarizesthelatesttrendsincontemporaryinternationalsocietyor international relations, and also implies the Chinese government's judgment on global governance and the direction of international rule of law. The members of the 'human community with a shared future' remain states, and the 'national standard' of international law will not undergo fundamental changes; however, an awareness of security and commonality will lead international law to the direction of international community. The idea of a 'human community with a shared future' can only be realized by translating it into an international legal system. During this process, efforts should be undertaken to popularize the discourse, transform domestic legislation as appropriate, harness the law-making functions of international organizations and also facilitate the role of non-governmental organizations.

Xu (2018) holds the view that the concept of building a 'human community with a shared future' falls in line with the trend for the development of contemporary international law, and contains rich elements of China's traditional legal culture. It demonstrates the strong sense of responsibility of the Chinese Communist Party in promoting international rule of law in the new era. It provides new values and objectives for the development of international law, particularly in placing humankind at the center of international law while pursuing the collective interests and the shared future of the international society. This idea has significant implications in relation to international law. It builds upon and advances the Five Principles and other basic principles of international law and the contemporary international legal regime. Therefore, it clearly constitutes an integral and systematic concept in international law, resonates with the theme of the times, and is geared toward practice. China has been consistently preserving and contributing to the international rule of law. Building a community with a shared future for mankind will require keen sensitivity toward international law, strengthened capacity in international law, transformation of this idea to global consensus, and eventually, international rules and legal regimes. Xiao (2019) proposes that the international legal community is a common rule system existing within the interdependent international society. It can simultaneously expand the intersection of national interests, form a community of common interests, implement the common responsibility of international actors, and advance humanity toward becoming a community with a shared future.

3. Controversy over the concept and system of international law

Chinese international law scholars have paid close attention to new concepts and theories emerging in the field. For these new concepts and new theories, there are two different views: one view seems to actively accept and support those concepts and theories, but the other view seems to be rather critical: scholars taking this view would not accept views emerging from other regions without considering the cultural background and national views of China.

3.1. Fragmentation of international law

Fragmentation of international law is a characteristic of international law that scholars such as Martti Koskenniemi introduced in the 20th Century. It was discussed at the UN International Law Commission (2006), and a report was issued to summarize and put forward opinions. After the UN began to pay attention to this issue, Chinese scholars held discussions and published several papers explaining the state of fragmentation of international law and possible solutions.

Fragmentation is a situation that exists in the reality of international law mainly due to the anarchic status of international society. Establishing a normative order of international law to solve the problem is the main idea to have been proposed and widely accepted (Gu, 2007). At this point, there are other theoretical issues involved. First, is international law a horizontal system; or a system that can be vertically oriented to a certain extent? Second, can international law be understood in a sense as a constitutional system? Third, are there any requirements in the international society for state behaviors as obligations *erga omnis*, and such norms as *jus cogens*? By combining these issues for comprehensive observation, we can make arrive at a more realistic analysis and accurate understanding of the proposition of the fragmentation of international law.

While fragmentation of international law is *prima facie* a theoretical issue, the proposition also contains a series of practical issues such as the possible compulsory nature of international law, the normative hierarchy of international law, and the duties of states. Therefore, it is a problem that extends to a wide range of practical nodes. In the perspective of China, the main concerns include: will international law be integrated and hence China must comply with it as a whole? If not, are there any obligations that states must seriously assume in international law? What international legal regulations does China have to comply with? The exploration of these issues means to examine the possible costs and benefits of China's participation in international transactions.

3.1.1. Constitutionalization of international law

The interaction between the disciplines of constitutional law and international law has promoted the constitutional interpretation of international law (Petersmann, 2004). If international law can form a constitutional structure as a whole – or in a certain part – then a normative system can be formed to a certain level (Chen, 2011). That is to say, the constitution is the highest, and other rules are under the constitution and guided by it. Optimistic scholars believe that in the process of evolution, international law has gradually overcome the situation of anarchy and decentralization, and has entered an organizational status (Chen, 2009). There are two possibilities for the constitutionalization and systemization of international law: the most ideal one may be the system of global integration. For this reason, a majority of scholars agree that the UN Charter can be used as a constitutional rule. The second possibility is to form a small-scale constitutional system within a specific field. There are suggestions that within the international economic arena, the WTO can be used as a constitutional system, and its legitimacy may be reshaped considering the requirements of members, individuals and international trade institutions (Cai, 2006). The result of this orientation is not to make international law more systemic, but to exacerbate its fragmentation. Of course, constitutional thinking can legitimize the pattern and process of global governance, but pessimistic scholars argue that this kind of thinking could be characterized as Eurocentric or a form of new imperialism (Cheng, 2017). If we compare these constitutional views of international law with the actual situation of the international society, it is not difficult to see that it has only academic significance, and that there is no possibility to establish such a constitutional system in international relations for a long time.

3.1.2. Obligations erga omnes and jus cogens

The solution to the fragmentation of international law could be normative hierarchy based on states' obligation *erga omnes* (to all) and *jus cogens* (peremptory law), closely related to it. From the perspective of historical development, the concept of obligation *erga omnes* and the idea of *jus cogens* appeared in the middle of the 20th Century. In view that international law was based on states' consent; idealistic scholars suggested that there should be rules that have effect without the consent of the state. The premise of these rules is that the state has obligation *erga omnis*. The concept of *jus cogens* was later incorporated into the Vienna Convention on the Law of Treaties (Qiu, 2005). In response to this concept, Chinese scholars conducted a systematic study to analyze its background, its possibilities, its criteria of recognition, its special features, its scope, the relationship between the *jus cogens* and the basic principles of international law, and its areas of existence and methods of implementation in international law (Zhang, 1995). The case of Germany vs. Italy, concerning state immunity, as examined by the International Court of Justice, fully demonstrates that an overly optimistic estimate of *jus cogens* and a discussion on obligations *erga omnis* may lead to misjudgment of the status quo of international law (Liang and Wenwu 2013). The attention on *jus cogens* has been paid for more than 20 years, and has achieved a series of results. But its consequences for international politics need further inquiry. In reality, the obligation and *jus cogens* do not really change the actual situation of the fragmentation of international law. Therefore, it is still a very important task to critically observe the obligation *erga omnis* and *jus cogens* and consider incorporating Chinese wisdom into it (He, 2018b).

3.2. Responsibility to protect

When the concept of 'responsibility to protect' emerged at the UN level in 2001, the views of many Chinese scholars were consistent with the opinions of the International Commission on Intervention and State Sovereignty (ICISS). They stressed that each state should be responsible for human rights within its territory, and measures should be taken against the human rights abuses in many states. Therefore, they welcomed the concept of 'responsibility to protect' and looked forward to it becoming an important component of international law. Yet consideration was given to its influence upon the internal affairs of affected states. What happens if the concept of 'responsibility to protect' enters the international legal system? If 'responsibility to protect' is not well defined and its standards and codes of conduct are not well thought out, could this principle become another manifestation of hegemony? Under such thinking, especially after the Western military intervention in Libya, Chinese scholars are increasingly skeptical and reflective on the concept. Chinese scholars believe that the theoretical basis of 'responsibility to protect' could be accepted by the international society, and also believe that the international society should take appropriate measures when some situations of human rights abuses exist. However, when deciding upon armed interventions to deal with so-called humanitarian crises or human rights issues within a country, actors must be very cautious. It is necessary to respect the principle of non-interference widely accepted in international law and take responsible protective measures. States must not arbitrarily use the principle to subvert a government (Huang, 2012). At the same time, scholars have also given a clear explanation of China's position: that the first thing to consider on the issue of human rights is sovereignty; in other words, the rights and obligations of a state. Then, human rights are first and foremost a state's internal affairs, and the intervention from the international society must abide by the principle of the rule of law (Qu 2012).

3.3. Studies on international rule of law

The international rule of law is a theoretical and practical topic that has appeared in Chinese academia on international law in the early 21stCentury (Che, 2000). Although decades ago, there were theoretical discussions and practical opinions on this issue in the West (Calvert, 1958), this view was not recognized and was even opposed by Chinese scholars (Ying, 1960). At the dawn of the new century, Chinese scholars paid greater attention to the issue of international rule of law. From the perspective of its theoretical origins, the main themes of China's study on international rule of law stemmed from the issues of 'globalization of law' and 'rule of law'. In the process of the UN beginning to promote the rule of law at the domestic and international levels in 2006, Chinese scholars paid closer attention and actively followed up with their own investigations.

Chinese scholars discussed the context of the international rule of law in the current era, and regarded economic globalization and political multipolarization as the background of international rule of law. Many of these writings tried to clearly define its connotation, analyze its social context and social goals, explore its key actors, examine its nature as a goal or just means, Inquire as to its necessity and future possibilities, and analyze its role in the international system.

Of particular concern is the fact that authors have different views on whether international rule of law should emphasize both substantive standards and procedural standards, or just procedural and formal legitimacy. Huang (2009) proposed that the trend of globalization and historical processes have jointly promoted the rule of law from the way of state governance (domestic rule of law) to the way of global governance (international rule of law). Starting from the concept of formal rule of law, the (international) rule of law mainly includes three basic elements: (1) the predictability of law, (2) the universal application of law, and (3) the effective settlement of legal disputes. The main difference between international rule of law and domestic rule of law lies in the fact that international rule of law is a contractual, pluralistic, and decentralized rule of law. Domestic rule of law is a compulsory rule of law and a unity rule of law. The international legal zone can be divided into global and regional levels –the WTO rule of law and the EU rule of law are examples of international rule of law operating at the two levels. He (2014b) held that although rule of law could be understood as formal in certain states, at the macro level, rule of law should not be limited to the formal area, but should also pursue the substantive requirements of justice. *Ius estars boni et aequi* (Law is the art of justice and virtue); substantive justice should always be in lawyers' minds. Since the international legal system is still in a primary, immature legal state, emphasize must be placed both on sound law and good governance. Because international law is not systematic, it will be impossible to put in place a formal rule of law system at present – in other words, because the procedures of international law are insufficient, the establishment of formal rule of law would be rootless. The dual system of law at the international and national levels makes laws at the international level less effective; hence, a formal rule of international law might be a failure. This is a reflection of the distinction between 'thin rule of law' and 'thick rule of law' from legal theory on international law.

In addition, there are discussions on the relationship between the international rule of law and the domestic rule of law in China. Concerning China's participation in the maintenance and construction of the international rule of law, as a key member of the international society, the views of Chinese academics and the government tend to be consistent (Wang, 2014). Both believe that the goals and requirements of the international rule of law are in parallel with China's 'harmonious world' concept, and complement the 'human community with a shared future' idea advocated by the new generation of leaders. In practice, China has made many important contributions to the international rule of law. At the same time, scholars suggest that in the field of international rule of law, China should propose more of its own plans and outwardly express its opinions at the global level with regard to in international law.

At present, although there remains a debate among Chinese scholars about whether China should advocate an international rule of law, the concept of 'international rule of law' is widely accepted as an important term, and has become a mainstream of field of within international law studies. Detailed studies have been carried out into various branches of international law, the standard of international rule of law, which has widened the horizon of international rule of law. (Xiao 2014)

Chinese scholars have studied the international rule of law for nearly 20 years. During this time, researchers have not regarded 'international rule of law' merely as a slogan, but have studied the concept in depth. Studies have touched upon the content of the international rule of law, expected governance goals, the main means and models to achieve international rule of law, and the ways in which it is implemented. Studies have also established a series of standards by which to measure international legal and political affairs (He, 2016). In terms of specific areas and evaluation criteria, studies have covered economic cooperation and development, intellectual property rights, cyberspace governance, human rights affairs, international humanitarian law, anti-corruption and international criminal law. A considerable number of books and articles have been published and more in-depth studies have also been carried out. It can be said that the study of the international rule of law is a topic to which the Chinese academia has paid great attention. Moreover, the academic depth of studies on the topic in China is considerable. In this respect, the quantity and quality of Chinese scholars' research is not inferior to that of scholars abroad.

3.4. Controversy on the status of international law in China's rule of law

Since 1978, the Chinese government has begun to attach significance to the role of the law. One substantial step forward came in 2014, when the Chinese Communist Party and the Chinese government put forward the idea of comprehensively governing states according to law, and building a socialist state rule of law. International lawyers have expressed concern that China does not stipulate the status of international law (including international treaties, international customs and the general principles of law) in its constitutional documents. At the same time, when the Chinese legislature (National People's Congress) announced the socialist legal system was essentially completed in 2011, it did not contain international law.[4] This has produced a strong response within the circle of international law studies. Most scholars believe that it is not appropriate to exclude international law from China's legal system. The Chinese legislature and a few domestic law experts argued that the international legal rules by which China should abide have already been incorporated into various areas of domestic law. Therefore, there is no specific need for international law to be singled out. International law scholars do not agree with this argument. Many international law scholars have clearly proposed that international law is an indispensable part of law in China's system of "governing states according to law". However, this kind of proposition has been transformed into 'international law is a part of the law in China's rule of law process' (inclusive view) by some influential scholars. Gu (2015) believes that in the process of comprehensively advancing the rule of law, the question of whether 'international law is a part of the law in the rule of law process in China' should be affirmatively answered. Appropriate institutional arrangements should be made, which will not only help improve China's influence in the international rule of law, but assign it a proper role within the construction of the socialist rule of law system.

Such assertions (could be named as "the inclusive view") have been criticized and opposed by a number of mainstream international law scholars in China. Since international law is a broad and decentralized system, many rules are irrelevant to a specific state. It must be very carefully examined whether a certain rule is binding for China. Because the scope of international law mentioned in "the inclusive view" is not clear, it is easy to over-contain the scope of the rules that states should follow in China's system of "governing states according to law", and this situation will increase states' obligations inappropriately (Che, 2015). The following expression may be more acceptable: 'to comprehensively govern states according to law and promote a new era of building a human community with a shared future, it is necessary to attach importance to international law. It is necessary to regard the construction of international rule of law as an integral part of the rule of law in socialist socialism with Chinese characteristics, realize the coordination between domestic law and international law, and promote the interaction between the international rule of law and the domestic rule of law' (Xiao, 2018).

The frontier issues of international law on a global scale are followed closely in China. This reflects the desire of Chinese international lawyers to integrate with the global international legal community. In addition, different voices demonstrate the desire of international law scholars to think independently and attempt to put forward the theory of international law from a Chinese perspective.

4. General observations

Based on the discussions above, the following observations can be made:

First, the theoretical consciousness among Chinese international lawyers is increasing. When the overall situation of theoretical research on Chinese international law is comprehensively examined from a historical perspective, it is not difficult to find such a developing process: (1) In the initial study of international law, the initial focus was on introducing and explaining the meaning of legal rules. That is to be in the primary stage of positive law. China gradually gained accurate cognition in relation to the concepts, rules and principles of international law. (2) Later, Chinese scholars attempted to provide interpretations on global frontier theory, and on China's practical advocations and perspectives related to international law. On the one hand, these efforts followed new international law theories and ideas from abroad. On the other hand, they reflected concepts put forward by China at the diplomatic and international political level. This follow-up approach is helpful for gradually developing Chinese theories of international law; however, it *per se* is not the Chinese theory of international law. (3) After a clear understanding of the dynamics of the theory of the state and practice of international law, China's international lawyers began to gradually carry out their own theoretical investigations, and put forward theoretical concepts and theoretical interpretations. It can be said that the creation of such theories is essential for further development and improvement of China's international law theorizing and practice in the future.

Second, as the interaction between China and international law at the practice level increases, frontier concerns are emerging. Enriching the knowledge of international law and enhancing the effectiveness of international law are aspects recognized by contemporary Chinese scholars. Such recognition is based on the understanding that international law is important to the international structure and China's development. The role of international law in shaping the world order and enhancing states' influence has been widely accepted by Chinese international law scholars. China should be widely recognized and supported with regard to its in-depth understanding and proficiency in the application of international law. However, there are differing views within the academic community on how international law should be observed and evaluated; especially the significance of international law for China. Most scholars believe that China should actively learn to understand and apply international law. International law is the dominant set of rules of the world today. China has an obligation to fully understand, profoundly grasp and actively apply it. It should be applied not only in international relations, but also in relevant domestic legislation and domestic administrative affairs, demonstrated by obeying and conscientiously following the requirements of international law for states. However, another point of view is that international law must be carefully measured and treated differently. Most international laws reflect the common will of all countries and are in China's interests. Many such laws can be enthusiastically recognized and actively followed by China; but there are also many rules unsuitable for China. They do not conform to China's national conditions and do not fully consider China's specific circumstances. Directly applying such rules would be harmful to states like China. Therefore, it is necessary to check whether international law is suitable for China firstly, and then to consider China's attitude, China's position, and China's response measures based on this evaluation.

Third, while many Chinese scholars just following the overall international law position of the world, there are studies highlighting independent thinking. It is widely believed within Chinese academia, that a negative evaluation of China's international law practice and attitude toward international law is not only inconsistent with China's reality, but also operationally unfeasible. Therefore, among the published academic papers and works, the evaluation of China's international law practice is generally positive. Based on this consensus, there are two ways to view the proposals and measures of the government: one is to expressly agree with the government's measures and positions, that is, to provide an academic endorsement, annotation or interpretation. The other is to make suggestions related to specific aspects, to influence future actions. This approach is more meaningful to the government and more valuable to academic development in this field.

Fourth, although there is a correlation between theory and practice; the depth of dialogue is still insufficient. International law studies should be based on practice, focused on practice, and serve practice. For decades, the theoretical and practical circles of Chinese international law have become more and more intimate, and many important efforts have been made in knowledge sharing and personnel collaboration. However, because the relationship between the Chinese government and academia is essentially controlled by the government, academic criticism is often inadequate. Due to problems associated with this reality, such as the government providing insufficient information, the practical concerns and theoretical needs of the government are not always clear. Therefore, on many occasions, China's international law community has failed to respond to questions the government has raised. In the theoretical circle, due to the limitations of their own vision, scholars have not been able to conduct forward-looking discussions on macroscopic and frontier issues. This leads to the theoretical study of Chinese international law, which generally follows the Chinese government's claims and appears to be lagging behind other states. Sincere and profound theoretical disputes and academic criticism among international law scholars in China must be encouraged. Only in this way can the level of Chinese international law theory be further enhanced, improving its ability to dialogue with international law scholars of various countries, and its ability to engage with the Chinese international law practice community.

Notes

1. Due to China's traditional cultural characteristics and the current cultural development pattern, especially since the financial support for scientific research mainly comes from the government, China's academic research is largely government-led. This kind of government-led color has both positive and negative consequences. The positive significance is mainly that people can clearly find the mainstream and trend of Chinese academic research; its negative significance is that the theoretical controversies in Chinese academic circles is relatively small, and the academic research is basically very close in discourse mode and ideological orientation. China's international law research also presents a government-led color. Therefore, Chinese scholars' research on the

theory and practical issues of international law is often closely related to the government's position.

2. After the mid-19th century (China was in the late Qing Dynasty), China conducted extensive and systematic contacts with international law. Government officials and intellectuals in China began to discuss whether these international legal rules were just for the world, even for weak powers, or mainly represented the will of great powers. Liu, Baogang (1993) '*Lun wanqing shidafu gongfa guannian de yanbian*', (On the Evolution of the Concept of Public Law of Scholar-officials in the Late Qing Dynasty) *Zhejiang xuekan* (Zhejiang Academic Journal) No. 3.

3. The original term "peaceful rising" was replaced by "peaceful development" because there were voices worrying the strong word "rising" may result in neighboring states' fear and cause the rumor of China threat.

4. On March 10, 2011, the Standing Committee of the National People's Congress announced that the socialist legal system with Chinese characteristics includes seven parts: The Constitution, civil and commercial law, administrative law, economic law, social law, criminal law, litigation and non-litigation procedure. Three levels of legal norms are laws, administrative regulations, local regulations and autonomous regulations.

Disclosure statement

No potential conflict of interest was reported by the author.

Funding

China National Office for Philosophy and Social Sciences.

References

Cai, C. (2006). Guojifa yujing zhong de xianzheng wenti yanjlu (Constitutional issues in the context of international law). *Fashang yanjiu (Studies in Law and Business)*, *23*(2), 85–91.

Cai, G. (2009). Daguo jueqi yu guojifa de fazhan (The rise of great powers and the development of international law). *Xiangtan daxue xuebao (Journal of Xiangtan University)*, *33*(4), 61–65.

Calvert, H. (1958). The rule of law in international Affairs. *Australian Outlook*, *17*, 11–32. doi:10.1080/10357715808444024

Che, P. (2000). Guoji fazhi chutan. (A probe into the international rule of law). *Qinghua fazhi lunheng(Tsinghua Forum of Rule of Law)*, *1*, 122–134.

Che, P. (2009). Guoji zhixu de guojifa zhicheng (International law support for international order). *Qinghua faxue (Tsinghua Law Review)*, *3*(1), 6–20.

Che, P. (2015). Guojifa kefou zuowei zhiguo zhi fa (Can international law be used as a law of governance?). *Guangmingribao (Guangming Daily)*, 2015-05-16.

Che, P. (2016). Guojifa de huayujiazhi (Discourse value of international law). *Jilin Daxue shehui kexue xuebao (Jilin University Journal Social Sciences Edition)*, *56*(6), 35–44.

Che, P. (2018). Renlei mingyun gongtongti linian de guojifa sikao (International jurisprudence on the concept of a human community with a shared future). *Jilin daxue shehui kexue xuebao (Jilin University Journal Social Sciences Edition)*, *58*(6), 15–24.

Che, P. (2019). Shi ni quanqiuhua haishi zai chongsu quanqiu guize (Is it "de-globalization" or is it reshaping global rules?). *Zhengfa luncong (Journal of Political Science and Law)*, *26*(1), 15–23.

Chen, H. (2011). Guojifa xianzheng wenti yanjiu (A study on constitutional issues in international law). *Taipingyang xuebao (Pacific Journal)*, *19*(3), 26–32.

Chen, X. (2009). Guojifa zizu zhidu: Zai bucheng tixi he shehui xianzhengz hijian (Self-contained regimes in international law: Between fragmentation and social constitutionalism). *Guowai shehui kexue (Social Sciences Abroad)*, *31*(4), 125–132.

Cheng, P. (1989). Xifang guojifa shouci chuanru Zhongguo de tantao (A discussion on the first introduction of Western international law into China). *Beijing daxue xuebao (Journal of Peking University)*, *25*(5), 105–113.

Cheng, X. (1984). Lun heping gongchu wuxiang yuanze (On the five principles of peaceful coexistence). *Zhongguo faxue (Chinese Legal Science)*, *1*(3), 145–152.

Cheng, W. (2017). Lixiang zhuyi haishi xindiguo zhuyi: Dangdai guojifa xianzheng hua lilun pipan (Idealism or new imperialism? Critique of constitutionalization theory in contemporary international law). *OuzhouYanjiu (Chinese Journal of European Studies)*, *35*(5), 1–15.

Gong, Y. (2006). Lun guojifa yu hexie shijie (International law and harmonious world). *XiandaiFaxue (Modern Law Science)*, *28*(6), 158–164.

Gu, Z. (2007). Xiandai guojifa de duoyang hua, suipian hua yu youxu hua (Diversification, fragmentation and ordering of modern international law). *Faxue yanjiu (Chinese Journal of Law)*, *42*(1), 135–147.

Gu, Z. (2015). Zhiguozhi fa zhong de guojifa: Zhongguo zhuzhang he zhidu shijian', (International law in the law of ruling the state: Chinese propositions and system practice). *Zhongguo shehui kexue (Social Sciences in China)*, *36*(10), 147–158.

He, Z. (2010). Zhongguo guojifa yanjiu fansi (Reflections on China's international law studies). *Zhengfa luntan (Tribune of Political Science and Law)*, *28*(4), 16–28.

He, Z. (2011). Cong heping yu fazhan dao hexie fazhan: Guojifa jiazhi guan de yanjin yu lichang tiaoshi', (From peace and development" to "harmonious development": The evolution of the values of international law and the adjustment of China's position). *Jilin Daxueshehuikexuexuebao (Jilin University Journal Social Sciences Edition)*, *51*(4), 115–123.

He, Z. (2014a). Lun zhongguo guojifa xintai de goucheng yinsu (On the constitutive factors of the mentality of China's international law). *Faxuepinglun (Law Review)*, *35*(1), 82–91.

He, Z. (2014b). Liangfa he shanzhi heyi tongyang zhongyao: Guoji fazhi biaozhun de shensi (Why are "sound law" and "good governance" equally important? thoughts on the criteria of international rule of Law). *Zhejiang daxue xuebao (Journal of Zhejiang University)*, *44*(3), 131–149.

He, Z. (2016). Guojifazhilun (International rule of law). Beijing: Peking University Press.

He, Z. (2018a). Yingshili de ruanyueshu he ruashili de yingzhicheng: Guojifa gongneng chongsi, (Soft constraint of hard power and hard support of soft power: The function of international law revisited). *Wuhan daxue xuebao (Wuhan University Journal)*, *71*(4), 104–115.

He, Z. (2018b). Piaofu de guoji qiangxingfa (The floating international jus cogens). *Dangdai faxue (Contemporary Law Review)*, *32*(6), 106–122.

He, Z., & Sun, L. (2014). Daguo zhilu de guojifa dianji (International law foundation of the way to great power). *Fashang yanjiu (Studies in Law and Business)*, *38*(4), 22–32.

Huang, Y. (2012). Cong shiyong wuli fa kan baohu de zeren lilun (The theory of responsibility of protection from Jus in Bello). *Faxue Yanjiu (Chinese Journal of Law)*, *47*(3), 195–208.

International Law Commission. (2006). Conclusions of the work of the study group on the fragmentation of international law: At difficulties arising from the diversification and expansion of international law.

Jiang, G. (2000). Guojifa yu guoji tiaoyue de jige wenti (Several issues of international law and international treaties). *Waijiao xueyuan xuebao (Journal of Foreign Affairs College)*, *17*(3), 8–17.

Jiang, S. (2009). Daguo qingjie yu guojifa yanjiu de xueshu xintai. (The great state complex and the academic mentality of international law research). *Shandong Shehui Kexue (Shandong Social Sciences)*, *23*(2), 33–36.

Lauterpacht, H. (1933). *The function of law in the international community*. Oxford: Oxford University Press.

Li, B., & Xie, W. (2013). *Yetan guoji qiangxingfa yu guojia huomianquan de chongtu* (The conflict between International Jus Cogens and State Immunity. *Falü Kexue (Science of Law)*, *31*(6), 178–183.

Liang, X. (2004). Guojifa de weiji. (Crisis of International Law). *Faxue Pinglun (Law Review)*, *25*(1), 3–9.

Liu, B. (2001). Guojifa de shuru yu Zhongguo waijiao jindai hua de qibu (The entry of international law and the beginning of modernization of Chinese diplomacy). *Tianjin Shehui Kexue (Tianjin Social Sciences)*, *21*(1), 85–88.

Liu, G. (1990). Heping gongchu wuxiang yuanze shi baozhang heping yu fazhan de guojifa jiben yuanze (The five principles of peaceful coexistence are the basic principles of international law guaranteeing peace and development). *Faxue yanjiu (Chinese Journal of Law)*, *25*(6), 88–94.

Liu, H. (1984). Heping gongchu wuxiang yuanze shi woguo dui xiandai guojifa de zhongyao gongxian (The five principles of peaceful coexistence are China's important contributions to modern international law). *Xibei zhengfa xueyuan xuebao (Journal of Northwest College of Political Sciences and Law)*, *2*(2), 42–46.

Liu, W. (1984). Lun heping gongchu wuxiang yuanze zai xiandai guojifa shang de huashidai yiyi (The epoch-making significance of the five principles of peaceful coexistence in modern international law). *Waijiao xueyuan xuebao. (Journal of Foreign Affairs College)*, *1*(2), 3–8.

Liu, W. (1994). Lun heping gongchu wuxiang yuanze zai dangdai guojifa shang de huashidai yiyi (The epoch-making significance of the five principles of peaceful coexistence in contemporary international law). *Guoji wenti yanjiu (International Studies)*, *21*(3), 13–19.

Liu, Z. (2003). Shilun dangdai guoji guanxi lilun zhong de guojifa juese dingwei', (The status of international law in international relations). *Xiandai guoji guanxi (Contemporary International Relations)*, *23*(2), 30–35.

Liu, Z. (2011). Guoji guanxi yuguojifa de xueke jiehe (The combination of international relations and international law: China's current situation, existing problems and solutions). *Guoji zhengzhi yanjiu (International Politics Quarterly)*, *32*(3), 68–80.

Lu, S. (1997). Zai guoji guanxi zhong fahui guojifa de zuoyong (Play the role of international law in international relations). *Xuexi yu Shijian (Study and Practice)*, *14*(3), 11–12.

Lu, S., Liu, W., & Qin, X. (1997). Guojifa zai guoji guanxi zhong de zuoyong (The role of international law in international relations). *Waijiao xueyuan xuebao (Journal of Foreign Affairs College)*, *14*(1), 6–15.

Pan, B. (1984). Heping gongchu wuxiang yuanze he dangdai guojifa (Five principles of peaceful coexistence and contemporary international law). *Faxue yanjiu (Chinese Journal of Law)*, *19*(2), 84–90.

Petersmann, E.-U. (2004). *Constitutional functions and constitutional problems of international economic law*. Beijing: Higher Education Press.

Qin, Y. (1998). Guoji zhidu yu guoji hezuo: Fansi xin ziyou zhidu zhuyi (International system and international cooperation: Rethinking new liberal institutionalism). *Waijiao xueyuan xuebao (Journal of Foreign Affairs College)*, *18*(1), 41–48.

Qin, Y. (2010). Shijie geju, guoji zhidu yu quanqiu zhixu. *(World Pattern, International System and Global Order) Xiandai Guoji Guanxi (Contemporary International Relations)*, *30*(s1), 10–17.

Qin, Y. (2014). Cong quanli zhengzhi zouxiang quanli zhengzhi (From power politics to rights politics) *Shijie jingji yu zhengzhi (World Economics and Politics)*, *18*(5), 1.

Qiu, D. (2005). Lun guoji qiangxingfa de yanjin (On the evolution of international jus cogens). *Xiamen daxue falü pinglun (Xiamen University Law Review)*, *8*, 124–149.

Qiu, R. (1984). Heping gongchu wuxiang yuanze de qiangda shengmingli (The vitality of the five principles of peaceful coexistence). *Zhengzhi yu falü (Political Science and Law)*, *3*(4), 54–58.

Qu, X. (2012). Lianheguo xianzhang, baohu de zeren yu Xuliya wenti. (UN Charter, Responsibility to Protect and Syria). *Guoji Wenti Yanjiu (International Studies)*, *39*(2), 6–18.

Shao, S. & Huang, Y. (2011). Xin duobianzhuyi shidai Zhongguo guojifa de shiming (The mission of China's international law in the era of new multilateralism). *Jinan xuebao (Journal of Jinan University)*, *33*(1), 29–34.

Su, C. (2014). Heping gongchu wuxiang yuanze yu Zhongguo guojifa lilun tixi de sisuo (The five principles of peaceful coexistence and the theoretical system of China's international law). *Shijie jingji yu zhengzhi (World Economics and Politics)*, *18*(6), 4–22.

Tian, T. (2000). 19 shiji xiabanqi Zhongguo zhishijie de guojifa guannian (The concept of international law of Chinese intellectuals in the second half of the 19th century). *Jindaishi Yanjiu (Modern Chinese History Studies)*, *22*(2), 108–135.

Tian, Y. (2006). Qingdai houqi guojifa zai Zhongguo de chuanbo xinlun (The spread of international law in China in the late Qing dynasty). *Shidai faxue (Present day Law Science)*, *8*(4), 98–107.

Vos, J. A. (2013). *The function of public international law*. Berlin: Springer.

Wang, C. & Wang, M. (2000). Heping gongchu wuxiang yuanze tuidong zhe dangjin guojifa de fazhan (The five principles of peaceful coexistence drive the development of today's international law). *Xinan zhengfa daxue xuebao. (Journal of Southwest University of Political Sciences and Law)*, *2*(2), 32–38.

Wang, Y. (2014). Zhongguo shi guoji fazhi de jianding weihuzhe he jianshezhe (China is a staunch defender and builder of the international rule of law). *Guangming ribao (Guangming Daily)*, 2014-10-24.

Wang, Y. (2015). Zhongguo ren weishenme tebie xuyao zunzhong guojifa. (Why do Chinese people particularly need to respect international law?) *Shijie zhishi (World Affairs)*, *68*(21), 58–61.

Huang, W. (2009). Quanqiuhua shidai de guojifazhi: Yi xingshi fazhi gainian wei jizhun de kaocha (The international rule of law in the era of globalization: A study based on the concept of formal rule of law). *Jilin Daxue shehui kexue xuebao (Jilin University Journal Social Sciences Edition)*, *49*(4), 21–27.

Xi, J. (2014). Carry forward the five principles of peaceful coexistence to build a better world through win-win cooperation (Address at meeting marking the 60th anniversary of the initiation of the five principles of peaceful coexistence). *People's Daily Online*. Retrieved from http://en.people.cn/n/2014/0710/c90883-8753393.html

Xiao, Y. (2015). Lun fazhi zhongguo jianshe beijing xia de Zhongguo guojifa yanjiu, (On China's study of international law under the background of the construction of rule of law China). *Fazhi yu shehui fazhan (Law and Social Development)*, *21*(5), 5–12.

Xiao, Y. (2018). Quanmian yifa zhiguo de xinjieduan: Tongchou tuijin guonei fazhi yu guojifa fazhij ianshe, (A new stage of ruling states by law: Promoting the rule of law and the construction of the international rule of law). *Wuda guojifa pinglun (Wuhan University International Law Review)*, *2*(1), 1–19.

Xiao, Y. (2019). Lun maixiang renlei mingyun gongtongti de guoji falü gongtongti jianshe (On the construction of an international legal community with a shared future for humankind). *Wuhan Daxue Xuebao (Wuhan University Journal)*, *72*(1), 135–142.

Xu, C. (2006). Tixi wai guojia de xintai yu Zhongguo guojifa lilun de pinkun (The mentality of "outside states" and the poverty of Chinese international law theory). *Zhengfa luntan (Tribune of Political Science and Law)*, *24*(5), 33–36.

Xu, H. (2018). Renlei mingyun gongtongti de guojifa (A human community with a shared futureand international law). *Guojifa yanjiu (Chinese Review of International Law)*, *5*(5), 3–14.

Xu, H. (2019). Qinli guojifa fengyun, dianzan Zhongguo gongxian (Experience the practices of international law and praise China's contribution). *Wuda guojifa pinglun (Wuhan University International Law Review)*, *3*(1), 29–40.

Yang, Z. (1999). Jindai guojifa shuru Zhongguo jiqi yingxiang (The importation of modern international law into china and its influence). *Faxue yanjiu (CASS Journal of Law)*, *34*(3), 122–131.

Ying, T. (1960). Cong jige jiben gainian renshi zichan jieji guojifa de zhen mianmu (The true face of bourgeois international law from several basic concepts). *Guoji Wenti Yanjiu (International Studies)*, *2*(1), 42–51.

Yu, M., & Liu, H. (2010). Lun guojifa zai zhongguo de fazhan zouxiang. (The Development Trend of International Law in China). *Wuhan Daxue Xuebao (Wuhan University Journal)*, *63*(5), 705–722.

Zeng, L. (2006). Lun zhongguo heping fazhan yu guojifa de jiaohu yingxiang he zuoyong', (On the interaction and role of China's peaceful development and international law). *Zhongguo faxue (China Legal Science)*, *23*(4), 110–119.

Zhang, X. (1995). *Guoji Qiangxingfa Lun (On international jus cogens)*. Beijing: Peking University Press.

Zhao, L. (1990). Heping gongchu wuxiang yuanze shi guoji guanxi de jiben zhunze (The five principles of peaceful coexistence are the basic norms of contemporary international relations). *Faxue zazhi (Law Science Magazine)*, *10*(4), 2–3.

Zhao, J. (2014). Heping gongchu wuxiang yuanze yu Lianheguo xianzhang de guanxi (The relationship between the five principles of peaceful coexistence and the charter of the United Nations). *Dangdai Faxue (Contemporary Law Review)*, *28*(6), 32–40.

Zhou, G. (1955). Cong guojifa lun heping gongchu de yuanze (Principle of peaceful coexistence from international law). *Faxue yanjiu (Chinese Journal of Law)*, *2*(6), 37–41.

Zhou, Z. (2004). Zhongguo de heping jueqi xuyao jiaqiang dui guojifa de yanjiu (China's peaceful rise needs to strengthen research on international law). *Faxue yanjiu (CASS Journal of Law)*, *39*(2), 131–132.

Zhu, Q. (1995). Heping gongchu wuxiang yuanze shi jianli guoji xinzhixu de genben zhunze (The five principles of peaceful coexistence are the fundamental principles for establishing a new international order). *Xiandai Faxue (Modern Law Science)*, *17*(1), 7–11.

Index

Note: Page numbers followed by "n" denote endnotes.

For Product Safety Concerns and Information please contact our EU
representative GPSR@taylorandfrancis.com
Taylor & Francis Verlag GmbH, Kaufingerstraße 24, 80331 München, Germany